THE MERSEY ESTUARY: A TRAVEL GUIDE

Places to visit, walks and cycle rides along
the Liverpool, Wirral, Cheshire, Runcorn,
Widnes and Warrington shores

*Plus insights into the history,
environment and wildlife of the estuary*

Kevin Sene

Matador
9 Priory Business Park
Wistow Road, Kibworth Beauchamp
Leicestershire, LE8 ORX
Tel: 0116 279 2299
Email: books@troubador.co.uk
Web: www.troubador.co.uk/matador
Twitter: @matadorbooks

ISBN: 978 1838591 908

All photographs © Kevin Sene unless otherwise stated.

Maps contain OS data © Crown copyright (2019).
Maps are indicative only; refer to OS maps for more details.

British Library Cataloguing in Publication Data.
A catalogue record for this book is available from the British Library.

Printed and bound by CPI Group (UK) Ltd, Croydon, CR0 4YY

Matador is an imprint of Troubador Publishing Ltd.

MIX
Paper from
responsible sources
FSC
www.fsc.org FSC® C013604

THE MERSEY ESTUARY: A TRAVEL GUIDE

Acknowledgements

Author, design and layout: Kevin Sene
www.meteowriter.com
Copy editing: Helen Fazal
Cover
Design: Jack Wedgbury
Front cover: Liverpool waterfront
Cartography: Kevin Sene
Maps contain OS data © Crown copyright (2019)
Typesetting: Joshua Howey

About the author

Kevin Sene is a scientist who specialises in issues related to water and climate. However, the idea for this guide arose from many enjoyable cycle rides and days out around the Mersey Estuary. This sparked an interest in the maritime history, environment and wildlife of the area, which all feature in this guide. He is a Fellow of the Royal Geographical Society and has worked extensively in Europe, Africa and Asia.

Credits

All photographs are by the author, except for the following images:
- Colin Simpson, Page 81
- Dr Paul Thomas, Page 219
- Historic England, Pages 118, 188
- Laver Publishing, Page 158
- Liverpool Record Office, Pages 177, 183
- Natural England, Page 22
- National Museums Liverpool, Pages 176, 207
- National Tidal and Sea Level Facility, Pages 159, 161
- The Daniel Adamson Preservation Society, Page 17
- U.S. Fish and Wildlife Service, Page 224
- Warrington Museum & Art Gallery, Pages 117, 176, 192

Much has been written about the Mersey Estuary and the Further Reading sections in each chapter note publications that were particularly useful. Websites, museums, and interpretation panels were other useful sources of information. Where possible, original sources are cited, although we apologise if there have been any unintentional errors.

Thanks also to representatives from the following organisations who kindly provided comments on excerpts of the text:

- ATYLA Ship Foundation
- Cumbria Wildlife Trust
- Forest Hills Hotel, Frodsham
- Fort Perch Rock, New Brighton
- Friends of Bidston Hill
- Friends of Hilbre
- Friends of Pickerings Pasture
- Friends of Warrington Transporter Bridge
- Laver Publishing
- Liverpool Cathedral
- Marketing Liverpool
- Mersey Ferries, Liverpool
- Merseyside Maritime Museum, Liverpool
- Moore Nature Reserve, near Warrington
- Museum of Liverpool
- National Tidal and Sea Level Facility, Liverpool
- National Trust, Formby
- National Trust, Speke Hall
- Old Hall Hotel, Frodsham
- Panoramic 34, Liverpool
- Peel Ports
- Risley Moss Local Nature Reserve
- RNLI New Brighton
- Royal Albert Dock Liverpool
- Speke Aerodrome Heritage Group
- St George's Hall, Liverpool
- The Daniel Adamson Preservation Society
- Warrington Borough Council
- Warrington Museum & Art Gallery
- Western Approaches Museum, Liverpool
- Wirral Museums Service
- World Museum, Liverpool

Also to Dr Stephen Pickles (www.bidstonlighthouse.org.uk) and Sally Tapp for their comments, Jane Tyler and Peter Smart for help with bird identification, and to the RNLI, RSPB, Sustrans and The Ramblers for allowing website text to be reproduced.

For more information on the Mersey Estuary and more general river, estuary and coastal news, see www.meteowriter.com. This includes links to higher resolution versions of selected photographs from this book for editorial and personal use. If you have found this book useful, please leave a review on Goodreads (www.goodreads.com).

A view across the mouth of the estuary towards New Brighton Lighthouse, with Formby Point on the opposite side just visible in the distance

INTRODUCTION

The Mersey Estuary has a rich maritime history and its attractions include nature reserves, heritage sites and coastal resorts.

Other highlights include spectacular views of the waterfront in Liverpool and watching the activity at one of the country's busiest ports.

Several waterside festivals are held each year, along with sports events and fireworks displays.

There are also many opportunities for waterside walks, cycle rides and boat trips around the estuary shores.

FORMBY

Formby
Point

Alt
Estuary

Sefton Coast

Crosby
Coastal
Park

The Mersey
Estuary

Outer Estuary

The Narrows

NEW
BRIGHTON

Egremont

Seacombe

LIVERPOOL

Pier
Head

Hoylake

Bidston Hill

BIRKENHEAD

Woodside
Birkenhead
Priory

Liverpool
Marina

West Kirby

New
Ferry

WIRRAL

Otterspool
Promenade

Garston

Speke a
Garston
Coastal
Reserve

Port Sunlight /
River Park

Eastham
Country
Park

Inner Estu

M53

ELLESMERE PORT

M57

Maps are indicative only and contain OS
data © Crown copyright (2019)

THE MERSEY ESTUARY

The Mersey Estuary is hugely varied. Docks and industrial works sit alongside nature reserves and waterside parks. Even its appearance is transformed during the day as mudflats and sandbanks are covered by the incoming tide.

The headwaters lie in the hills of the Peak District, but the tidal influence begins in Warrington. Here a tidal bore arrives on the highest tides, and there are many signs of the town's seafaring past.

Approaching Widnes and Runcorn, sandstone outcrops force the Mersey through the Runcorn Gap, site of the impressive Silver Jubilee Bridge. Nearby are medieval Norton Priory and Halton Castle, while the Catalyst Science Discovery Centre explores the more recent industrial past.

The wide areas of mudflats beyond are important feeding grounds for migrating birds and are best seen from reserves on the northern shores. There are more expansive views from hills to the south.

The estuary then narrows again between Liverpool and Birkenhead where sights include Albert Dock, Birkenhead Priory and the iconic Three Graces, along with the Mersey Ferry.

The coast is first reached at the seaside resort of New Brighton and the estuary finally ends at Formby Point, an area of sand dunes, beaches and pinewoods, with a population of red squirrels.

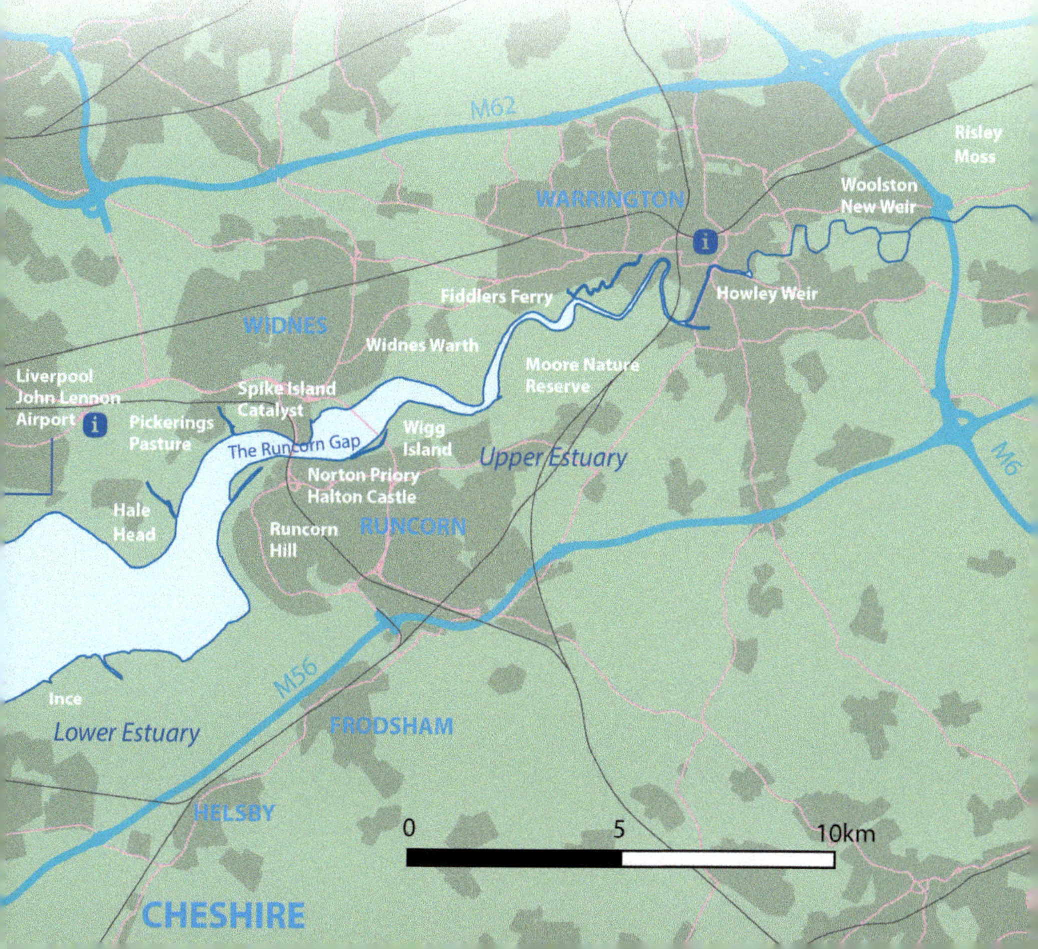

M62

Risley Moss

WARRINGTON

Woolston New Weir

Fiddlers Ferry

Howley Weir

WIDNES

Widnes Warth

Moore Nature Reserve

Liverpool John Lennon Airport

Pickerings Pasture

Spike Island Catalyst

The Runcorn Gap

Wigg Island

Upper Estuary

M6

Norton Priory Halton Castle

Hale Head

Runcorn Hill

RUNCORN

M56

Ince

FRODSHAM

Lower Estuary

HELSBY

0   5   10km

CHESHIRE

About this guide

This guide suggests places to visit around the estuary with a maritime theme, from its uppermost reaches in Warrington to the coast at New Brighton and Formby Point. As well as the better known attractions, it includes a host of destinations relating to the history, environment and wildlife of the area. These will be of interest to local residents and visitors alike. The Listings sections later highlight some examples.

The book is divided into two main sections, each with three chapters. Part One, **Places to Visit**, describes sights along the Liverpool, Wirral and Cheshire shorelines and in the Upper Estuary between Runcorn, Widnes and Warrington. It includes indicative route maps and descriptions for fifteen walks and cycle rides, ranging from trips of a couple of hours to a full day out. Brief summaries appear throughout on topics of general interest, such as the histories of the Mersey Ferries, Liverpool John Lennon Airport, and the three transporter bridges which once spanned the Mersey.

Part Two, **Estuary Themes**, describes the natural and maritime history of the estuary. Chapter 4, **Rivers and Tides**, considers topics related to the natural environment, such as the underlying geology, efforts to clean up pollution, and the pioneering work on tidal

> **STAY SAFE!**
> As in any estuary, there are risks from the tides and from soft mud and quicksand at the waterside, even when strolling along the beach. The Royal National Lifeboat Institution (RNLI) publishes some excellent advice on water safety, which is reproduced later in this chapter.

prediction in the region. Visit suggestions include trips to the source of the Mersey and one of the lost rivers of Liverpool. It also has useful tips on estimating tide times and viewing the Mersey Tidal Bore.

Chapter 5, **Maritime Connections**, looks at the history of the Port of Liverpool and the various docks upstream at Ellesmere Port, Runcorn, Widnes and Warrington. It also describes canal links to other towns and cities, including the Manchester Ship Canal. Current operations are also considered, such as the popularity of Liverpool as a cruise ship destination and the navigational challenges in the estuary. Suggestions for places to visit include former lighthouses and reminders of the overhead railway that once stretched the length of the docks.

Chapter 6, **Wildlife**, considers the marine life and waterbirds found around the estuary and the habitat and nature reserves on its

A Mersey Ferry departs from the waterfront at Pier Head in Liverpool ▼

▲ The world-famous *Another Place* artwork created by Sir Antony Gormley lies to the north of the Port of Liverpool; a hundred life-size cast-iron statues looking out to sea

shores. Insights are also included into the life cycle of the salmon, spectacular bird displays called murmurations, Liverpool's famous Liver Birds and the peat bogs that once lined the valley floor. As well as ideas for places to visit, it includes tips on birdwatching, bird photography and spotting seals, dolphins and porpoises around Liverpool Bay.

The Further Reading sections at the end of each chapter suggest places to look for more information, including the original sources for the quotations that appear throughout.

▲ **Upper to Lower:** Liverpool and the mouth of the estuary viewed from the Summit at Port Sunlight River Park on the Wirral / Birkenhead Docks and Liverpool waterfront viewed from Radio City Tower, with a Mersey Ferry en route to Pier Head and the hills of north Wales just visible in the distance

Aerial view of the estuary between Fiddler's Ferry near Warrington and Liverpool John Lennon Airport ▼

Manchester Ship Canal

rs Ferry

Runcorn

Widnes

Manchester Ship Canal

Liverpool John Lennon Airport

LISTINGS

GOOD PLACES FOR INSIGHTS INTO MARITIME AND LOCAL HISTORY
- Museum of Liverpool, p44
- Merseyside Maritime Museum, Liverpool, p45
- World Museum, Liverpool, p52
- Fort Perch Rock, Wirral, p70
- Birkenhead Priory, Wirral, p82
- Port Sunlight Museum, Wirral, p89
- National Waterways Museum, Wirral, p92
- Norton Priory Museum, Runcorn, p104
- Catalyst Science Discovery Centre, Widnes, p105
- Warrington Museum & Art Gallery, Warrington, p116

GOOD PLACES FOR A BIRD'S EYE VIEW
- Liverpool Cathedral, p54
- Radio City Tower, Liverpool, p54
- Panoramic 34, Liverpool, p54
- Bidston Hill, Wirral, p78
- Birkenhead Priory, Wirral, p82
- Port Sunlight River Park, Wirral, p88
- Overton Hill, Frodsham, p96
- Halton Castle, Runcorn, p104
- Runcorn Hill Park, Runcorn, p104
- Trans Pennine Trail, near Widnes, p124

*Liverpool waterfront viewed at twilight
from near New Brighton*

◀ **Upper to Lower:** Liverpool has two cathedrals, seen here from the opposite shores of the Mersey: Liverpool Cathedral (left) and the Metropolitan Cathedral (right) / Halton Castle in Runcorn lies on a sandstone outcrop and is a good viewpoint for the Upper Estuary / Liverpool waterfront on a misty day

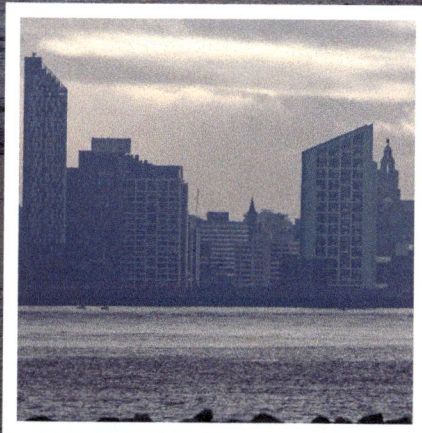

LISTINGS

GOOD PLACES TO SEE WILDLIFE

- Formby Point, p42
- Speke and Garston Coastal Reserve, p56
- Pickerings Pasture, near Widnes, p57
- Port Sunlight River Park, Wirral, p88
- Eastham Country Park, Wirral, p92
- Wigg Island, Runcorn, p105
- Spike Island, Widnes, p105
- Widnes Warth, Widnes, p114
- Moore Nature Reserve, near Warrington, p115
- Risley Moss, Warrington, p116

GOOD PLACES FOR WATERSIDE DINING

- Matou, Liverpool, p44
- Merseyside Maritime Museum, p48
- Panoramic 34, Liverpool, p54
- Britannia Inn, Liverpool, p58
- Chung Ku, Liverpool, p58
- Floral Pavilion, Wirral, p71
- The Ferry, Wirral, p72
- Woodside Terminal café, Wirral, p82
- The Mersey Hotel, Widnes, p111
- The Ferry Tavern, Fiddler's Ferry, p114

GOOD PLACES FOR SCENIC WALKS

- *Another Place* artwork, Crosby Beach, p36
- Speke Hall, Liverpool, p56
- Hale Head Lighthouse, p60
- New Brighton Lighthouse, p70
- One O'Clock Gun, Birkenhead, p80
- Port Sunlight Garden Village, p88
- Fiddler's Ferry, p114
- Head of the estuary, Warrington, p128
- Source of the Mersey, Stockport, p140
- Headwaters of the Mersey, Peak District, p140
- See Walks #1 to #9 also

Telephoto view of Hale Head Lighthouse from Runcorn Hill Park

▲ Red squirrels thrive in the pinewoods at the National Trust reserve at Formby Point

Oystercatchers and redshanks are common types of wading bird found around the estuary ▼

WHAT IS THE MERSEY ESTUARY?

An estuary is the part of a river where water levels are affected by the tides. In the Mersey the tidal influence normally ends at Howley Weir close to Warrington town centre and water levels here can vary several metres in a day. In Liverpool, which has one of the highest tidal ranges in the world, they sometimes exceed ten metres.

Howley Weir in Warrington ▶

On the highest tides, water flows over the top of Howley Weir and the tidal fluctuations reach the eastern parts of the town. This then is the true upper limit of the estuary, about thirty miles from the sea. As discussed in Chapter 6, Wildlife, seals occasionally make it this far as they chase fish upstream on the incoming tide. Schooners, steamships and barges were once built in the town and thousands of tons of freight were carried each year to and from Liverpool, Ellesmere Port, Runcorn and Widnes.

◀ A sand dune near Formby Point with Blackpool Tower and a roller coaster just visible in the distance through the heat haze

At the opposite end of the estuary, the Mersey first meets the sea at New Brighton, while Formby Point is often considered the boundary on the other shoreline to the east, close to where ships leaving the estuary turn out into Liverpool Bay. There is however some debate about exactly where the estuary ends and Chapter 4, Rivers and Tides, examines this further.

The estuary is normally considered to consist of the Upper Estuary upstream of the Runcorn Gap and the Lower Estuary further downstream, whose components are the Inner Estuary, The Narrows and the Outer Estuary. As discussed later, each has its own distinct types of landscape and habitat.

Tourist information

There are several tourist information centres around the estuary, providing information on accommodation, transport and places to visit. In Liverpool, the main centre is at the Central Library, near Lime Street Station. Others include the New Brighton Heritage & Information Centre, just a short walk from the main station, and an information desk at Warrington Market.

Most tourist destinations have leaflets on local attractions, as do larger bus and railway stations, and the following websites are also good sources of information:

- Liverpool and surroundings: www.visitliverpool.com; www.cultureliverpool.co.uk
- Royal Albert Dock: www.albertdock.com
- The Sefton Coast, north of Liverpool: www.visitseftonandwestlancs.co.uk
- Wirral: www.visitwirral.com
- Frodsham, Helsby and surrounding areas: www.visitcheshire.com
- Widnes, Runcorn and surrounding areas: www.visithalton.me
- Warrington and surrounding areas: www.warrington.gov.uk
- Manchester and surroundings: www.visitmanchester.com

▲ Some much-photographed statues of the Beatles at Pier Head in Liverpool

One feature worth looking out for is the option to register for email or text notifications of special events such as festivals (www.cultureliverpool.co.uk).

In Liverpool, several companies operate guided walks and bus tours. Popular topics include the Beatles and the cultural heritage of the city. Many begin at the waterfront – see Chapter 1 for suggestions with a maritime theme. Most of the boat trips described later also include entertaining commentaries.

A distant view of Fiddler's Ferry from the opposite shores of the Mersey ▼

When to go

The main tourist season around the estuary is from March to October, but many places are open year-round. Out of season, destinations are often quieter, and this is a good time to watch wildlife. The crystal-clear air of a fine winter's day is hard to beat for waterside views.

The maritime influence means that the weather can be changeable, with the coast sometimes enveloped in sea mist and fine weather inland, or it may be raining inland with clear weather further west. It therefore helps to be flexible when deciding where to go. The state of the tides is another important consideration, particularly for photography, birdwatching or seeing the tidal bore. Chapter 4, Rivers and Tides, and Chapter 6, Wildlife, give tips on when and where to go. As in any activity near water, it is important to consider your safety, and the RNLI advice reproduced later provides some common-sense guidelines.

Around the estuary, there are many festivals and special events throughout the year, particularly in Liverpool, and the table opposite lists some with waterside views. Others include the international carnivals of Brazilica and Brouhaha, and the Chinese New Year celebrations. The city is also a

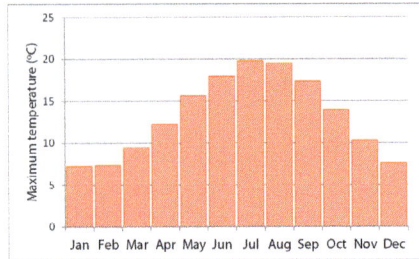

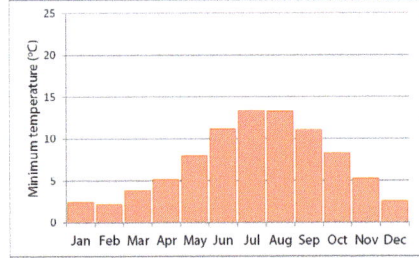

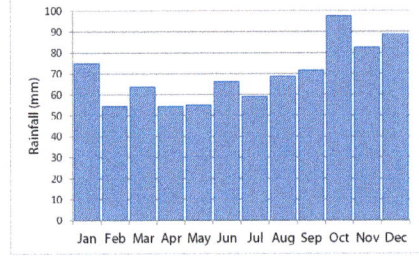

▲ Monthly average maximum and minimum air temperatures, and monthly average rainfall, for the Met Office meteorological station at Crosby, north of Liverpool, in the period 1981-2010 (data from www.metoffice.gov.uk; contains public sector information licensed under the Open Government Licence v1.0)

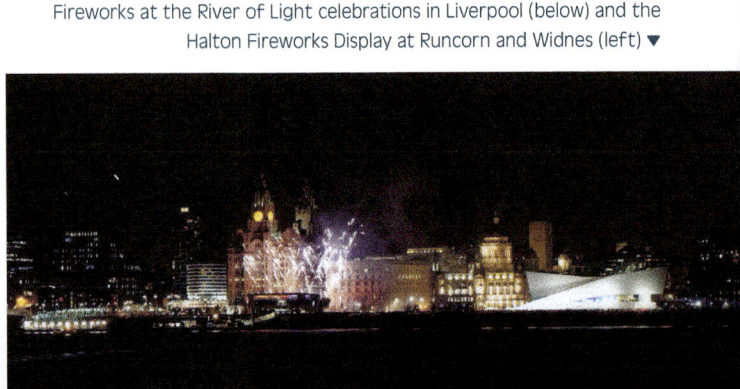

Fireworks at the River of Light celebrations in Liverpool (below) and the Halton Fireworks Display at Runcorn and Widnes (left) ▼

SOME ANNUAL HIGHLIGHTS

LOCATION	HIGHLIGHTS
Albert Dock, Liverpool www.albertdock.com	Summer on the Dock festival: film, sports, health and wellbeing activities
Egremont, near New Brighton www.visitwirral.com	Egremont Festival: waterside festival
Otterspool Promenade, Liverpool www.visitwirral.com	Fusion Festival: live music
Hoylake, Wirral www.hoylakelifeboat.org.uk	Hoylake & West Kirby Lifeboat Open Day: funfair, mock rescues
Pier Head, Liverpool www.theriverfestival.co.uk	River Festival Liverpool: maritime heritage, culture, music, food and wine events
Liverpool, selected locations www.cultureliverpool.co.uk	Armed Forces Day, Reserves Day
Liverpool, city wide www.lightnightliverpool.co.uk	Light Night: art, culture, live music
Pier Head, Liverpool www.visitliverpool.com	Liverpool Christmas Ice Festival and Festive Markets: ice rink, ice slide, street food
Northern docks, Liverpool www.liverpoolsoundcity.co.uk	Liverpool Sound City: film, live music
Warrington, town wide www.culturewarrington.org	Warrington Festival: art, culture, live music

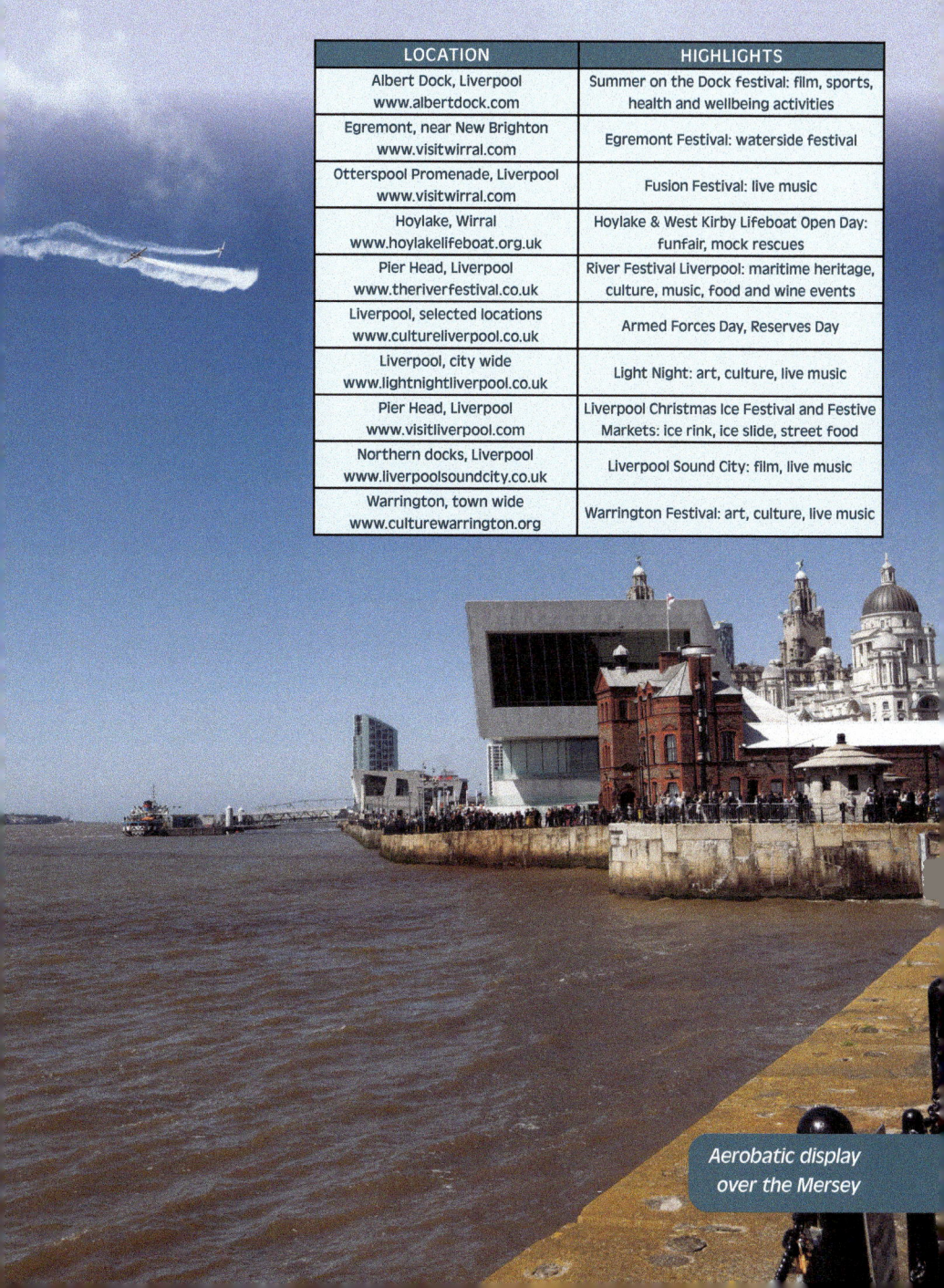

Aerobatic display over the Mersey

▲ Dragon Dance at the Chinese New Year celebrations in Chinatown in Liverpool

▲ The Red Arrows occasionally visit Liverpool for major events, and here are seen passing over Pier Head (above) and heading into the distance over the Mersey Ferry (left)

favoured start point for the Clipper Round the World Yacht Race and Tall Ships Regatta. In November, the Bonfire Night celebrations include two spectacular waterside displays: the River of Light between Liverpool and the Wirral and the Halton Fireworks Display between Runcorn and Widnes.

For history enthusiasts, the Wirral Walking Festival in May (www.visitwirral.com) and the Heritage Open Days in September (www.heritageopendays.org.uk) both include tours of churches and other historic buildings that may not always be open to the public. Most museums around the estuary also have regular programmes of talks and exhibitions; see websites for details. For runners and cyclists, there are several waterside events, including two that feature a trip through one of the tunnels beneath the Mersey: the Mersey Tunnel 10k run and the Liverpool to Chester Bike Ride.

The Mersey Tidal Bore viewed from Wigg Island in Runcorn, soon after passing the Silver Jubilee Bridge. The bore is a low wave that travels inland from near Hale Head to Warrington on the highest tides ▼

The Parade of Sail before the start of the Clipper 2017–18 Round the World Yacht Race

Getting around

Most places around the estuary are accessible by public transport. Many operators offer daily or weekly passes and some allow travel by train, bus and – in some cases – ferry.

The Mersey Ferries provide a commuter service between Liverpool and the Wirral, while their longer River Explorer Cruises are one of the most popular tourist attractions in the region. Some tickets include entry to tourist destinations (www.merseyferries.co.uk).

If travelling by train, there are major stations at Liverpool, Widnes, Runcorn and Warrington, with links to nearby Chester, Crewe, Wigan and Manchester. Locally, the excellent Merseyrail network provides connections to many locations around the estuary, including Formby, New Brighton and Port Sunlight, all about a half hour train ride from Liverpool (www.merseyrail.org). In the city, other stops include the mainline station at Liverpool Lime Street and the major interchange at Liverpool South Parkway, which is also the departure point for buses to Liverpool John Lennon Airport.

Other bus services include those between Liverpool and Birkenhead via

▲ A City Explorer bus near Albert Dock

the road tunnels beneath the Mersey, and by bridge between Runcorn and Widnes. Bus operators include Arriva, Stagecoach and Network Warrington: see websites for timetables. In Liverpool, hop-on hop-off buses run between the main sights, such as the cathedrals, Cultural Quarter, Pier Head and Albert Dock (www.visitliverpool.com). Other useful sources of information include the national route planner service Traveline (www.traveline.info) and the Merseytravel website (www.merseytravel.gov.uk).

Schematic map of the rail network around the Mersey Estuary ▼

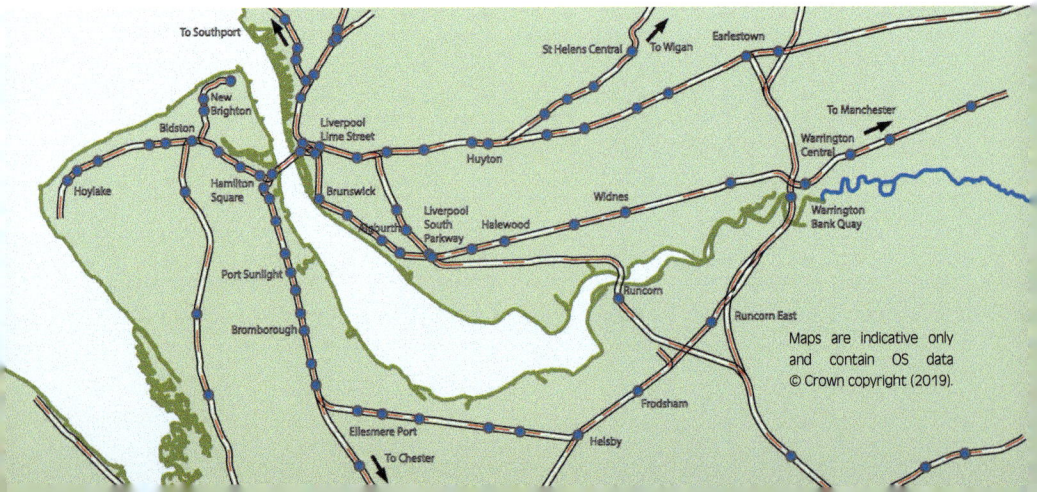

To Southport · New Brighton · Bidston · Hoylake · Hamilton Square · Port Sunlight · Bromborough · Liverpool Lime Street · Brunswick · Liverpool South Parkway · Huyton · Halewood · St Helens Central · To Wigan · Earlestown · Widnes · Runcorn · Runcorn East · Frodsham · Helsby · Ellesmere Port · To Chester · To Manchester · Warrington Central · Warrington Bank Quay

Maps are indicative only and contain OS data © Crown copyright (2019).

Boat trips

Another fine way to explore the estuary is by boat. In Liverpool, the Mersey Ferries are a top attraction and their River Explorer Cruises include a commentary on the main sights. During the tourist season, they also operate a wide variety of special cruises, including themed summer evening cruises and trips to Salford along the Manchester Ship Canal: see www. merseyferries.co.uk for dates.

Within the docks south of Pier Head, two other companies run tours: on board the *Skylark* motor vessel and a floating restaurant, *The Floating Grace* (www. floatinggrace.co.uk). Both depart from Salthouse Quay close to Albert Dock, and sometimes include a tour of the dock.

Further afield, a restored steam ship, the *Daniel Adamson* – the *Danny* for short – offers a choice of cruises along the Weaver Navigation between Frodsham and the spectacular Anderton Boat Lift near Winsford, and sometimes from Ellesmere Port and Liverpool (www. thedanny.co.uk). Some highlights of the Weaver trips include the many spectacular locks, swing bridges and viaducts along the Navigation. Other options include themed cruises and family fun days, plus tours of the *Danny* itself, including its Art Deco saloons.

Nearby, in Ellesmere Port, the National Waterways Museum offers narrowboat cruises along the Shropshire Union Canal during the tourist season (www. canalrivertrust.org.uk), while in Manchester two companies operate canal tours in the city: City Centre Cruises and Manchester River Cruises (www.citycentrecruises.com; www.manchesterrivercruises.com).

▲ **Upper to Lower:** The Mersey Ferries' *Royal Iris of the Mersey* on the Manchester Ship Canal in Warrington / The *Danny* on a Weaver Navigation cruise (© The Daniel Adamson Preservation Society)

With the exception of the River Explorer Cruises, most of these trips are only offered in the tourist season, so check websites for details. For more of a seafaring experience, the scheduled ferry services to the Isle of Man and Ireland are another possibility, with departures from Liverpool or Birkenhead. The main ferry operators are P&O Irish Sea Ferries, Stena Line and the Isle of Man Steam Packet Company.

During the summer, pleasure cruises are sometimes offered from Liverpool along the north Wales coast on board the historic paddle steamer *Waverley* and the coastal cruise ship *MV Balmoral* (www.waverleyexcursions. co.uk; www.whitefunnel.co.uk).

Watching the ships go by

Viewed from close quarters, a modern cargo or cruise ship is an impressive sight.

Cruise ship passengers board and disembark at Liverpool Cruise Terminal near Pier Head. When a ship is in port, viewpoints include the waterfront around Pier Head and, on the opposite shoreline, the promenades alongside Seacombe and Woodside ferry terminals. Walks #2 and #4 and Cycle Route #3 pass these areas. The Mersey Ferry is another good viewpoint and the dates of trips to coincide with cruise ship visits are shown on the Mersey Ferries website (www.merseyferries.co.uk). Visit dates also appear on the cruise terminal website (www.cruise-liverpool.com).

The high-speed catamaran ferries of the Isle of Man Steam Packet Company also operate from the waterfront. Further afield, locations for ship-watching include the Sefton Coast (Walk #1 and Cycle Route #1), Liverpool Marina (Cycle Route #2), the promenade between Seacombe and New Brighton (Walk #4 and Cycle Route #3) and the former ferry pier next to Eastham Country Park (Cycle Route #4). Elevated viewpoints such as Liverpool Cathedral, Radio City Tower, the Wheel of Liverpool and the Panoramic 34 restaurant can also provide interesting distant views of ships arriving and departing the estuary; see Chapter 1 for details.

▲ Yachts, tall ships, tugs and a naval vessel at the Three Festivals Tall Ships Regatta on the Mersey in 2018

Chapter 5, Maritime Connections, gives more information on the types of ships seen around the estuary. For the largest vessels, the busiest time tends to be around high tide when the water is deepest.

On a smaller scale, the events held by local rowing clubs can offer great photographic opportunities: examples include the Head of the Mersey races run by Warrington Rowing Club and dragon boat races in Warrington and at Princes Dock in Liverpool. Most of the sailing clubs around the estuary organise regattas, including those at Blundellsands, Fiddler's Ferry, Tranmere and Wallasey, and the Liverpool, Royal Mersey and Wallasey yacht clubs: see websites for dates.

New Brighton's lighthouse, Victoria Tower and the mouth of the estuary viewed from Radio City Tower ▶

Queen Mary 2 berthed at the Cruise Terminal in Liverpool, photographed from the Mersey Ferry ▼

Walking and cycling

Another popular way to tour the estuary is to walk or cycle around its shores. Later chapters include suggestions for fifteen walks and cycle routes over a mix of terrain from flat riverside paths to steeper ascents along unmade paths. See overleaf for a summary of the routes and some running and cycling events that may be of interest.

Trips range from an hour or two to several hours, and ideas for extending the route are often included. Most begin at railway stations, avoiding the need to travel by car, sometimes with the option to make a one-way trip and return from another station. Some of the cycle rides follow long distance routes for part of the way. The best known is the 215-mile coast-to-coast Trans Pennine Trail, which stretches from Southport in the west to the coastline east of Hull. In Liverpool, it connects to Pier Head via National Cycle Route 56. Cycle Routes #2 and #5 make use of these trails.

On the Wirral, Route 56 continues around the coastline and then cuts inland to Chester, overlapping with the Wirral Circular Trail, a 37-mile route around the peninsula. Cycle Routes #3 and #4 follow these trails some of the way. To the north of Pier Head, Cycle Route #1 follows National Cycle Route 810 alongside the Leeds & Liverpool Canal and then joins the Sefton Circular Trail to the coast.

For walkers, one of the longest footpaths in the area is the Sandstone Trail, extending for 34 miles from the historic town of Frodsham to Whitchurch in Shropshire. Initially there are superb views of the estuary and the early stages of the trail are followed on Walk #6. Heading in the other direction, the 22-mile long Mersey Valley Timberland Trail runs west along the Mersey Valley from

▲ **Upper to Lower:** Liverpool waterfront from near New Brighton / The Citybike stand at Pier Head

Runcorn Hill to Lymm near Warrington and is followed briefly during Walk #7.

Another 22-mile walk, the Mersey Way, lies on the opposite shoreline and runs from the head of the estuary in Warrington to Garston in south Liverpool, overlapping with the Trans Pennine Trail some of the way. Walks #3, #8 and #9 and Cycle Routes #5 and #6 follow the trail in places.

If travelling by train, most operators allow cycle carriage although reservations are sometimes required; see train company websites for details. Hiring a bike is another possibility. In Liverpool, the citybike scheme allows hire by the hour, day or week, and the many collection points include Pier Head and Otterspool Promenade (www.citybikeliverpool.co.uk). Bikes can be carried on the Mersey Ferries if there is space available.

WALKS, CYCLE ROUTES & EVENTS

WALK	NAME	DISTANCE	TERRAIN	HIGHLIGHTS	PAGE
Walk #1	Crosby Coastal Park	6–7 miles	Flat/unmade paths	Coastal views, Another Place statues, Marine Lake	38-39
Walk #2	Liverpool Waterfront	Various	Flat/tarmac	Pier Head, Three Graces, Albert Dock	49
Walk #3	Hale Head Lighthouse	~3 miles	Flat/well-graded paths	Hale village, lighthouse	60-61
Walk #4	New Brighton to Seacombe	3–4 miles	Flat/tarmac	New Brighton, Mersey Ferry	76-77
Walk #5	Bidston Hill	~3 miles	Hilly/unmade paths	Lighthouse, windmill and observatory	78-79
Walk #6	Frodsham Heights	~3 miles	Hilly/unmade paths	Far-reaching views, historic Frodsham	96-97
Walk #7	Runcorn Hill	~3 miles	Hilly/unmade paths	Woodland walks, sandstone edges	108-109
Walk #8	Widnes Promenade	~2 miles	Mainly flat/tarmac	Spike Island, Victoria Promenade, Catalyst Science Discovery Centre	110-111
Walk #9	Warrington Navigation	3–4 miles	Flat/unmade paths	Howley Weir, Victoria Park	120-121

Runners pass along the promenade near Albert Dock

ROUTE	NAME	DISTANCE	TERRAIN	HIGHLIGHTS	PAGE
Cycle Route #1	Pier Head to Crosby Beach	19–20 miles	Flat/tarmac/ unmade paths	Pier Head, Another Place artwork, Leeds & Liverpool Canal	40-41
Cycle Route #2	Sitting Bull	9–10 miles	Flat/tarmac	Liverpool waterfront, Otterspool Promenade	58-59
Cycle Route #3	Tour of the Proms	~11 miles	Flat/tarmac	New Brighton, Mersey Ferry	80-81
Cycle Route #4	Port Sunlight	6–7 miles	Flat/tarmac	Port Sunlight Village, Eastham Country Park	94-95
Cycle Route #5	Mersey Route 62	19–20 miles	Flat/tarmac/ unmade paths	Fiddler's Ferry, Spike Island, Pickerings Pasture	124-127
Cycle Route #6	Warrington Waterways	~11 miles	Flat/tarmac/ unmade paths	Head of the Estuary, Manchester Ship Canal	128-129

RUNNING AND CYCLING EVENTS	LOCATION	MONTH	WEBSITE
Liverpool Half Marathon	Liverpool	March	www.btrliverpool.com
Rock 'n' Roll Marathon	Liverpool	May	www.runrocknroll.com
Wirral Coastal Walk	Wirral	June	www.wirralcoastalwalk.org
Mersey Tunnel 10K	Liverpool/ Wirral	June	www.btrliverpool.com
Port Sunlight 5K and 10K	Wirral	June	www.btrliverpool.com
Liverpool to Chester Bike Ride	Liverpool to Chester	July	www.liverpoolchesterliverpool.com
Wirral Half Marathon and 10K	Wirral	September	www.btrliverpool.com
English Half Marathon	Warrington	September	www.motivrunning.com
Santa Dash Fun Run	Liverpool	December	www.btrliverpool.com

The dates of events can change; check websites for the latest details

Walking and cycling guides

The Further Reading sections in later chapters list several guidebooks that may be useful, and the following websites are another source of walking and cycling information:

- Liverpool: www.liverpool.gov.uk
- Merseytravel: www.merseytravel.gov.uk
- The Sefton Coast, north of Liverpool: www.visitseftonandwestlancs.co.uk
- Wirral: www.visitwirral.com
- Widnes and Runcorn: www.halton.gov.uk
- Warrington: www.warrington.gov.uk

Most include free-to-download maps, in some cases with area-wide cycle maps that can be viewed in incredible detail by zooming in on the image on a computer or smartphone screen. Tourist information centres may also have paper copies available.

Other useful sources of information include the websites for the Trans Pennine Trail (www.transpenninetrail.org.uk), the Sandstone Trail (www.sandstonetrail.com) and Sustrans, whose range of cycling guides includes one for Merseyside and Manchester (www.sustrans.org.uk).

ROAD SAFETY FOR CYCLISTS

The cycling charity Sustrans notes that:

If you follow some simple road safety advice the roads don't have to be a dangerous place to cycle. Many people say they are put off cycling because they don't like the idea of cycling in traffic, but many cyclists use busy roads every day without any problems. That's because they cycle safely and make sure drivers know they're there. Once you know the basics of road cycling, you can start to enjoy using a bike for everyday journeys to work, school or to visit friends.

Some key tips on cycling safely are reproduced later in this chapter and more information is available from the Sustrans website (www.sustrans.org.uk).

When walking or cycling it is essential to be aware of the risks and go prepared; see the Ramblers and Sustrans advice later in this chapter. The excellent advice on water safety from the RNLI there should also be heeded.

More generally, the Countryside Code published by Natural England provides recommendations in three main areas: respect for other people, protecting the natural environment and enjoying the outdoors. The full version of the code is available from www.gov.uk/natural-england whilst the bookmark below provides a useful summary.

The Countryside Code

Respect
Protect
Enjoy

Respect other people
- Consider the local community and other people enjoying the outdoors
- Leave gates and property as you find them and follow paths unless wider access is available

Protect the natural environment
- Leave no trace of your visit and take your litter home
- Keep dogs under effective control

Enjoy the outdoors
- Plan ahead and be prepared
- Follow advice and local signs

Produced jointly with Natural Resources Wales

NATURAL ENGLAND

www.gov.uk/natural-england

▲ A bookmark summarising key points from The Countryside Code (contains public sector information licensed under the Open Government Licence v3.0)

TOUR D'ESTUARY?

The Mersey Estuary reaches the coast at New Brighton to the west and Formby Point to the east, nearly seven miles away across the water and visible on a clear day.

By linking together some of the cycle routes suggested in this guide, it's possible to make a tour of the estuary, a distance of 60–70 miles, starting from either New Brighton or Formby.

▲ Woolston New Weir in Warrington, at the top of the estuary

▲ The promenade from Seacombe Ferry Terminal to New Brighton, part of the Wirral Circular Trail

Much of the route has good waterside views, although some sections are inland, such as on the southern shores between Warrington and Ellesmere Port and around the docks and airport in Liverpool. The busy roads in south Liverpool, around Ellesmere Port and between Runcorn and Frodsham could be avoided by choosing a quieter route further inland, although this would lengthen the trip.

On the northern and eastern shores of the estuary, navigation is straightforward as the Trans Pennine Trail and National Cycle Routes 56 and 810 can be followed much of the way, as described in Cycle Routes #1 and #5. On the opposite shores, more map reading would be required, except along the Wirral Circular Trail between Eastham Country Park and New Brighton, as described in Cycle Routes #2 and #4.

Between Frodsham and Ellesmere Port, National Cycle Route 5 provides a way across the marshes to the south of the estuary. Initially this follows largely unmade paths to Ince and then skirts round Stanlow Oil Refinery to join busy roads in the town. It then heads inland so some route finding would be required between Ellesmere Port and Eastham Country Park.

Fort Perch Rock and the lighthouse at New Brighton ▼

Water safety

The Mersey Estuary has one of the highest tidal ranges in the world and currents reach several miles an hour in places. Sandbanks and areas of soft mud and quicksand add to the risk particularly around the Runcorn Gap, the Inner Estuary, New Brighton and along the Sefton and North Wirral coastlines.

Most water rescues in these areas are carried out from the RNLI station at New Brighton using *Charles Dibdin*, an inshore lifeboat, and – in collaboration with the neighbouring Hoylake Station – the hovercraft *Hurley Spirit* (www.newbrightonlifeboat.org.uk). The area of operation is from the Runcorn Gap down to the coast and joint rescues are sometimes performed with neighbouring RNLI stations, HM Coastguard and/or the Marine Rescue Unit at Pier Head, part of Merseyside Fire & Rescue Service.

The hovercraft is used for rescues from the mud and sands. In these types of rescue, the time pressure is always huge due to the need to free people before the tide comes in.

There are several RNLI lifeguard posts along the Wirral and Sefton coastlines, including at New Brighton and around the *Another Place* statues at Crosby Beach, an all-too-common place for people to become trapped on the sands. Dog walkers are another frequent source of call-outs due to owners trying to rescue pets when it would be safer to call for help.

As a voluntary organisation the RNLI relies on donations, and ways to provide support include becoming a member, helping with fundraising, and using the gift shops at lifeboat stations. The New Brighton Lifeboat Station also holds an annual open day, as do the other stations on the Wirral, in the form of the Hoylake & West Kirby Lifeboat Open Day, which includes mock rescues and a funfair (www.hoylakelifeboat.org.uk).

The next page provides some safety advice from the RNLI on a particular risk around the estuary: tidal cut-off. The RNLI's website contains a wealth of information on this and other risks, such as rip tides, waves and quicksand, with videos, safety tips, and real-life stories (www.rnli.org/safety/respect-the-water). At times of heavy rainfall and/or high tides it is also important to check the Environment Agency's website for the latest flood alerts and warnings (www.gov.uk).

Launching the RNLI lifeboat *Charles Dibdin* at New Brighton at the start of a training exercise ▼

The RNLI inshore rescue hovercraft *Hurley Spirit* passing Pier Head ▼

Tidal cut-off

Swimming and other watersports aren't the only ways that people get into trouble at the beach. Getting cut off by the tide also contributes to a significant number of RNLI rescues every year.

Because tide times and heights vary throughout the month, a beach that was clear yesterday at 5pm might be completely covered in sea at the same time today.

Tides have a reputation for being unpredictable, but really they follow a timetable more reliable than most trains! There are two different types: spring and neap.

Spring tides have greater depth range between high and low water, so at high tide the water comes in further up the beach.

Neap tides have less variation, so at high tide the water won't come in as far.

Check the tide conditions and your surroundings.

The UK and Ireland have some of the biggest tidal ranges in the world.

To avoid getting cut off by the tide:
- Before you head out, make sure it's safe. Check the tide tables.
- While you're out, be aware of your surroundings and the tide's direction.

A beach can seem like a vast playground but the tide can come in surprisingly quickly.

As the tide moves up and down the beach, the depth of the water changes throughout the day, sometimes by as much as 10 metres.

As the tide comes in, simply walking further up the beach and away to safety might not be an option.

If you've walked round to another cove at low tide, or walked around an outcrop of rocks, the water can soon block your way back as the tide turns. If

▲ RNLI warning flags on the sands at New Brighton

the cove you're in doesn't have steps or access of its own, you could be in trouble.

Don't get cut off by the tide, check them.

You can find out more information about tides in your area through tide tables, apps, weather news or local websites.

You can also get local tidal information from the Harbour Master, tourist information centre and some seaside retail outlets.

- Check forecasts and tides at RNLI lifeguarded beaches (www.rnli.org/find-my-nearest/lifeguarded-beaches).
- Or find tide tables and surf reports for the UK and Ireland at www.magicseaweed.com.

Reproduced from www.rnli.org/safety

Walking Safety

Walking is a great way to explore the countryside and towns and cities, but like any outdoor activity is not entirely without risk. The Ramblers website offers the following excellent personal safety advice:

General safety rules

Walking isn't without risk, but statistics show it's safer walking in the countryside than on a city street. Personal attacks and assaults from strangers are rare, however you should take care and follow these basic rules to keep safe:

- Make sure you've got plenty of food and drink and wear suitable clothing
- Check the weather forecast before you set out, take a waterproof and keep an eye on the sky
- Don't take risks by attempting long or difficult routes without preparation
- Take a map and know how to read it
- Be aware of any 'escape routes' if you're walking long-distance paths and need to cut the walk short
- Tell someone when you expect to be back and where you are going

If you're worried about security when walking alone in quiet places, this advice may help:

- Change your route if you feel unsafe for any reason
- Consider taking a personal alarm
- Avoid using headphones to listen to music if this stops you from remaining alert
- Make sure someone is aware when you plan to be back and where you are going

Walking on roads

Stick to the Highway Code (www.gov.uk) when walking on roads, and always use the pavement, if there is one. Cross at a designated point and make sure drivers can see you.

If the road has no pavement, try to walk on the right, facing oncoming traffic and cross to the other side when on sharp right-hand bends. Try to be more aware when walking on country roads, because traffic may be moving very fast. Take special care with young children, pushchairs and non-powered wheelchairs.

Mobile phones

It's always a good idea to carry a mobile with you, which you should fully charge before setting out. If you have to call the emergency services, make sure you keep your mobile on, so they can call you back. However remember that there may be no coverage in some hilly and remote areas.

Group walking

Group walking is a good option if you're new to walking and not yet ready to walk independently. If you do walk in a group, don't just follow the person in front; try to look around you and be aware of what's going on. It's important to take responsibility for your own safety.

The Ramblers

The Ramblers is a leading walking charity that promotes the benefits of walking, including helping to maintain rights of way and keep footpaths clear. There are several hundred local groups across the country that organise regular group walks led by experienced Walk Leaders; walks are also organised through the Walking for Health programme (www.walkingforhealth.org.uk). For more information on safety, navigation, access rights, walking gear, local groups and the work of the association see www.ramblers.org.uk.

Cycling Safety

As with walking, cycling is a great way to explore, and the Sustrans website offers the following excellent tips for cycling on roads:

1. Cycling safely
- Follow the Highway Code (www.gov.uk) – don't jump red lights and don't cycle on the pavement unless it's a designated cycle path.
- In wet weather watch your speed as surfaces may be slippery and it will take you longer to stop.
- Ride positively, decisively, and well clear of the kerb.
- Consider wearing a helmet.
- Keep your bike roadworthy.

2. Make sure motorists can see you
- Ride in a position where you can see and be seen.
- Use lights and consider wearing bright or reflective clothing, especially in towns, at night and in bad weather.
- Make eye contact with other road users, especially at junctions, then you know they've seen you.
- Signal clearly at all times.
- Use your bell – not all pedestrians can see you.

3. Be aware of vehicles
Many collisions occur when a cyclist is on the inside of a vehicle which is turning left. Don't assume the vehicle is going straight ahead just because it isn't signalling left. Always avoid 'undertaking' any vehicle in this situation – it's better to hang back until the vehicle has moved off.

Never cycle along the inside of large vehicles, such as lorries and buses, especially at junctions, where most accidents happen.

When turning left, a lorry will often pull out to the right first, creating a wide gap between the vehicle and the kerb. Many cyclists think it's safe to ride into this space, but this is a dangerous place to be as the gap quickly disappears when the lorry swings around to the left.

Cycle training
Cycle training is a good option if you are new to cycling or haven't cycled for a while. It will help you develop skills and increase your confidence to tackle busier routes. To find out about local courses, phone the National Cycle Training Helpline on 0844 736 8460/8461.

Tips for motorists
To make roads as safe as they can be, motorists need to be aware of cyclists too:
- When turning left watch for cyclists coming up on your near side and don't cut them up.
- Give cyclists a wide berth when overtaking.
- At night, dip your headlights when approaching cyclists.
- In wet weather, allow cyclists extra room as surfaces may be slippery.
- Remember, cyclists and motorists are equally entitled to use and share the same road space. Respecting all road users helps everyone to benefit from travelling by road.

Sustrans
Sustrans is a charity that makes it easier for people to walk and cycle, through education, improving cycle safety, and developing cycle routes; in particular the National Cycle Network. See the Sustrans website for information on cycle routes, bike maintenance, setting up your bike, policy and services, plus a number of free downloads such as the leaflet 'Check your bike is safe to ride' (www.sustrans.org.uk).

USING SHARED-USE PATHS

Shared-use paths away from the road help many people make their everyday journeys safely and they are also important for leisure. Sustrans offer the following advice on using shared-use paths (www.sustrans.org.uk):

- Many people including young, elderly and disabled people benefit from shared paths, which provide valuable opportunities to travel in a traffic-free environment, and to relax, unwind and play.
- All users of shared use paths have responsibilities for the safety of others they are sharing space with.
- People riding bikes tend to be the fastest movers on these paths and particularly need to consider their speed so as not to startle other people, particularly those who are frail or who have reduced sight, hearing or mobility.

TOP TIPS FOR SHARING THE SPACE

- Use the path in a way that is considerate to the comfort and safety of others.
- If there is a dividing line segregating cyclists from pedestrians, keep to the appropriate side; this is normally indicated on blue and white road signs and by logos on the road surface.
- When it's dark, or in dull conditions, make sure you are visible to others, use lights at night.
- Be particularly careful at junctions, bends, entrances onto the path, or any other 'blind spots' where people could appear in front of you without warning.
- When riding a bike, travel at a speed appropriate to the conditions and ensure you can stop in time.
- Be courteous and patient with other path users who are moving more slowly than you and slow down as needed when space is limited or if you cannot see clearly ahead.
- Please be aware, especially of more vulnerable users such as older people, people with small children, people in wheelchairs, or the hearing or visually impaired.
- Give way to slower users and wheelchair users and take care around horse riders leaving them plenty of room.
- When riding a bike, ring a bell well in advance if approaching people from behind.
- Keep your dog under control which may require a short lead

Further reading

Much has been written about the Mersey Estuary and the Port of Liverpool and the following books provide many useful insights:

> Both sides of the river: Merseyside in poetry and prose, Gladys Mary Coles (ed.), (Headland, 1993)
> Liverpool: the story of a city, National Museums Liverpool, (Liverpool University Press, 2012)
> Mersey: the river that changed the world, Ian Wray (ed.), photography by Colin McPherson, (The Bluecoat Press, 2007)
> River Mersey from source to sea, Phil Page and Ian Littlechilds, (Amberley Publishing, 2014)
> Schooner Port: two centuries of upper Mersey sail, H.F. Starkey, (Avid Publications, 1998)
> The River Mersey, Ron Freethy, (Terence Dalton, 1985)

Many of the websites listed in this guide also give useful background. The following are of particular interest:

> www.allertonOak.net The Allerton Oak website has fascinating insights into both local history and the environment. It includes a series of suggested walks and a section on the lost rivers of Liverpool.
> www.merseybasin.org.uk The Mersey Basin Campaign was a 25-year campaign to clean up the river system and had a major impact on water quality and waterside development in the estuary. The campaign ended in 2010 and this legacy website is a treasure-trove of information on the history, wildlife and environment of the Mersey, and the history and achievements of the campaign. The campaign is described in more detail in Chapter 4, Rivers and Tides. See www.merseyrivers.org.uk also.
> www.gerryco23.wordpress.com is a blog entitled 'That's how the light gets in'. Here you will find a series of beautifully written posts on a huge range of subjects, including waterside and canal walks and historical insights into Liverpool and the surrounding region.
> www.mywarrington.me.uk mywarrington is a website which covers a wide range of topics on Warrington and the surrounding areas, including the Mersey and its canal network.

Later chapters have many suggestions for books, reports and websites with more background on the wildlife, environment and maritime history of the estuary.

Warehouses at Albert Dock in Liverpool.

part one

PLACES TO VISIT

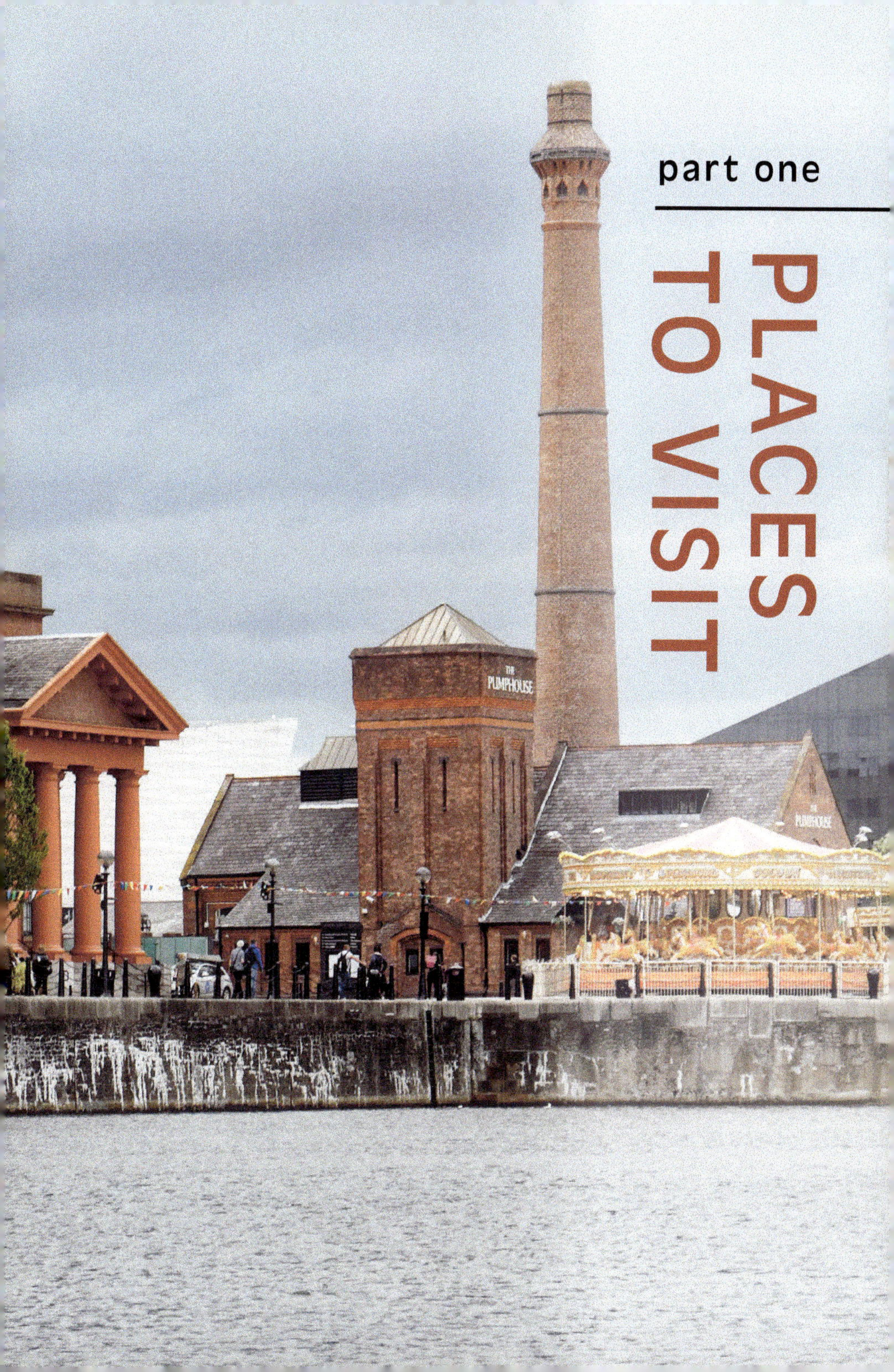

Tall ships in Canning Dock
at Liverpool Waterfront

chapter 1

LOWER ESTUARY
LIVERPOOL AREA

The sand dunes, beaches and pinewoods at Formby Point mark the end of the Mersey Estuary.

A coastal trail then leads to the Port of Liverpool and the Another Place statues: a hundred iron men looking out to sea, submerged twice daily by the tide.

The waterfront at Liverpool lies beyond the docks and is one of the most spectacular in the world; its sights include Albert Dock, the Mersey Ferry and the Three Graces.

Further south the Mersey widens to form an inland sea, with nature reserves and historic Speke Hall on its northern shores.

VISIT IDEAS

See the following chapters for more sights in the Liverpool area on different themes:

Chapter 4 – Rivers and Tides

- Otterspool Park, Liverpool
- Tide prediction machines, Liverpool
- Tidal fountain memorial, Liverpool

Chapter 5 – Maritime Connections

- Remains of the Liverpool Overhead Railway
- Liverpool Castle plaque
- Former White Star Lines headquarters, Liverpool
- One O'Clock Gun, Liverpool

Chapter 6 – Wildlife

- Seal-watching locations, Cumbria
- Martin Mere Wetland Centre, Ormskirk
- Liver Bird history and motifs, Liverpool
- Wading bird exhibits, Liverpool
- Birdwatching reserves, several locations

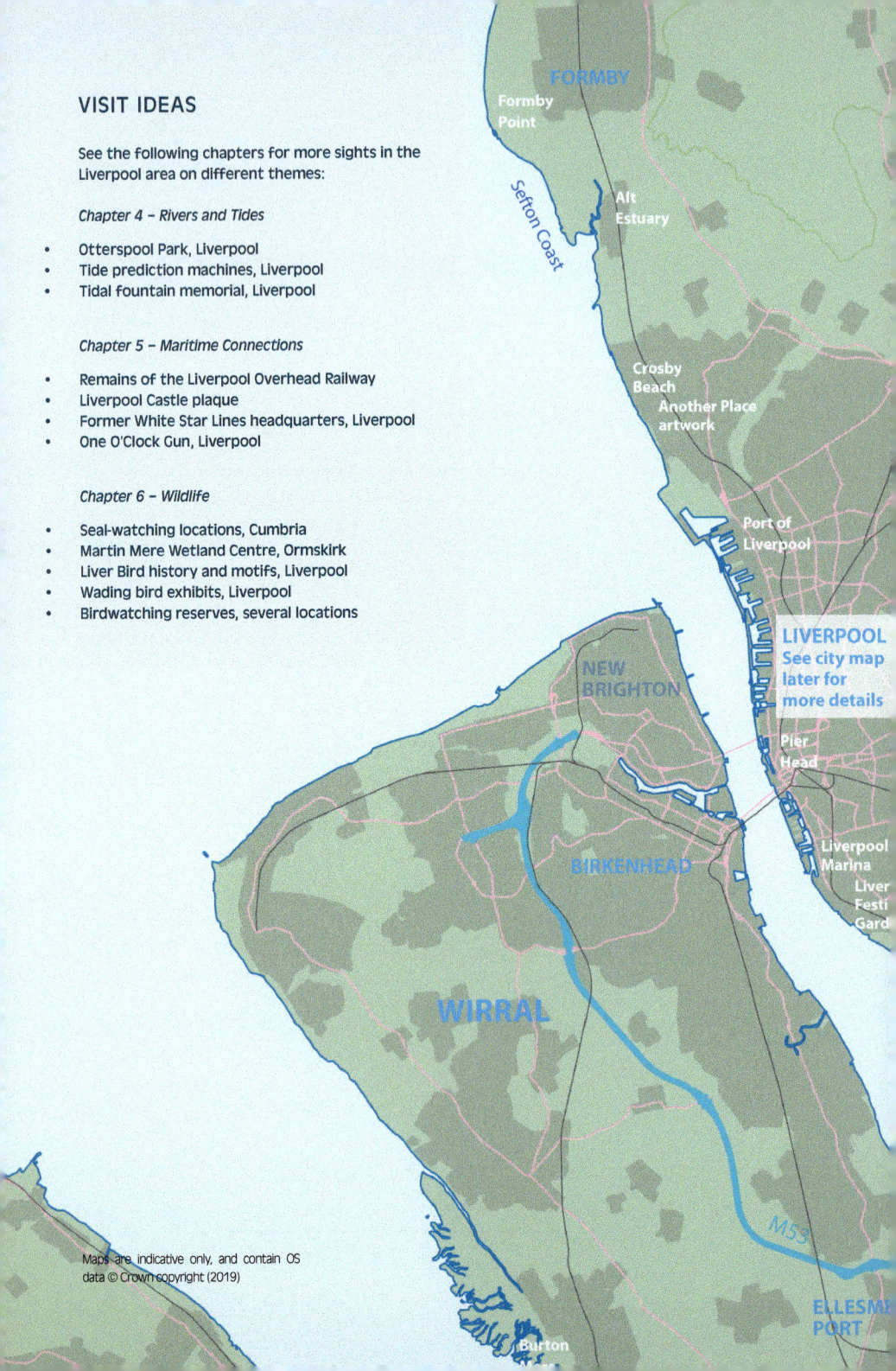

FORMBY

Formby Point

Sefton Coast

Alt Estuary

Crosby Beach
Another Place artwork

Port of Liverpool

LIVERPOOL
See city map later for more details

NEW BRIGHTON

Pier Head

Liverpool Marina

Liver Festi Gard

BIRKENHEAD

WIRRAL

M53

ELLESME PORT

Burton

Maps are indicative only, and contain OS data © Crown copyright (2019)

LIVERPOOL AREA

The distinctive curve of Formby Point marks the northernmost limit of the Mersey Estuary. Wide sandy beaches lead to the world-famous *Another Place* statues and the start of the Port of Liverpool, from where the Leeds & Liverpool Canal provides a scenic route to the heart of the city.

Visitor attractions at the waterfront include museums, Albert Dock and the iconic Three Graces. The waterfront is also the departure point for the Mersey Ferry. For a bird's eye view of the city, Radio City Tower further inland is a great vantage point, as is the magnificent Liverpool Cathedral.

Heading upstream, a wide promenade extends past Liverpool Marina and Liverpool Festival Gardens with fine views towards the Wirral; a short detour inland then leads to the Speke and Garston Coastal Reserve and a Tudor mansion, Speke Hall.

Beyond Liverpool John Lennon Airport, the coastal path passes the lighthouse at Hale Head, a reminder of the days of steamships and sail. The Trans Pennine Trail passes nearby en route to Pickerings Pasture and the Runcorn Gap, which is spanned by the distinctive Silver Jubilee Bridge and marks the start of the Upper Estuary.

0   5   10km

WARRINGTON

WIDNES

Otterspool Promenade

Speke and Garston Coastal Reserve

Speke Hall

Liverpool John Lennon Airport

Hale Head

Pickerings Pasture

The Runcorn Gap

RUNCORN

M62

M56

Formby Point to Liverpool

The Mersey Estuary ends at **Formby Point**, the westernmost point on a long line of beaches that extend northwards towards Southport and south to the Port of Liverpool. This stretch of coastline is known as the Sefton Coast.

The trails nearby pass through sand dunes, pinewoods and farmland, including the Asparagus Route, named after a crop that thrives in the sandy soils here. Much of the land is part of National Trust Formby where the team are often on hand to provide advice, while information boards at Lifeboat Road and Victoria Road car parks show the main walking routes (www.nationaltrust.org.uk). The pinewoods provide shelter for red squirrels and the views from the dunes are truly spectacular. To travel by train, use Freshfield Station for Victoria Road or Formby Station for Lifeboat Road, both about a mile away (www.merseyrail.org). Arriving on foot is highly recommended during hot weather as the car parks fill up early in the day.

Heading south, the coastal path detours inland briefly before reaching the sea again close to the mouth of the

Looking towards Formby Point from offshore ▶

Just one of the *Another Place* statues; each is made from cast iron and stands more than six feet tall ▼

THE ANOTHER PLACE ARTWORK

The *Another Place* statues, 100 in total, extend for more than two miles along Crosby Beach and were created by Sir Antony Gormley, whose other creations include the *Angel of the North* statue near Gateshead. A quotation from the artist on an information board at Crosby Beach says:

In this work, human life is tested against planetary time. This sculpture exposes to light and time the nakedness of a particular and peculiar body, no hero, no ideal, just the industrially reproduced body of a middle-aged man trying to remain standing and trying to breathe, facing a horizon busy with ships, moving material and manufactured things around the planet.

◄ **Upper to Lower:** A red squirrel at the National Trust reserve at Formby Point / Yachts from the local sailing club moored in the Alt Estuary / A container ship heading for the Port of Liverpool viewed from the Sefton Coast near the Alt Estuary

Alt Estuary, a scenic spot where wading birds congregate in winter to feed on the mudflats. Beyond, the north Wirral and Welsh coastlines soon come into view, with ships passing surprisingly close to the shoreline as they follow the main shipping lane into the Port of Liverpool.

The coastal path ends at Crosby Beach and **Walk #1** visits the main sights in this area, including a marine lake and the *Another Place* artwork. The docks prevent further progress along the coast, but options for reaching the city centre include Merseyrail trains from nearby Waterloo Station (see Walk #1) or, for cyclists, following the Leeds & Liverpool Canal as described in **Cycle Route #1**.

TAKE CARE NEAR THE WATER!

As in many other places around the estuary, the dangers from soft sand and the fast-moving tides are real, as shown by the frequent rescues of walkers along this part of the coastline and the need for a lifeguard presence. These are therefore non-bathing beaches and the warning signs along the promenade should be heeded, particularly regarding the risks of walking alongside the *Another Place* statues. If visiting the coast it is worth reading the excellent advice on water safety from the Royal National Lifeboat Institution (RNLI) that appears in the Introduction to this book.

Crosby Coastal Park

The starting point for this walk is **Waterloo Station**, about twenty minutes by train from Moorfields Station in Liverpool. From the main entrance head left along South Road and cross Marine Terrace into Crosby Coastal Park (**A**), turning left after passing a café and refreshments kiosk to reach **Crosby Lakeside Adventure Centre**: a water sports, lodge and fitness centre with a bar and bistro overlooking the marine lake.

From the centre, follow the approach road and turn right at the second car park, signed Crosby Promenade, crossing this to reach a wide path that leads past the marine lake to the coast (**B**). Signs for the Sefton Circular route indicate the

▲ New Brighton seen from Crosby Beach with the radar tower and two Another Place statues in the foreground

way. The security fence to the left is for Royal Seaforth Dock, the main container terminal for the Port of Liverpool, while the distinctive slab-sided radar tower at the end once housed the control centre for the port.

On reaching the coastal path (**C**), the first statues come into view. From here head towards **Crosby Leisure Centre** (**D**), a distinctive grey-domed building set back from the shoreline with a café open to the public. The statues then continue for another mile or so to end near the former coastguard station at Crosby, which marks the end of the outward part of this route.

For the return journey, retrace your steps and beyond the leisure centre turn left onto a narrower path that passes a wooden-framed waste bin (**E**). This leads through sand dunes to the

Continue to the former coastguard station

Leisure Centre

Boating Lake

South Road

Waterloo Station

Lakeside Adventure Centre

Marine Lake

Cycle Route #1

Dinghies on the Marine Lake ▶

▲ The marine lake and Bar & Bistro at Crosby Lakeside Adventure Centre.

WALK 1

👣 👣

Distance: 6-7 miles on reasonably flat terrain
Start/end: Waterloo Station
Key features: Great coastal views, a marine lake and the *Another Place* artwork are the highlights of this walk. The route is generally flat with easy terrain. The coast is exposed to the wind and, on the highest tides, there is a risk that some of the path may be flooded, although the statues are best seen around low tide. See Chapter 4, Rivers and Tides, for sources of information on tide times and 'Take Care near the water' at the start of this chapter for safety advice at the beach.

marine lake and adventure centre, passing a smaller boating lake on the way. It is then a short walk back to **Waterloo Station**.

To extend the walk, continue along the coastal path from the coastguard station for about a mile. The path then turns inland and leads through a housing estate. Another mile or so beyond on Alt Road, to the right just before a junction, is **Hightown Station** from where there are train services back to Waterloo or Liverpool; Cycle Route #2 gives more details.

You may also wish to visit the Alt Estuary, which is a short walk away. Sefton Council and West Lancashire Borough Council publish some excellent maps of these and other trails in this area (visitseftonandwestlancs.co.uk).

Pier Head to Crosby Beach

From Liverpool, this ride can be done as a one-way trip of 13 to 14 miles, returning by train from Waterloo Station, or an out-and-return journey of 19 to 20 miles. Note that the canal towpath is narrow in places so it is important to take care and dismount where the signs indicate. Also, as with Walk #1, be sure to read the safety notices at the coast about the risks of going onto the beach.

The starting point is the Mersey Ferries' terminal at **Pier Head (A)** from where a short walk across the pedestrianised area leads to Water Street, between the Royal Liver and Cunard buildings. Near the end, dismount and walk left alongside the busy road, crossing at the traffic lights. A short walk then leads past **St Nicholas'**, **Liverpool Parish Church (B)**, to Chapel Street. The church is easily recognised by its elegant open-lantern bell tower and is one of the oldest in the city.

Now cycling again, continue right past the Mercure Hotel along Chapel Street to Tithebarn Street and turn left into **Vauxhall Road (C)** at a junction with a large yellow-painted statue by the roadside, known as a superlambanana.

Continuing along Vauxhall Road, after passing a major crossroads turn left after the second traffic lights into Burlington Street, a blue sign for the Leeds & Liverpool Canal indicating the way. Turn right again on reaching a mini roundabout then continue following the cycleway signs through side streets to reach **Stanley Locks (D)**, on a branch of the canal. The towpath, which is part of National Cycle Route 810, is then reached via a footbridge over the uppermost lock. The map of Liverpool overleaf indicates the route to this point.

The canal initially runs roughly parallel to the docks before turning inland, with cranes and warehouses sometimes visible in the distance. The route follows the canal for about 4 miles, crossing to the opposite bank for part of the way, before taking a left turn **(E)** at a metal gate across the towpath, with a blue-painted footbridge just beyond.

The cycleway now leads into Rimrose Valley Country Park, an attractive park that follows this section of the canal. On reaching a T-junction, turn left, leaving NCR 810, and then turn right shortly before an entrance barrier to the park. The path then passes through woods to reach a road. Here, cross this into Brooklands Avenue where signs for Crosby Coastal Park indicate the way ahead. A short way along the avenue, take a footpath on the left which passes between two houses. Dismount to pass through two gates and again a few hundred metres later, bearing left to cross a busy main road at traffic lights.

Great George's Road is just beyond and the route now follows this to its end, at a sharp bend that marks the start of Marine Terrace. Leave the road here, continuing straight on along a path to reach the approach road to **Crosby Lakeside Adventure Centre (F)**. Turn left, with signs for the Sefton Circular route now indicating the way.

At the second car park on the right, signed Crosby Promenade, cross this to follow a wide path past Crosby Marine Lake to the coast. On reaching the coastal path, the first statues come into view. Continue northwards

▲ Stanley Locks descend into Stanley Dock allowing boats to reach the southern docks via a tunnel beneath Pier Head

until they end, more than two miles away, close to a former coastguard station. This is the northernmost point on the route.

For the return journey, options include following the outward route back to Pier Head or returning by train from **Waterloo Station**. The station is about a quarter mile along South Road, which is reached by retracing the route to Marine Terrace and following this left, then turning second right into South Road.

Alternatively, to extend the route, from the coastguard station you could continue northwards. Initially the cycleway follows the coast, then after about a mile turns inland through a housing estate, passing close to **Hightown Station** a mile or so beyond, with frequent train services to Liverpool, which is on the right on Alt Road, just before a junction.

More ambitiously, you could carry on to Formby Point at the end of the estuary, about four miles from Hightown, although this would involve riding along some busy roads. From here the closest station for trains back to Liverpool is Freshfield, about a mile away. The walking and cycling guides published by Sefton Council and West

A bridge over the Leeds & Liverpool Canal ▼

CYCLE ROUTE 1 🚲

Distance: 19-20 miles (13-14 miles return by train)
Start/end: Pier Head/Pier Head or Waterloo Station
Key features: This ride goes from Pier Head in Liverpool to Crosby, ending alongside the famous *Another Place* statues at Crosby beach. It follows the Leeds & Liverpool Canal for part of the way. The return journey can then be made by retracing the route or taking the train. The terrain is generally flat and along tarmac or well-graded paths, although the coastal path is sometimes affected by deep drifts of windblown sand.

Lancashire Borough Council are an excellent source of information on routes in this area (www.sefton.gov.uk). The description for Walk #1 gives more details on the section from Waterloo Station to Crosby Beach.

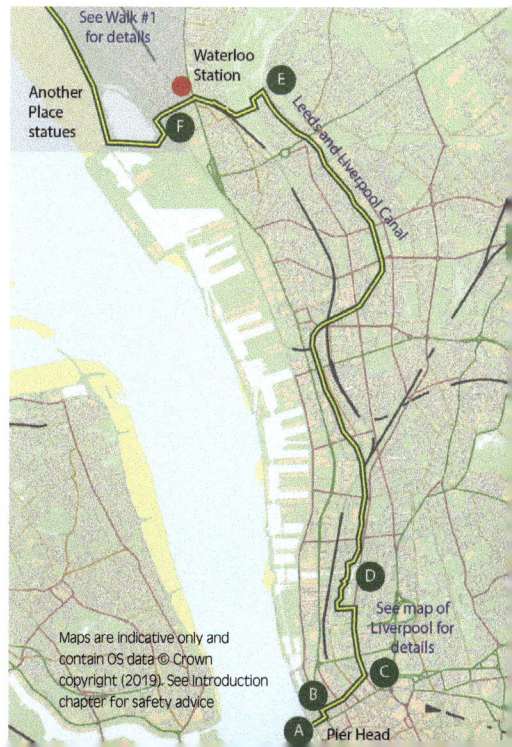

Maps are indicative only and contain OS data © Crown copyright (2019). See Introduction chapter for safety advice

Liverpool waterfront

The waterfront in Liverpool extends for several miles along the Mersey and its focal point is the **Three Graces** at Pier Head: three grand buildings that were once the headquarters for the Mersey Docks and Harbour Board, the Cunard Steamship Company and the Royal Liver Friendly Society. The tallest of the three is the Royal Liver Building where the clock faces are almost a metre wider than the clock at London's Big Ben. Its towers are topped by the famous Liver Bird statues, possibly representing a cormorant or eagle, although there are several other contenders (see Chapter 6, Wildlife).

The Three Graces are now used mainly for office accommodation and may only be visited on guided tours as described in **Walk #2**. Since 2017 the Cunard building has housed the **British Music Experience**, which is located in what was once the first-class lounge for transatlantic steamship passengers and is dedicated to the history of British popular music. Visitors can see costumes, instruments and memorabilia

from famous artists, and try out guitars, keyboards and drum kits.

In front of the Three Graces is the main terminal for the Mersey Ferries. In addition to providing a commuter service to Woodside and Seacombe on the Wirral, longer River Explorer Cruises are one of the most popular tourist attractions in the region. The ferries were immortalised

THE RIVER MERSEY
The River Mersey is the lifeblood of Liverpool, shaping not just the waterfront contours but the very soul of the city. It stretches for 70 miles from Stockport to Liverpool Bay and for centuries marked the boundary between the historic counties of Lancashire and Cheshire. It gave its name to Merseybeat, the sound of Liverpool bands in the 1960s, and the hit single 'Ferry Cross the Mersey' by Gerry and the Pacemakers. *From the website of the Liverpool Echo (www.liverpoolecho.co.uk).*

The Liver Birds ▶

Liverpool waterfront viewed from New Brighton, with from left to right the Three Graces, Liverpool Cruise Terminal, the Museum of Liverpool and Albert Dock ▼

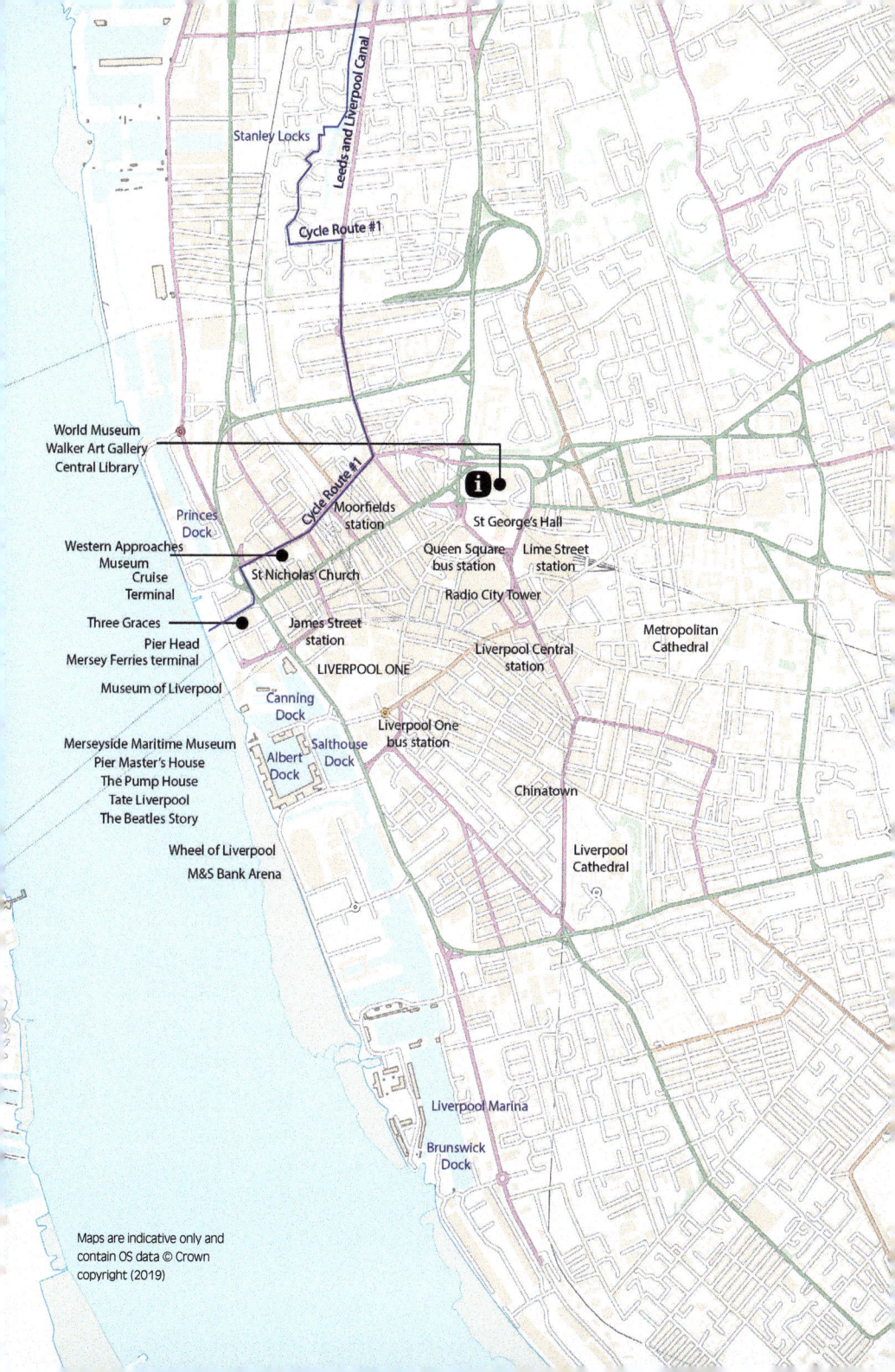

Stanley Locks

Leeds and Liverpool Canal

Cycle Route #1

World Museum
Walker Art Gallery
Central Library

Cycle Route #1

Moorfields
station

Princes
Dock

St George's Hall

Western Approaches
Museum
Cruise
Terminal

Queen Square
bus station

Lime Street
station

St Nicholas Church

Radio City Tower

Three Graces

James Street
station

Liverpool Central
station

Metropolitan
Cathedral

Pier Head
Mersey Ferries terminal

Museum of Liverpool

LIVERPOOL ONE

Canning
Dock

Liverpool One
bus station

Merseyside Maritime Museum
Pier Master's House
The Pump House
Tate Liverpool
The Beatles Story

Salthouse
Albert   Dock
Dock

Chinatown

Liverpool
Cathedral

Wheel of Liverpool
M&S Bank Arena

Liverpool Marina

Brunswick
Dock

Maps are indicative only and
contain OS data © Crown
copyright (2019)

by the 1965 hit single 'Ferry Cross the Mersey' by Gerry and the Pacemakers and this is played on departure, followed by an entertaining commentary on the main sights. On some days in the main tourist season, there are evening cruises on the Mersey and trips to Salford along the Manchester Ship Canal.

All three terminals have attractions in their own right. At Pier Head there is a Beatles-themed store and café (www.beatlesstory.com), plus a new (for 2019) exhibit at Seacombe and a U-boat exhibit at Woodside. The café at Woodside and Matou restaurant at Pier Head are fine viewpoints for the estuary.

Pier Head is often busy with festivals and music events. In the summer, the Pier Head Village festival takes over the waterfront with street food, live music, and fairground rides, while in the winter months there is an ice festival with a skating rink, ice slide and market stalls. In summer, the River Festival Liverpool is one of the highlights of the year. The

Introduction to this guide and the Visit Liverpool website give information on other festivals in the city.

Another must-see sight at Pier Head is the **Museum of Liverpool**, a distinctive addition to the skyline since it was opened in 2011. The museum is dedicated to the cultural, industrial and natural history of the city, including the Beatles and its two famous football clubs. Maritime-themed exhibits include displays on the Port of Liverpool and the overhead railway that once ran the length of the docks. There are great views of the waterfront and the Three Graces from its panoramic windows. Further information on the museum and its exhibition programme is available at www.liverpoolmusems.org/mol.

To the south, the docks extend a mile or so to the entrance to Liverpool Marina. **Albert Dock**, renamed Royal Albert Dock Liverpool in 2018, is perhaps the most famous and since redevelopment in the 1980s has become a major tourist attraction. The main branch of the Beatles Story

These larger-than-life statues at Pier Head are just one of the many links to the Beatles around Liverpool; others include Penny Lane, the Cavern Club on Mathew Street and the Beatles Story exhibition at Albert Dock ▶

GUIDED TOURS IN LIVERPOOL
Liverpool has an excellent network of qualified tour guides. There are over 100 blue badge, green badge and official Beatles tour guides, who offer a wide range of services from individual walking tours to large coach tours. There is a huge selection of special interest tours on offer too, including photography, architecture, ghost tours and pub tours. *From the Visit Liverpool website (www.visitliverpool.com).*

exhibition is here, as is **Tate Liverpool**, which is dedicated to British and international art (www.tate.org.uk). The former warehouses also contain offices, hotels, bars and restaurants. A lively programme of events includes the month-long Summer on the Dock festival, with film, sports, health and wellbeing activities, and a food and drink festival (www.albertdock.com).

Merseyside Maritime Museum

Another attraction at the dock is the **Merseyside Maritime Museum** where there are displays on the history of the port and landmark events such as the Battle of the Atlantic and the sinking of the Titanic, which was registered in Liverpool.

Tucked away in the basement are mock-ups of a street in the port in Victorian times and the sleeping quarters on an emigrant ship, both complete with sound effects. The Seized! gallery, dedicated to the work of the Border Force, includes interesting examples of contraband seized. Throughout the building there are many

The remains of the Old Dock are reached down a flight of stairs beneath the Liverpool ONE retail and shopping complex (www.liverpool-one.com); the yellow-red sandstone bedrock underlies much of the city ▶

Sailing ships berthed alongside Merseyside Maritime Museum ▼

scale models on display, ranging from the days of sail to modern-day container vessels and support ships. This includes several examples of vessels built at the Cammell Laird shipyard, whose huge buildings are a distinctive feature on the opposite shoreline.

Here also is the **International Slavery Museum**, which describes the history of the slave trade in Liverpool as well as topical issues related to slavery around the world. Exhibits include an audio-visual display with insights into the horrors of the transatlantic trade and a full-size replica of a family compound from an African village.

At the quays and dry docks nearby, several restored vessels are on display, including a 1960s tug, *Brocklebank*, and a 1950s pilot cutter, *Edmund Gardner*, and are sometimes open to the public. Across the entrance to Royal Albert Dock is the former **Piermaster's House**. Built in 1852, it has been restored to illustrate the way of life in Liverpool during World War 2.

On some weekdays museum staff lead informative and entertaining tours to the nearby remains of the first dock in

The Mersey Ferries' Royal Iris of the Mersey approaching Pier Head

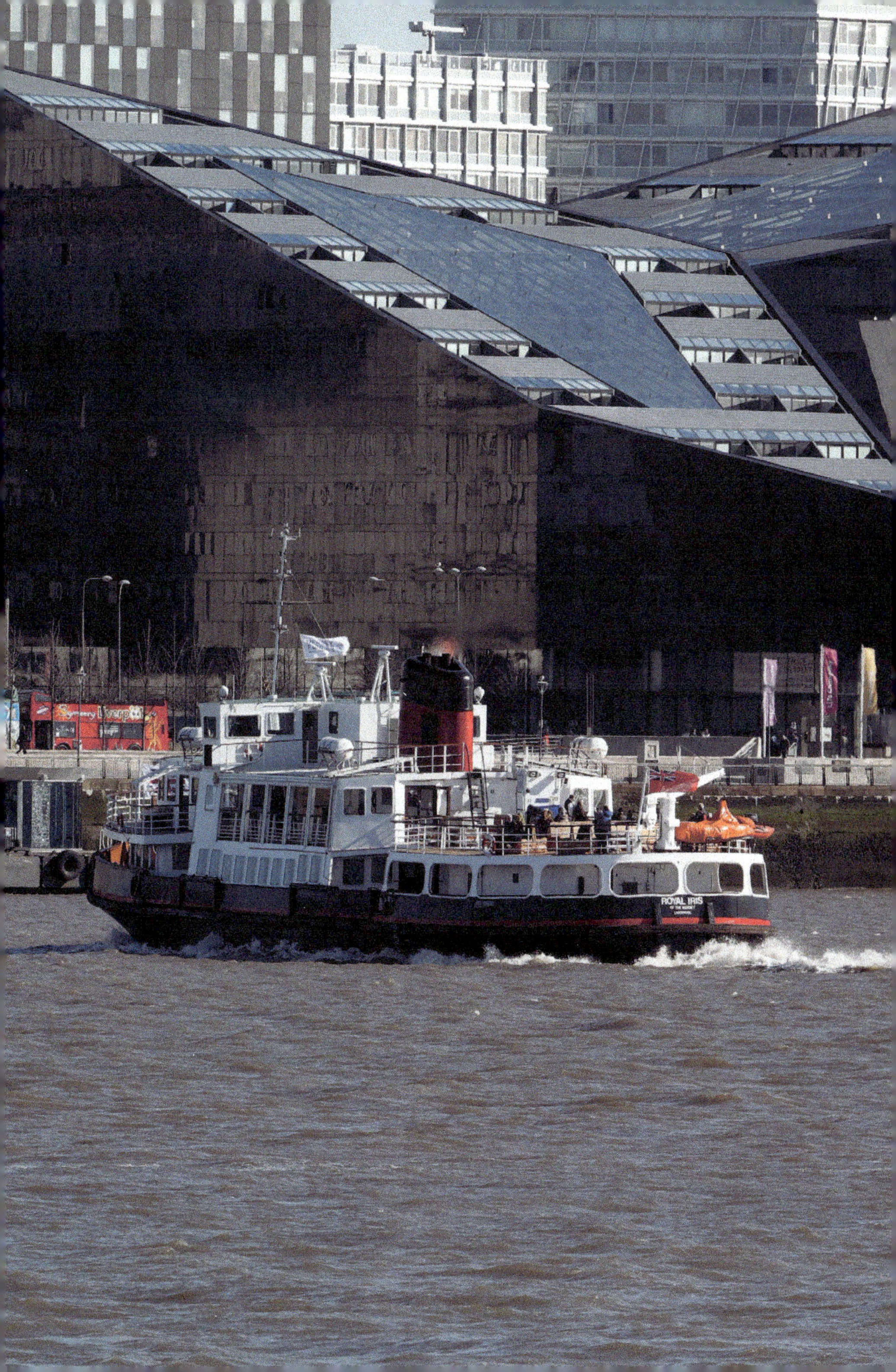
ROYAL IRIS

the port, the Old Dock. Built in 1715, it was constructed in a tidal inlet known as the Pool, from which Liverpool's name probably derives. It had the distinction of being the first commercial wet dock in the country, allowing water levels to be controlled so that ships could be loaded and unloaded while sheltered from the tides. See Chapter 5, Maritime Connections, for more information on the history of the port and these fascinating tours.

The tours of the Old Dock are just one of the guided walks available in this area. See **Walk #2** for more suggestions. Another great way to see the southern part of the docks is by boat, on board the *Skylark* motor vessel, or *The Floating Grace*, a restaurant and bar. Both depart from Salthouse Quay and often include a brief tour of Albert Dock. Check the operators' websites and signs at the quay for departure dates and times (www.floatinggrace.co.uk). Other attractions nearby include the Wheel of Liverpool for views of the city and M&S Bank Arena Liverpool for shows and sports events.

Merseyside Maritime Museum and the Museum of Liverpool are just two of those managed by National Museums Liverpool (www.liverpoolmuseums.org.uk). Others include the World Museum and Walker Art Gallery in the Cultural Quarter, described later in this chapter; Sudley House, a restored Victorian merchant's mansion in the city; and Lady Lever Art Gallery, home to one of the finest art collections in the country (see Chapter 2). All have gift shops and cafés, which provide valuable additional income, and the restaurant at the Maritime Museum has particularly fine views of the waterfront. Entrance is normally free but donations to help with running the sites are always welcome.

Upper: The Three Graces from the top-floor restaurant at Merseyside Maritime Museum; the multi-coloured vessel in the foreground is the *Edmund Gardner*, a cutter once operated by Liverpool Pilotage Service that is sometimes open to the public / **Lower:** A builder's model from 1910 at Merseyside Maritime Museum that was subsequently configured to represent the *Titanic* ▼

Liverpool Waterfront

Guided tours

On Liverpool's UNESCO World Heritage Waterfront, there are various guided walks and tours on offer and the *Three Graces and Waterfront* tours in particular give some great insights into the history of the port.

These tours begin at the Pier Head and on weekdays normally include a visit to the Three Graces, including the Cunard Building, which is usually closed to the public. See www.liverpoolcitywalks.com for tour dates. The Royal Liver Building 360 tours include a trip up one of the clock towers, plus a digital show on the history of the building and city; pre-booking is essential (www.rlb360.com). RIBA North also organises walking tours to points of architectural interest in the city (www.architecture.com/liverpoolcitytours).

Another option is to take a tour of one of the two road tunnels beneath the Mersey (www.merseytunnels.co.uk). These tours start from the George's Dock building behind the Three Graces, its distinctive art deco tower housing a ventilation shaft for the tunnel. Tourist offices can provide details on these and other guided walks, and nearby are pick-up and drop-off points for bus tours (see the Visit Liverpool website for operators).

The Royal Liver Building viewed from Princes Dock ▶

Liverpool Marina from near the entrance lock to Brunswick Dock ▼

WALK 2 👣👣

Distance: Various options up to 4-5 miles
Start/end: Pier Head
Key features: This page suggests several ideas for guided tours and self-guided trips along Liverpool Waterfront.

Self-guided walks

If exploring on your own, a popular approach is to visit Pier Head and Albert Dock and take a trip on the Mersey Ferry. For an easy self-guided walk from Albert Dock, follow the promenade southwards to Liverpool Marina about 1.5 miles away or Liverpool Festival Gardens, another mile or so beyond. Either walk back or take the train from Brunswick or St Michaels station, both of which are a short distance from the waterfront. The Merseyrail website (www.merseytravel.gov.uk) gives train times and local maps for the stations; Cycle Route #2 has a more detailed description of this trip.

Heading in the other direction from Pier Head, the promenade extends northwards for about a half mile to the end of Princes Dock, a great way to have a closer look at any cruise ships in port. Making the return trip around the far side of the dock takes in some interesting views of the Three Graces and waterfront.

The northern part of Albert Dock, including the Tate Gallery (left) and Merseyside Maritime Museum (right)

The City of Liverpool

Liverpool is one of the world's great cities and beyond the waterfront there is much to see, including museums, art galleries, restaurants and shopping centres. In 2004 it was designated a World Heritage site by UNESCO, thereby joining other locations that have received this honour, such as the Taj Mahal in India and the Great Wall of China (www.whc.unesco.org).

Some of the grandest buildings are in the Cultural Quarter, part of St George's Quarter near Liverpool Lime Street Station. Here the Victorian architecture includes the Walker Art Gallery – part of National Museums Liverpool – and the magnificent Central Library, in recent years restored to include a glass-domed roof and rooftop viewing area. The Royal Court, Empire and Playhouse theatres are nearby.

This cluster of buildings includes the **World Museum**, a chance to learn about the history of our planet. In addition to an aquarium and a planetarium, the museum has several fascinating exhibits with a maritime theme, such as examples of the marine chronometers for which the region was famous and the astronomical regulator clock that once provided the time standard for the port. Perhaps also visit the bug house with its live insects, and the space technology exhibition. Also of interest are displays on the historical and cultural ties between Liverpool and the rest of the world. Further information on the museum and its imaginative programme of exhibitions and events is available at www.liverpoolmuseums.org/wml.

Perhaps the most impressive building of all is **St George's Hall**, which once housed the city's civil and crown courts and nowadays hosts an active programme of concerts, talks and exhibitions. Inside is the Heritage Centre from where visitors can take a guided tour to the former prison cells, courtrooms

▲ Liverpool's Chinatown was the first in Europe and the Chinese New Year celebrations are a highlight of the festival calendar in the city

▲ Looking along Mathew Street towards the Cavern Club where the Beatles once performed

and the magnificent Great Hall. See www.
stgeorgeshallliverpool.co.uk for tour dates and
opening times for the centre and café.

Elsewhere in the city, and closer to the
waterfront, is the **Western Approaches
Museum**, a bomb- and gas-proof labyrinth of
rooms beneath the city's streets that housed the
Western Approaches Command during World
War 2. Many of the original features have been
preserved, including the large operations room
where convoy routes and enemy locations were
plotted, and many examples of technology from
the 1940s, such as teleprinters, radios and the
telephone hotline to the War Cabinet in London.

The museum also pays tribute to the
sacrifices made during the Battle of the Atlantic
and explores the wartime damage in the city,
which was a prime target due to the role of
the port in the convoys. The self-guided tour
includes a surprise near the end: a mock-up of
a wartime street including a grocer's store and
sweet shop with examples of products from
that era (www.liverpoolwarmuseum.co.uk).

The Western Approaches Museum and
the Cultural Quarter are of course just a few
of the city's attractions and the Visit Liverpool
website (www.visitliverpool.com) provides more
information. The next section also discusses ways
of seeing the city from above, including from the
tower at the Anglican Cathedral.

To travel between the main sights, hop-on
hop-off bus services operate between Albert
Dock, Pier Head, the Cultural Quarter and
the two cathedrals. If travelling by train, the
closest railway stations are Lime Street for the
Cultural Quarter, Moorfields for the Western
Approaches Museum, and James Street for Pier
Head – all part of the efficient underground
system in the city (www.merseyrail.org). There
is a tourist information desk at Liverpool
Central Library.

▲ **Upper to Lower:** St George's Hall /
Mock-up of a 1940s street at the Western
Approaches Museum / Entrance to the
World Museum

A bird's eye view of the city

A great way to appreciate the sights of the city is from above and there are several ways to do this.

In the city centre, the viewing gallery close to the top of **Radio City Tower** – also known as St John's Beacon – provides panoramic views for miles around on a clear day and stands nearly 140 metres tall (www.stjohnsbeacon.co.uk).

Further south, **Liverpool Cathedral** is the largest Anglican cathedral in Europe and the fifth largest in the world. As well as a place of worship, it is a popular tourist destination. Reached via two lifts and 108 stairs, the 101m-high tower is open to the public and there are spectacular views from the top. A short film shown before setting off describes the history of the cathedral. On the way down, it is worth stopping at the Embroidery Gallery to see the exhibits and appreciate the huge scale of the building.

Twilight tours of the tower give views of the sunset over the city, while occasional 'bell nights' offer visitors the chance to meet the bell-ringers and try a bell simulator. Other highlights include the beautiful Holy Spirit and Lady chapel, the UK's largest organ, and a wide-ranging collection of paintings and sculptures. For visitors, there is a shop, café and restaurant, and the building is open

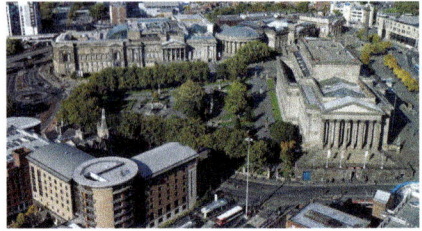

▲ St George's Hall, the World Museum, Central Library and the Walker Art Gallery from Radio City Tower

during normal working hours although with some restrictions on Sundays. Twilight tours are held on Thursdays during the main tourist season. See www.liverpoolcathedral.org.uk for dates and details.

Two other ways to see the city from on high are to visit the **Panoramic 34** restaurant, and the **Wheel of Liverpool**, alongside M&S Bank Arena Liverpool. Panoramic 34 is one of the tallest buildings in the city and again provides superb all-round views, with bar snacks and afternoon tea on offer, as well as meals. Always popular, it is advisable to book ahead (www.panoramic34.com). The closest railway station is Moorfields.

Around the waterfront, other places to dine with a view include the restaurants at the Merseyside Maritime Museum and Mersey Ferries terminal (see earlier).

A WORLD HERITAGE SITE

Six areas in the historic centre and docklands of Liverpool bear witness to the development of one of the world's major trading centres in the 18th, 19th and early 20th centuries. A series of significant commercial, civic and public buildings lie within these areas, including the Pier Head, with its three principal waterfront buildings – the Royal Liver Building, the Cunard Building, and Port of Liverpool Building; the dock area with its warehouses, dock walls, remnant canal system, docks and other facilities related to port activities; the mercantile area, with its shipping offices, produce exchanges, marine insurance offices, banks, inland warehouses and merchants houses, together with the William Brown Street Cultural Quarter, including St. George's Plateau, with its monumental cultural and civic buildings.

An extract from the 'Brief Synthesis' for the UNESCO World Heritage site Liverpool – Maritime Mercantile City (www.whc.unesco.org)

A twilight view looking north towards New Brighton from Liverpool Cathedral, including Radio City Tower

There are in fact two cathedrals in Liverpool. Viewed here from the opposite shores of the Mersey, they are the Anglican Cathedral (right) and the Metropolitan Cathedral (left) ▼

Interior of Liverpool Cathedral

Looking towards Liverpool Cathedral, the Mersey and the south of the city from Radio City Tower ▼

Liverpool to the Runcorn Gap

Heading southwards from Pier Head, the promenade alongside the Mersey is popular with walkers, cyclists and joggers, and provides fine views across the estuary. **Cycle Route #2** gives directions.

In addition to Albert Dock, sights along the way include the yachts in Liverpool Marina, and **Liverpool Festival Gardens**. The gardens were created for the 1984 Liverpool International Garden Festival, which attracted more than three million visitors, some arriving on a ferry service from Pier Head laid on for the event. The site has now been restored and highlights include woodland walks, lakes, a waterfall, a Chinese pagoda and a Japanese garden (www.liverpool.gov.uk).

The gardens lie at the northern end of **Otterspool Promenade**, an attractive waterside walk often thronged with people on a warm summer's day. Until the late 1940s, the gap between the sea wall and shoreline was used as a landfill site, including material excavated during construction of one of the Mersey road tunnels. The area was then landscaped to create the walkways and green areas we see today. Further south is an adventure centre and the unusual Sitting Bull statue visited during Cycle Route #2.

The promenade ends at Grassendale Park, a leafy residential area of large Victorian houses. About three miles beyond by road, the next place with public access to the shoreline is the **Speke and Garston Coastal Reserve**, where grassland and reeds lie above low cliffs.

During autumn and winter, this can be a good place to see wading birds feeding on the mudflats below. See Chapter 6, Wildlife, for more information. The reserve lies about a mile from the A561 Speke Road close to

▲ Sign at Speke and Garston Coastal Reserve

the New Mersey retail park and is signposted from the major crossroads nearby.

Immediately to the south lies **Speke Hall**, an elegant 16th century timber-framed Tudor manor house owned by the National Trust. There are several waymarked trails through the ancient woodlands in the grounds, including a path along an embankment with expansive views across the Mersey. Visitors can go on guided tours of the hall and there is a restaurant, café and play area. Check the National Trust website for opening times and the varied programme of events, which includes temporary exhibitions, family activities, outdoor cinema and theatre perfomances, fun runs and much more (www.nationaltrust.org.uk).

The hall is less than a mile from the approach road to Liverpool John Lennon Airport and the next easily accessible waterside trails lie beyond, at **Hale Head**. As described in **Walk #3**, highlights in this area include a

The main entrance to Speke Hall ▶

lighthouse and a statue of one of the village's former residents who stood more than 9 feet tall, the so-called Hale Giant. The lighthouse was one of several in this part of the estuary, although only one other remains, at Ellesmere Port. See Chapter 5, Maritime Connections, to find out more about some of the navigation techniques used in that era.

The next opportunity to access the waterside is at **Pickerings Pasture Local Nature Reserve**, an area of woodland walks, meadows and waterside paths between Hale Head and Widnes. By road, this is less than half a mile from Hale Bank, while cyclists can also reach it via the Trans Pennine Trail: see **Cycle Route #5** for details. In spring and summer look out for wild flowers in the meadows, and during the winter the reserve can be an excellent place to see wading birds; it is also a viewpoint for the Mersey Tidal Bore.

A visitor centre is open on one Sunday each month and is run by the Friends of Pickerings Pasture, whose website has a wealth of information on local wildlife, including recent sightings (www.thefriendsofpickeringspasture. org.uk). A Facebook page ('Pickerings Pasture Café') gives opening times and the homemade food menu. See Chapter 6, Wildlife, for more information.

From Pickerings Pasture, the Trans Pennine Trail continues alongside the Mersey. On leaving the reserve, it climbs a low hill via a wooden staircase, with some particularly fine views of this part of the estuary. The trail then passes alongside industrial works and a former dock at Widnes to go beneath the Silver Jubilee Bridge at the Runcorn Gap. With a magnificent steel-arched structure, this is of a similar design to Australia's Sydney Harbour Bridge. The bridge also marks the start of the Upper Estuary whose sights are described in Chapter 3.

▼ **Upper to Lower:** The Chinese pagoda at Liverpool Festival Gardens / The Mersey seen from Pickerings Pasture / Gables at Speke Hall

Sitting Bull

The round trip for this ride is about 9 to 10 miles and mainly along flat well-surfaced paths but with some short cobbled sections with steps to negotiate. The route takes its name from a most unusual sight towards the far end, a large fibreglass sculpture of a resting red bull looking out over the Mersey, created for the Liverpool International Garden Festival of 1984.

The starting point is the Mersey Ferries terminal at **Pier Head (A)**. Pass the Museum of Liverpool and dismount to cross the bridge over the entrance to Canning Dock. The promenade then passes Albert Dock, M&S Bank Arena Liverpool and the Liverpool Watersports Centre, detouring briefly inland around the Chung Ku restaurant, a popular spot to eat, with great waterside views.

About 1.5 miles from Pier Head is the entrance lock to **Brunswick Dock (B)**, a good place to see the boats in Liverpool Marina. Soon after, the promenade passes the Britannia Inn, which includes an outdoor dining area overlooking the estuary. **The Festival Gardens (C)** are a short way beyond and open to pedestrians only, so bikes need to be locked up securely and left outside. Follow the sign for St. Michael's Station. It is then about 2 miles to the **Sitting Bull statue (D)**, set back a short way from the waterfront. The play area and adventure park of Otterspool Adventure Centre is nearby, with an open-air terrace outside the café looking towards the Mersey. The end of the promenade is a short way beyond.

To return to Pier Head, either retrace the route or follow signs to **Aigburth Station**, about half a mile away, for trains back to the city centre. The closest stations to Pier Head are Moorfields and James Street, the latter reached by changing at Central Station (www.merseyrail.org).

To extend the route, once past the Festival Gardens make a detour about a mile inland to **Sefton Park (E)** along National Cycle Network Route 56. This is one of the largest and most scenic parks in Liverpool and has ornamental lakes, two cafés and the enclosed tropical gardens of the Palm House (www.liverpool.gov.uk). From there either return to the promenade or continue a further 3 to 4 miles to the junction

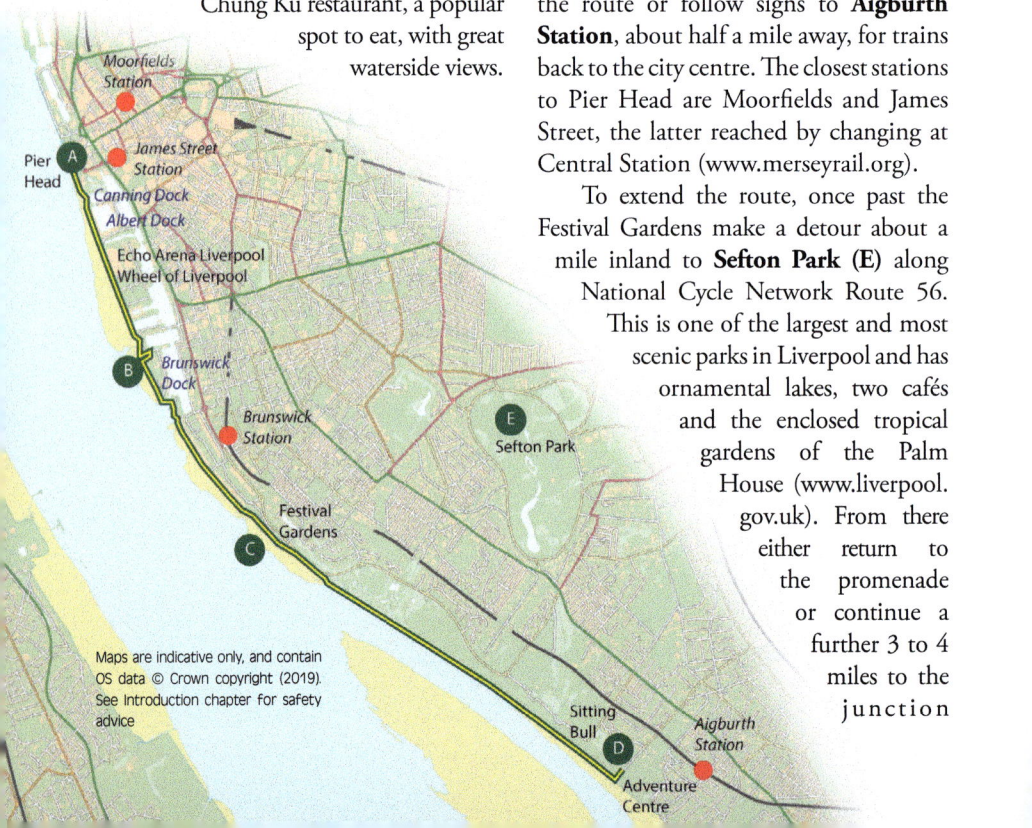

Moorfields Station

James Street Station

Pier Head

A

Canning Dock

Albert Dock

Echo Arena Liverpool
Wheel of Liverpool

B Brunswick Dock

Brunswick Station

E Sefton Park

Festival Gardens

C

Sitting Bull

D

Aigburth Station

Adventure Centre

▲ The Sitting Bull statue near Otterspool Promenade

CYCLE ROUTE 2 🚲

Distance: 9-10 miles (or 4-5 miles using the train)

Start/end: Pier Head/Pier Head or Aigburth station

Key features: This cycle ride heads southwards from Pier Head along the promenade, and features fine views of the Mersey, waterside dining, and the option for a walk around Liverpool Festival Gardens.

with the Trans Pennine Trail and follow this southwards for about three miles to Halewood for trains back to Liverpool via Liverpool South Parkway; however, be sure to check return train times before setting off.

Free maps showing the trail and national cycle route are available from the council's website (www.liverpool.gov.uk) and Cycle Route #5 describes the trail beyond Halewood as it passes through Widnes and Warrington.

▲ Two views of Otterspool Promenade with the Mersey at low tide ▼

Hale Head

A convenient place to start this walk is at the war memorial in the centre of Hale village, from where **Church End road (A)** leads towards the Mersey. En route, a life-size bronze statue commemorates John Middleton, the 'Childe of Hale', who is thought to have stood more than 9 feet tall. He was born in the village in 1578 and an information board outside the church of St Mary nearby describes his extraordinary life.

The road ends at a gate and a track then leads to low cliffs and the coastal path near the **lighthouse (B)**. This is now part of the Mersey Way, a long-distance walk from Warrington to south Liverpool that largely follows the Trans Pennine Trail between Hale and Warrington. Interpretation panels nearby describe the wildlife and maritime heritage in this part of the estuary

Heading left eastwards along the coastal path, next pass through a gate and around trees to arrive back at the cliffs and water's edge. The final estuary views are from another gate **(C)** about a mile beyond, where the path turns inland. The landscape here is more industrial with the chemical works on the opposite bank providing a stark contrast with the farmland on the northern shores.

The path soon reaches another gate and an interpretation panel nearby describes the history of Hale Ford. This ancient and highly dangerous point for crossing the Mersey fell into disuse in the 1800s due to the risks from the increasingly polluted water and completion of the railway bridge at the Runcorn Gap, which originally had a footbridge alongside. The Manchester Ship Canal was then built across the path of the ford in the 1890s, thereby preventing any further use of the crossing.

The path joins a wider track beyond the gate. Follow this straight on for about half a mile until it veers right towards farm buildings, instead continuing ahead along a narrower path. This leads to a side street – Within Way – that joins the outward route at a point close to the Hale Giant statue. From there it is a short walk back to the start.

For a longer walk, on reaching the lighthouse, turn right to follow the Mersey

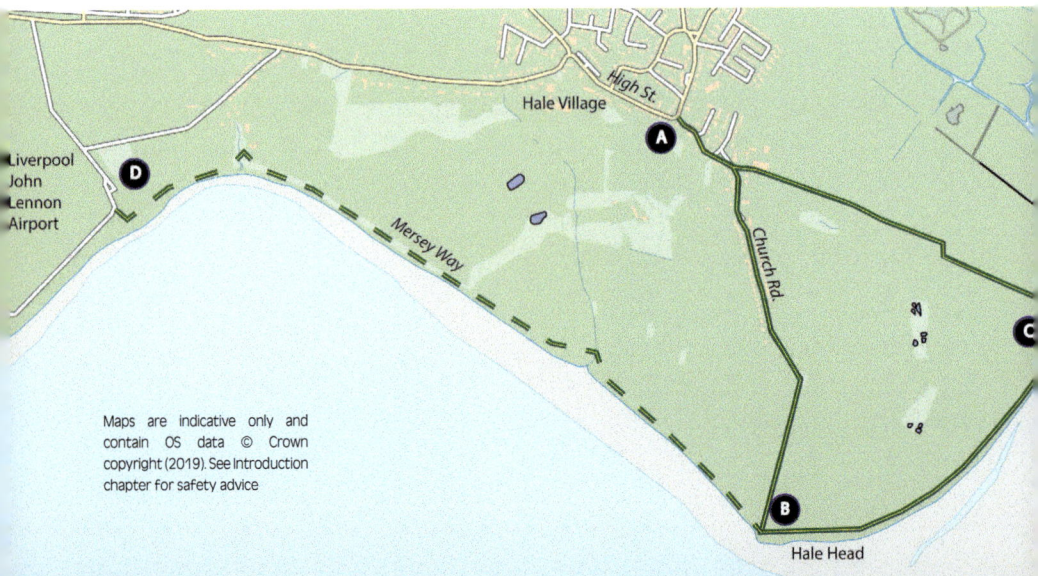

High St.

Hale Village

Liverpool John Lennon Airport

Mersey Way

Church Rd.

Hale Head

Maps are indicative only and contain OS data © Crown copyright (2019). See Introduction chapter for safety advice

▲ The statue of John Middleton in Hale

WALK 3

Distance: About 3 miles
Start/end: Hale village
Key features: The lighthouse at Hale Head is a distinctive landmark on the estuary shores, and the low sandstone cliffs nearby provide good views across the water to the hills beyond. This round trip from Hale village is about three miles long and mainly along pavements and flat, well-graded paths, although parts may be muddy at times. There are regular buses to Hale from Liverpool and Widnes (www.merseytravel.gov.uk).

Way in the opposite direction. The path initially continues alongside the cliffs and then passes through woods to emerge at a road near the boundary of Liverpool John Lennon Airport (**D**). From here retrace your steps to the lighthouse, either to continue with Walk #3 or return to the war memorial along the outward route. The additional distance for this detour from the lighthouse is about three miles.

▲ A sign for the Mersey Way

The lighthouse at Hale Head was completed in 1907 and remained in use until 1958, having replaced an earlier structure dating from 1838

ABOVE US, ONLY SKY

Liverpool John Lennon Airport lies on the banks of the Mersey and is one of the busiest in the country. Originally called Speke Aerodrome, it was renamed in 2001 in honour of John Lennon from the Beatles, with the great strapline 'Above us, only sky' taken from the lyrics of his song *Imagine*.

One of the first long-distance flights in the area was in 1909 by the barnstorming pilot Samuel Cody, who took off from Aintree Racecourse in an attempt to win a prize for the first flight from Liverpool to Manchester. He failed and it wasn't until two years later that Henry Melly gained that honour, starting from Waterloo Sands near Crosby, where he had recently established a flying school.

The first scheduled flights began from Aintree in the 1920s. A second airfield, Hooton Park near Ellesmere Port, then became the main airport in the region in the early 1930s (www. hootonparktrust.co.uk). In 1926 a flying boat service to Belfast was also briefly trialled on the Mersey, making use of a designated take-off and landing area extending across the water from Rock Ferry on the Wirral, near Birkenhead. However, later plans to develop a seaplane service from Speke never progressed.

The official opening of Speke Aerodrome was in 1933, and as RAF Speke it played an important role in World War 2. From the 1960s, operations were gradually transferred to the present site following construction of a new runway to the south, with the elegant terminal from the 1930s eventually replaced in 1986. The central part of the old terminal remains and now houses the Crowne Plaza hotel, a Grade II* listed building with an art deco restaurant. Outside, an unusual feature is a small collection of historic aircraft, under restoration by the Speke Aerodrome Heritage Group (www.spekeaero.org), which give a flavour of how the airport might have once been. Some of the original taxiways are still visible nearby, close to Speke and Garston Coastal Reserve.

From the modern-day terminal there are picturesque views of the estuary and hills beyond, but access is strictly for passengers. Another way to look around the airport is on the tours occasionally organised by the Friends of Liverpool Airport, which can be booked via the airport website (www. liverpoolairport.com). The airport is also a popular place to learn to fly, not least for its magnificent estuary setting. Flying school operators include Liverpool Flying School, Lomac Aviators, Merseyflight and Ravenair.

The former control tower of the old terminal at Speke ▼

An aircraft on final approach to Liverpool John Lennon Airport passing over the Mersey and Pickerings Pasture

The Royal Liver Building, Cunard Building and Mersey Ferries Terminal, seen at the start of the Clipper Round the World Yacht Race in 2017

Further reading

To learn more about the history, culture and sights around this part of the estuary, the following guides and reviews provide a fine introduction:

Albert Dock Liverpool: The Complete Guide, Ron Jones, (Liverpool History Press, 2013)

Both sides of the river: Merseyside in poetry and prose, Gladys Mary Coles (ed.), (Headland, 1993)

Discover Liverpool, Ken Pye, (Trinity Mirror Sport Media, 2008)

Liverpool: a history of the 'Great Port', Adrian Jarvis, (Liverpool History Press, 2014)

Liverpool: The First 1000 Years, Arabella McIntyre-Brown, Guy Woodland, (Garlic Press Publishing Ltd., 2001)

Liverpool World Heritage City, Ian Wray, John Hinchliffe, Rob Burns, edited by Peter de Figueiredo, (The Bluecoat Press, 2007)

Liverpool: The Story of a City, Museum of Liverpool, (Liverpool University Press, 2012)

Making the most of the Mersey: a leisure guide to your estuary, (Mersey Basin Campaign, 2007)

Mersey the river that changed the world, Ian Wray (ed.), photography by Colin McPherson, (The Bluecoat Press, 2007)

Merseyside Meanders: Country walks & town trails around Wirral, Liverpool and Southport, Michael Smout, (Sigma Leisure, 2002)

River Mersey from source to sea, Phil Page and Ian Littlechilds, (Amberley Publishing, 2014)

Riverside rambles along the Mersey, Ron Freethy, (Sigma Leisure, 2004)

The Insiders' Guide to Liverpool, (Trinity Mirror Sport Media, 2010)

The River Mersey, Ron Freethy, (Terence Dalton Ltd., 1985)

The various websites of National Museums Liverpool (www.liverpoolmuseums.org. uk) also include much useful information including links to a series of information sheets published by the Maritime Archives and Library. Chapters 4 to 6 suggest sources of further reading on the environment, maritime heritage and wildlife of the region.

Ellesmere Port Lighthouse

chapter 2

LOWER ESTUARY
WIRRAL, CHESHIRE

The coastal resort of New Brighton lies at the mouth of the Mersey Estuary.

A waterside promenade heads south, with spectacular views of Liverpool's waterfront; nearby Bidston Hill and historic Birkenhead Priory are also great vantage points.

Destinations beyond include the garden village of Port Sunlight, Eastham Country Park and the National Waterways Museum at Ellesmere Port.

The estuary then widens, with expansive views from the sandstone hills above Frodsham and Helsby.

VISIT IDEAS

See the following chapters for more sights in Wirral and Cheshire on different themes:

Chapter 4 – Rivers and Tides

- Anderton Boat Lift, near Winsford
- Tide Stones, Frodsham
- Brotherton Park and Dibbinsdale Nature Reserve, Wirral

Chapter 5 – Maritime Connections

- Optical telegraph station, Wirral
- Mersey Flat barge, Ellesmere Port
- Lighthouse, Ellesmere Port

Chapter 6 – Wildlife

- Wirral Country Park
- Seal watching, Wirral
- Burton Mere Wetlands, Wirral
- Gowy Meadows Nature Reserve, near Chester
- Birdwatching, various locations

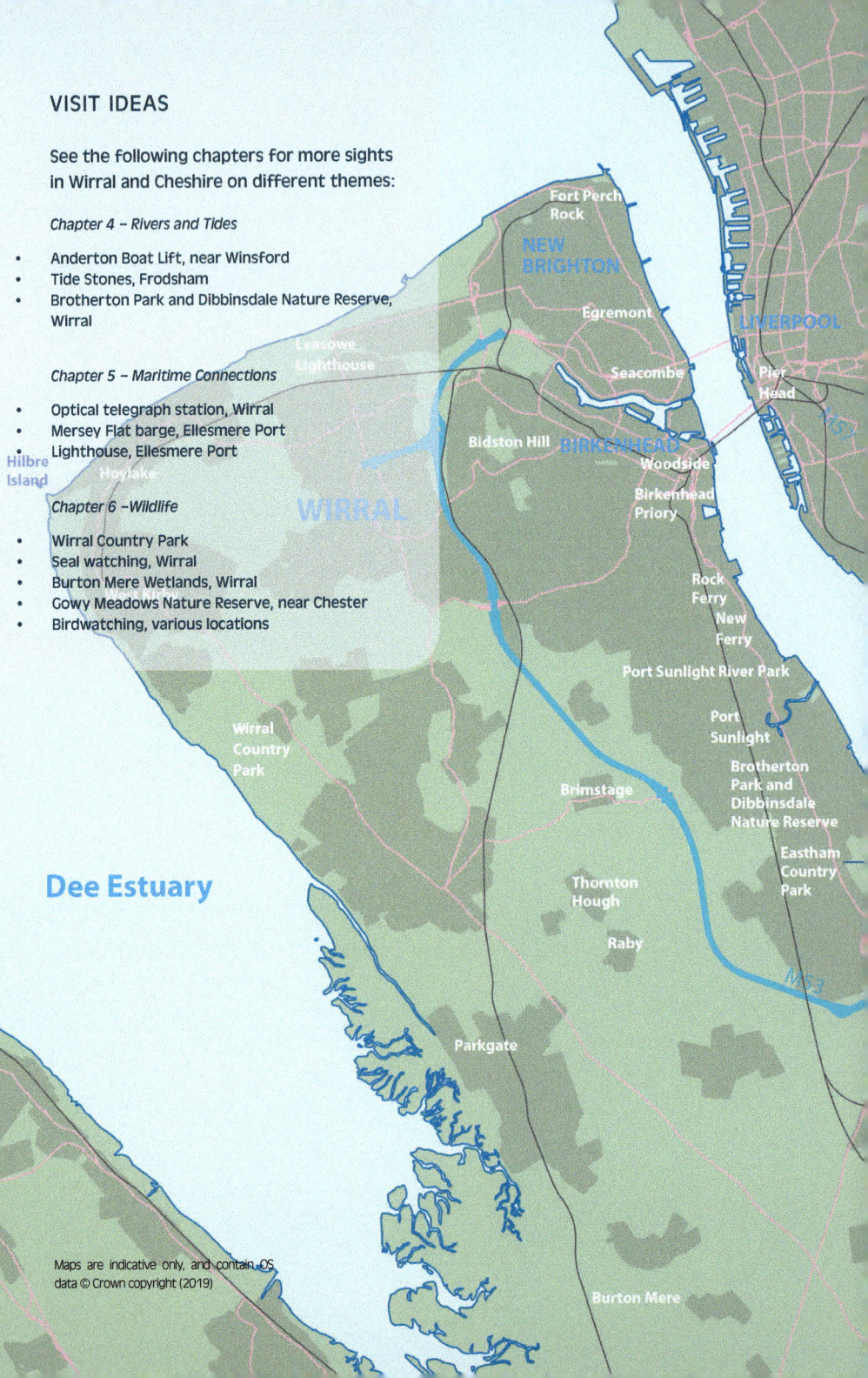

Fort Perch Rock

NEW BRIGHTON

Egremont

LIVERPOOL

Leasowe Lighthouse

Seacombe

Pier Head

Hilbre Island

Hoylake

Bidston Hill   BIRKENHEAD

Woodside

WIRRAL

Meols

Birkenhead Priory

Rock Ferry

New Ferry

Port Sunlight River Park

Port Sunlight

Wirral Country Park

Brimstage

Brotherton Park and Dibbinsdale Nature Reserve

Eastham Country Park

Dee Estuary

Thornton Hough

Raby

M53

Parkgate

Burton Mere

WIRRAL, CHESHIRE

The Mersey first reaches Liverpool Bay at New Brighton, where a lighthouse and fort are distinctive landmarks at the mouth of the estuary.

Heading upstream, a wide promenade leads to the Mersey Ferries' terminal at Seacombe with particularly fine views of the Liverpool waterfront. Further inland there are expansive views from Bidston Hill with the added interest of a lighthouse, observatory and windmill.

Beyond the docks, historic destinations in Birkenhead include Hamilton Square and Birkenhead Priory, while to the south the garden village of Port Sunlight is a popular tourist destination. Along the shores of the Mersey there are waterside walks at Eastham Country Park and Port Sunlight River Park.

In Ellesmere Port, the National Waterways Museum gives insights into the history of the region's canals, including the Manchester Ship Canal, which passes nearby. Perhaps the best views of this part of the estuary are from the tree-lined hills to the south, along the Sandstone Trail from Frodsham.

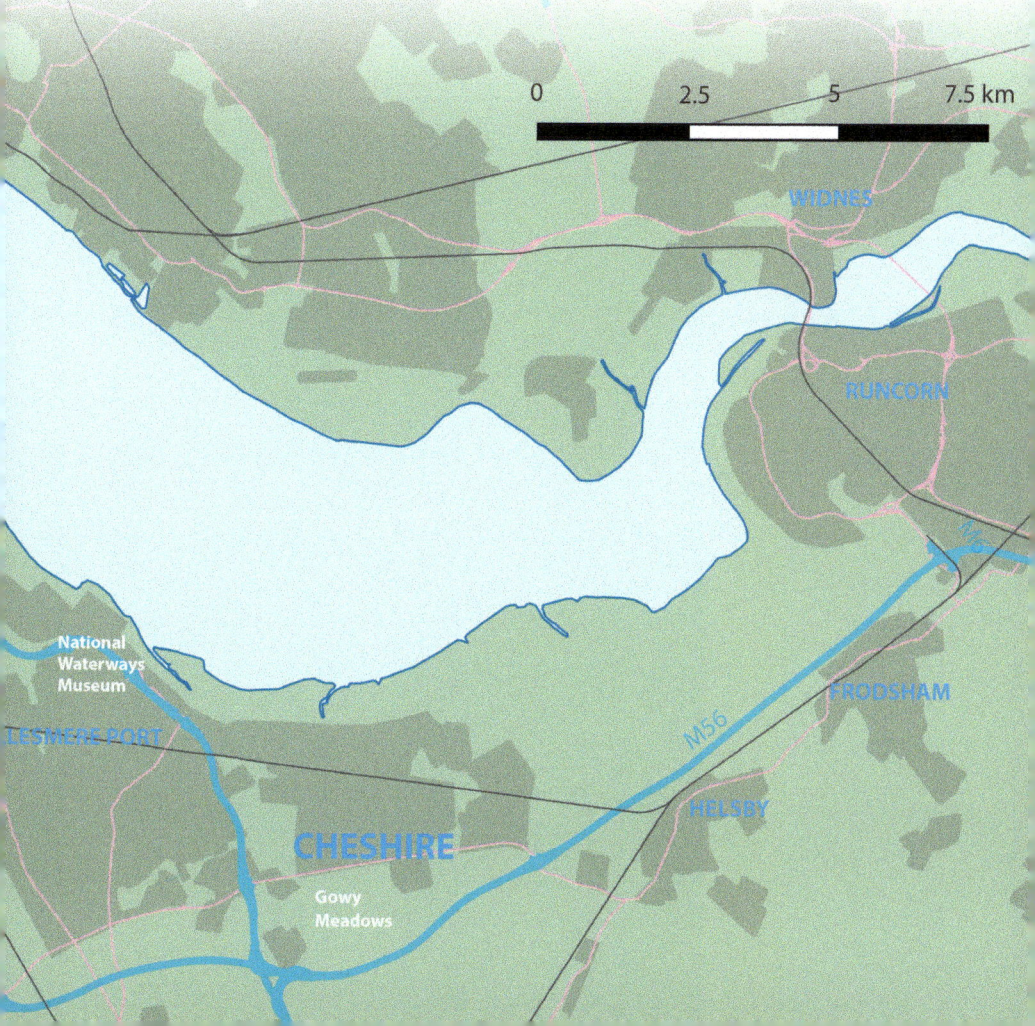

0   2.5   5   7.5 km

WIDNES

RUNCORN

National
Waterways
Museum

FRODSHAM

M56

ELLESMERE PORT

HELSBY

CHESHIRE

Gowy
Meadows

New Brighton to Seacombe

New Brighton is a traditional seaside resort with amusement arcades, ice-cream parlours, a marine lake and a funfair. The coastal promenades are popular with walkers and cyclists, and it's a great place to take in the sea air and watch the ships go by.

At the mouth of the estuary, **Fort Perch Rock** is a notable landmark. Built in the 1820s to help defend the Port of Liverpool, it was finally decommissioned in 1957. It is open at weekends and on school holidays and bank holidays (www.fortperchrock.org). Visitors can see several maritime and aviation exhibits, such as a mock-up of the radio signalling room on the Titanic, and examples of valve-driven maritime communications equipment, reminders of life in the days before satellites and computers. The rooftop walkways are a good vantage point for the mouth of the estuary, including the much-photographed **New Brighton Lighthouse**, once important for navigation around the estuary and operated until the 1970s; Chapter 5, Maritime Connections, gives more details.

> **A FLAVOUR OF WIRRAL**
> Set between the rivers Dee and Mersey and extending into Liverpool Bay and the Irish Sea, Wirral is blessed with stunning natural splendour and a rich heritage. From refined golf courses to wild and unspoilt coastline, it is a uniquely charming part of the world with plenty for the visitor to discover.
> *From Wirral: the Official Visitor Guide for 2016/17 (www.visitwirral.com)*

The popularity of the town as a resort dates from Victorian times. There was once a tower here, taller than Blackpool Tower, and a ballroom that drew acts as famous as the Beatles and the Rolling Stones. The **New Brighton Heritage & Information Centre** near the railway station includes an interesting exhibition on the history of the area as well as being a useful source of tourist information. Check the Visit Wirral website for opening hours (www.visitwirral.com).

The lighthouse at New Brighton on a stormy day ▼

▲ The fort viewed across the sands

◄ The entrance to Fort Perch Rock

Other attractions in the town include the marine lake and the restaurants and cinema at nearby Marine Point (www.marinepoint.co.uk). The Panoramic Lounge in the Floral Pavilion theatre is a fine place to take in the sea views while eating before a show (www.floralpavilion.com). During the winter, wading birds congregate along the coastline, and Chapter 6, Wildlife, suggests some viewing locations.

Heading upstream from New Brighton, a waterside promenade extends as far as the entrance to Birkenhead Docks. The unusual name of the first section, **Magazines Promenade**, dates from the 18th century when underground chambers were used to store gunpowder, which for safety would be dropped off or collected by ships using the port. Highlights here include **Vale Park**, with its bandstand and community-run café, and the *Black Pearl* art installation at the shoreline, built from driftwood to resemble a pirate ship.

▲ The bandstand at Vale Park, a popular venue for brass band and folk concerts (www.valehousecafe.co.uk)

▼ The *Black Pearl* art installation with Liverpool and Birkenhead in the distance

Continuing towards Birkenhead, a short platform jutting out from the shore is all that remains of Egremont Pier, a former stopping point for ferries on the Mersey. The Ferry pub nearby dates from that time and is a popular place to eat, with panoramic views of the estuary from the first floor restaurant. Not far beyond are two distinctive landmarks visible for miles around: **Wallasey Town Hall** and a block-shaped tower, one of six ventilation shafts for the two road tunnels beneath the Mersey. A grand flight of steps descends to the promenade from the town hall, although the main entrance on the other side of the building is a more modest affair.

From the town hall it is just a short walk to the ferry terminal at Seacombe in Wallasey where, in addition to a café, there is a new (for 2019) attraction; see www.merseyferries. co.uk for details. The promenade ends at a tree-lined area next to the entrance lock to

> **WIRRAL PENINSULA**
> Within a mere 20-minute train ride from Liverpool city centre you can be strolling on clean sandy beaches, breathing in the sea air and savouring distant views of the Welsh coast and mountains with only the screaming gulls for company.
> *From Making the most of the Mersey: a leisure guide to your estuary, Mersey Basin Campaign*

Birkenhead Docks for some of the finest views of the waterfront in Liverpool.

The descriptions for **Walk #4** and **Cycle Route #3** suggest ideas for excursions in this part of the estuary, including exploring the north Wirral coastline. **Bidston Hill** is also well worth a visit, with its urban farm, lighthouse and windmill as described in **Walk #5**.

▼ The Mersey Ferries' *Royal Iris of the Mersey* passing Wallasey Town Hall

THE WIRRAL BEYOND THE MERSEY

The Wirral Peninsula lies between the Mersey and Dee estuaries and has many visitor attractions.

On the western side, these include the picturesque village of Parkgate, the marine lake at West Kirby, Ness Botanic Gardens, Burton Mere Wetlands and Wirral Country Park. More generally, from autumn to spring the Dee Estuary is one of the finest birdwatching locations in the country due to the huge numbers of geese and wading birds that feed on the mudflats exposed at low tide.

Destinations inland include Brimstage Hall and Courtyard and the historic villages of Raby and Thornton Hough. Close to the village of Oxton, the Williamson Art Gallery & Museum houses internationally important paintings, ceramics and sculptures, with more than thirty exhibitions held a year. There is also a café and a shop selling craftwork from local artists (www.williamsonartgallery.org).

▲ Little Eye at low tide: the smallest of the Hilbre Islands. The Point of Ayr lighthouse at Talacre in north Wales is just visible, on the opposite side of the Dee Estuary

On the northern shores a coastal walk extends from New Brighton to Hoylake, passing through North Wirral Coastal Park. At low tide it is possible to walk to Hilbre Island from West Kirby, although due to the risks from the tides and quicksand be sure to read the warning signs at the marine lake first and the safety advice on the Friends of Hilbre website (www.deeestuary.co.uk).

For more information on these and other destinations, Wirral Council publishes an excellent visitor guide and a range of walking, cycling and nature guides (www.visitwirral.com). See Chapter 6, Wildlife, for more information on visiting Hilbre Island, and seal watching opportunities in the Dee Estuary.

▼ Sailing dinghies on the marine lake at West Kirby

Three landmarks in New Brighton viewed from offshore: the lighthouse, St James Church and the Dome of Home Catholic Church

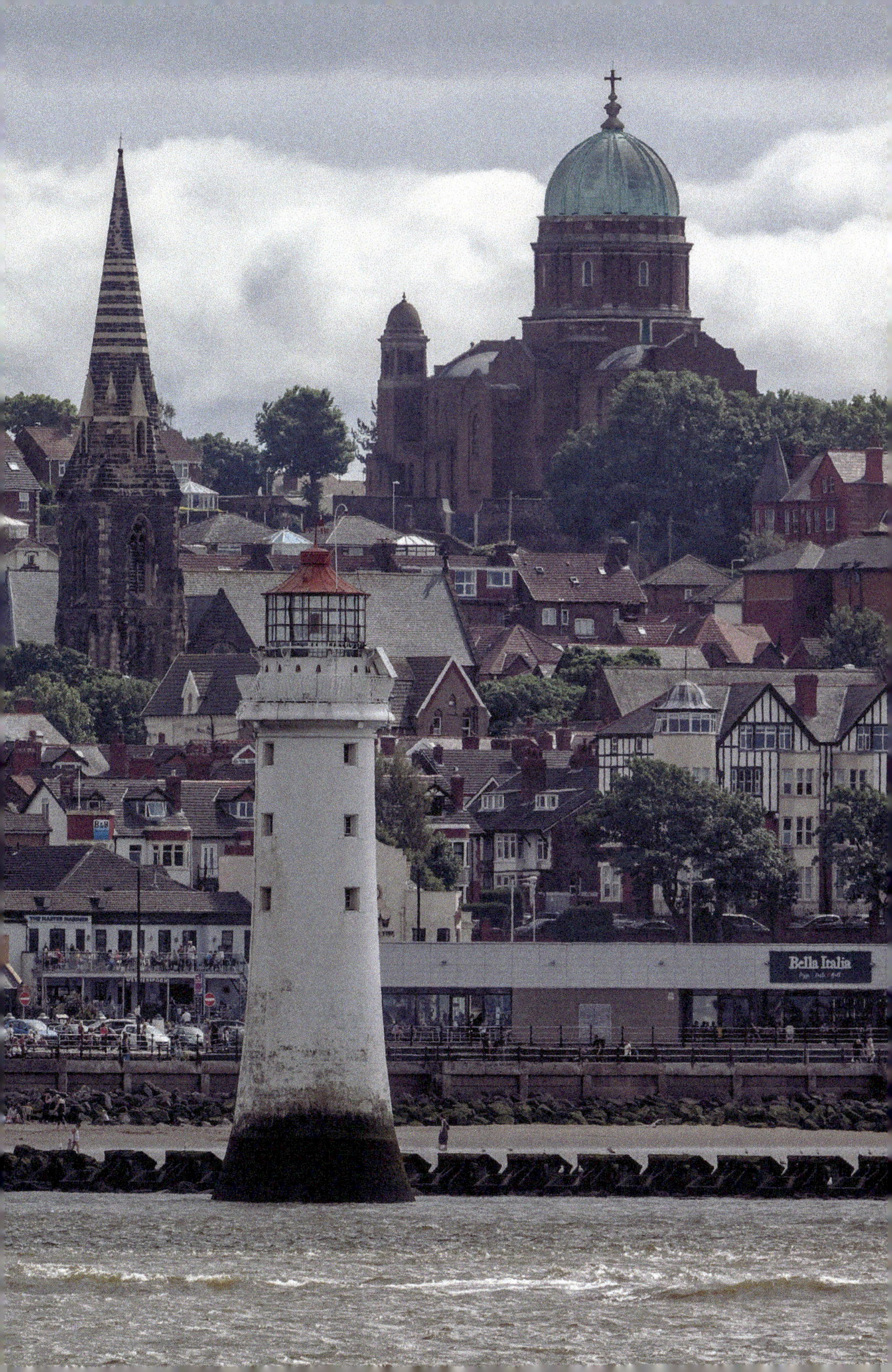
B&B
Bella Italia

New Brighton to Seacombe

This walk starts from the station in **New Brighton (A)**. On leaving the main entrance, head downhill and cross the coastal road at the traffic lights.

On reaching the waterside promenade, turn right to pass the shops, cinema and restaurants at **Marine Point (B)**, and continue past the marine lake to arrive at **Fort Perch Rock (C)**. The lighthouse is nearby and on the other shoreline are the huge red-painted cranes of Liverpool2, a deep-water container terminal opened in 2017. On a clear day, the northernmost point in the estuary at Formby Point about seven miles away is visible across the water as a long curving peninsula stretching out to sea.

From the fort follow the promenade the two miles or so to **Seacombe Ferry Terminal (D)**, on the way passing Vale Park, Wallasey Town

▲ Warning sign about the risks from the tides displayed on the promenade wall

Hall and the remains of Egremont Pier. For the best views of Liverpool, it is worth continuing to the end of the promenade – a round-trip of less than a mile – alongside the entrance to Birkenhead Docks. Attractions at the terminal itself include a café and exhibition.

Options for the return trip include walking back to the start or taking a bus from outside the terminal. However, if returning to Liverpool, perhaps the finest way of all is to return by ferry, having made the outward trip to New Brighton by train, although be sure to check ferry times before starting the walk (www.merseyferries.co.uk). In Liverpool, the closest station to Pier Head is James Street (www.merseyrail.org).

If taking the ferry, one way to extend the walk would be to disembark at Woodside Ferry Terminal at Birkenhead. The terminal houses an interactive exhibition, the U-boat Story, and has a café.

▲ A sign along the promenade: Guinea Gap Baths are at a leisure centre near the town hall

WALK 4

Distance: 3-4 miles
Start/end: New Brighton/Seacombe
Key features: The promenade south from New Brighton provides fine views of the estuary and Liverpool's waterfront. This walk begins in the town and ends at Seacombe Ferry Terminal, and is mainly on flat terrain. Highlights along the way include Fort Perch Rock, New Brighton Lighthouse, Vale Park and Wallasey Town Hall.

Cycle Route #3 describes the route from here to Birkenhead Priory. Other sights in the town include Birkenhead Park and Hamilton Square. In addition to the ferry, onward travel options from Woodside include buses to Liverpool and New Brighton from outside the terminal, and trains from Hamilton Square Station about a half mile away.

The waterfront in Liverpool seen from the promenade near New Brighton ▼

Bidston Hill

This walk starts from Bidston railway station (www.merseyrail.org) and is mainly along pavements and graded paths, although the unmade paths on the hill can be muddy and slippery, so suitable footwear is required.

On leaving the station (**A**), follow the approach road right to reach a dual carriageway. Cross over at the traffic lights and look for a sign for Cycleway 56. Follow this left along School Lane to **St Oswald's Church (B)** at a junction with a main road. Turn left and almost opposite Lennox Lane cross over to follow a wide public footpath that begins on the other side. This leads past houses to **Bidston Hall (C)**, where you should follow the boundary wall left onto a narrower path. Near the start, look out for a low marker post, which is the first of several on a heritage trail around the hill.

The path initially climbs between walls but soon emerges onto open ground, where a turn to the right leads along the crest of the hill. On reaching a walled compound, follow this right past **Bidston Lighthouse** and **Bidston Observatory (D)** to reach the hilltop. On a clear day, there are fine views towards Liverpool and Birkenhead, with even North Wales sometimes visible through gaps in the trees.

The observatory and lighthouse are now both privately owned, and had key roles in timekeeping and navigation respectively for the Port of Liverpool. Nearby stood a line of signalling masts, their role to alert ship owners

▲ **Upper to Lower:** Bidston Observatory / Bidston Lighthouse from where the views even extend to the mountains of Cumbria on a clear day

to approaching vessels. The rock cuttings that supported most of the masts are now hidden beneath gorse and brambles, although a drilled hole in the rock for one is a feature on the heritage trail. Chapter 4, Rivers and Tides, and Chapter 5, Maritime Connections, give more information on the lighthouse, signalling masts and observatory.

Landmarks in Liverpool visible from Bidston Hill on a clear day include the Three Graces, Albert Dock, Radio City Tower and the Anglican and Metropolitan cathedrals ▼

▲ There has probably been a windmill at Bidston Hill since the 16th century and the present structure was used for milling flour from 1800 to 1875

Bidston Windmill (E) is not far beyond and like the lighthouse is sometimes open to the public at weekends between spring and autumn; opening times vary so check www.bidstonhill. org.uk and www.bidstonlighthouse.org.uk for details. It is also the most distant point on this walk. The easiest way back is to retrace the route, but another option is to take a lower branch of the trail that leads around the opposite side of the observatory and then through woods to meet the outward route at Bidston Hall. Sights on this detour include the remains of a cock-fighting pit and some ancient rock carvings.

For a longer walk, the heritage trail continues across a footbridge to **Tam O'Shanter Urban Farm (F)** where areas open to the public include an animal house, café, play area and gift shop (www.tamoshanterfarm.org.uk). The round trip from the windmill is 1 to 2 miles. The website of the Friends of Bidston Hill includes a map of the trail and descriptions of the main sights along the way (www.bidstonhill.org.uk). Free guided walks are organised on Saturdays.

WALK 5

Distance: 3 miles with a 300 feet height gain
Start/end: Bidston railway station
Key features: Bidston Hill is an area of woods, heath and grassland about three miles from New Brighton and a great viewpoint for Liverpool and Birkenhead. There is plenty to see here, including a lighthouse, windmill and urban farm.

Maps are indicative only and contain OS data © Crown copyright (2019). See Introduction chapter for safety advice

Bidston Station

A

B   C

D

Bidston Hill   To lower route

E

F

Urban Farm

Tour of the Proms

The starting point for this ride is **Woodside Ferry Terminal (A)**. If travelling from Liverpool, this can be reached by trains to nearby Hamilton Square (www.merseyrail. org). Alternatively, if space is available, cycles can be carried on the ferries, although be sure to check departure times for the trip back before setting off (www.merseyferries.co.uk).

The route begins by walking the short distance left around the side of the ferry terminal past the U-boat Story exhibition and then riding to the end of the promenade at **Monks Ferry (B)**, where a waterside platform is all that remains of the old ferry pier. The priory is about a half mile inland and reached by following signs for the Wirral Circular Trail and then **Birkenhead Priory (C)**: its church spire clearly visible. For opening times check the website (www. thebirkenheadpriory.org).

To return to the terminal, retrace the outward route and continue towards the coast, passing a huge brick-built tower, a ventilation shaft for one of the Mersey road tunnels. The promenade then loops around the entrance to **Morpeth Dock (D)**, a disused part of Birkenhead Docks. A cannon on a plinth nearby is a replica of one

▲ The One O'Clock Gun near Morpeth Dock

that was used until the 1960s to provide a 1pm time signal for the port, as described in Chapter 5, Maritime Connections.

On reaching the 12 Quays Terminal, the cycleway detours inland to reach a main road at traffic lights. Dismount to cross the road bridges over the entrance channel to the docks, with surprisingly large ships often in view to the left. The cycleway then continues to **Seacombe Ferry Terminal (E)** where it rejoins the waterside.

The promenade now runs alongside the estuary to New Brighton – a route also followed in Walk #4. In addition to views of Liverpool, sights along the way include Wallasey Town Hall, Vale Park and the remains of Egremont Pier. On reaching **Fort Perch Rock (F)**, the promenade heads west along the coast past the marine lake, shops and restaurants of Marine Point to the

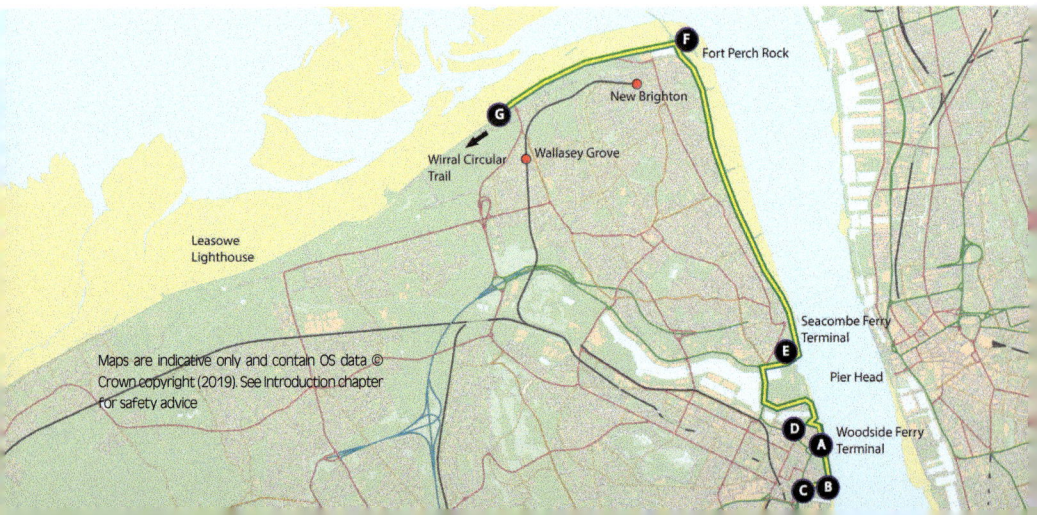

Maps are indicative only and contain OS data © Crown copyright (2019). See Introduction chapter for safety advice

end of **King's Parade (G)**, just beyond an RNLI lifeguard station. There are expansive views along the north Wirral coast from here, including to Leasowe Lighthouse, once a key navigation aid for shipping in the estuary, again as described in Chapter 5.

This marks the end of the outward route. For the return journey, one option is to retrace the route to Woodside. Alternatively, return by train from Wallasey Grove or New Brighton station, either to Hamilton Square for Woodside or to James Street in Liverpool, the closest station to Pier Head. Another way to Pier Head is by ferry from Seacombe Ferry Terminal.

For a longer ride, you could follow the Wirral Circular Trail west along the north Wales coast, although the route becomes rougher in places, with some unmade paths. The trail runs along the coast for about a mile before making a detour of about two miles inland, reaching the shoreline again close to Leasowe Lighthouse, from where it continues to Hoylake, 3 to 4 miles beyond. It then follows roads and a disused railway line inland before heading back across the peninsula to the shores of the Mersey at Eastham Country Park, a stopping point on Cycle Route #4. For those who only want to see the north Wirral coastline, the ride may be cut short by returning by train from Hoylake Station, within a mile of the western end of the seafront promenade.

For more information, guides and maps of the trail can be downloaded from the Visit Wirral website (www.visitwirral.com).

Upper to Lower: Guest Hall in the medieval Western Range building at Birkenhead Priory (courtesy of Colin Simpson) / Leasowe Lighthouse from the western end of King's Parade; the lighthouse is open to the public on some weekends (www.leasowelighthouse.co.uk) ▶

CYCLE ROUTE 3

Distance: 11 miles on mainly flat terrain
Start/end: Woodside Ferry Terminal
Key features: The promenade from Birkenhead to New Brighton provides fine views of the Mersey and continues along the coast to a good viewpoint for Leasowe Lighthouse. This out-and-return route from Woodside Ferry Terminal includes a visit to Birkenhead Priory and makes use of two longer trails on the peninsula: the Wirral Maritime Heritage Trail and the Wirral Circular Trail (www.visitwirral.com).

Birkenhead to the Runcorn Gap

Birkenhead is the largest town on the Wirral. The docks are major employers and the huge shipyard buildings of Cammell Laird are a distinctive feature of the waterfront. The company has built more than 1000 ships since it was founded in the 1820s, including aircraft carriers and cruise liners.

The docks were built along a tidal inlet during the 1800s. The area to the south was once a wooded headland, with a smaller inlet – also now enclosed – on the far side. Some of the earliest residents in this area were the Benedictine monks at **Birkenhead Priory**, which dates from the 12th century and remained in use until the dissolution of the monasteries in the 16th century. This is the oldest standing building on Merseyside and is tucked away in a quiet corner of the town alongside the shipyard, just a short walk or cycle ride from the promenade (see **Cycle Route #3**).

There are several listed buildings in the grounds, including a chapel and St Mary's Tower, which offers superb views towards Liverpool. Beneath the refectory, a covered area known as the Undercroft houses a museum dedicated to the history of the site. Opening times are typically weekends and Wednesday, Thursday and Friday afternoons, except Bank Holidays, although check the website for the latest information (www.thebirkenheadpriory.org).

▲ Birkenhead Town Hall in Hamilton Square

The priory is less than a mile from **Woodside Ferry Terminal** where there are good waterside views from the first floor café. It also features an exhibition called the U-boat Story, which describes the history of German submarine U-534 sunk by allied fire in the North Sea towards the end of World War 2. The almost complete, salvaged remains are part of the display (www.merseyferries.co.uk). On some days, a tram service operates to nearby **Wirral Transport Museum**, home to one of the UK's largest collections of vintage buses and trams, a model railway and several classic cars and motorcycles. There is a tea room and sales kiosk on site; check www.mtps.co.uk for opening times and the dates of tram operations.

The historic heart of Birkenhead is **Hamilton Square** with its impressive collection

Looking towards Liverpool waterfront from St Mary's Tower at Birkenhead Priory ▼

▲ St Mary's Tower at Birkenhead Priory

Upper to Lower: Woodside Ferry Terminal, with a tram departing for Wirral Transport Museum. The black-painted object to the left is a replica of a submarine built at a local shipyard, one of the first in the world / A figure of a monk in the priory museum; this area was probably once used as a storage cellar and perhaps as a dining room or parlour / The museum at Birkenhead Priory ▼

of Grade I listed buildings in Georgian and early Victorian styles commissioned by William Laird, of Cammell Laird fame. The square is about a half mile from Woodside and close to Hamilton Square Station (www.merseyrail. org). Another mile or so inland, **Birkenhead Park** has the distinction of being the world's first publicly funded park and influenced the design of Central Park in Manhattan; attractions include ornamental lakes, the Swiss Bridge, a visitor centre and a café (www. visitwirral.com). The closest rail connections are from Birkenhead Park Station.

From Woodside Ferry Terminal, the waterside promenade extends in both directions with fine views towards Liverpool. To the south it ends at the shipyard security fence, near the remains of a ferry pier, while to the north the first landmark is a large ventilation tower for one of the road tunnels beneath the Mersey. From here the path skirts around the entrance to a former dock to end at the 12 Quays Terminal, departure point for Stena Line ferries to Belfast. **Cycle Route #3** gives more details on routes in the Woodside area.

Queen Victoria Monument in Hamilton Square, Birkenhead

Ferry services across the Mersey

Before the road and rail tunnels were built, ferries were the only way to cross the Mersey between Liverpool and the Wirral. The first regulated service was operated by the Benedictine monks at Birkenhead Priory and started soon after the priory was built in the 12th century. As demand increased, Royal Charters were granted, initially to build lodgings and sell food (1318) and then to charge tolls for passengers and goods (1330), both valuable additional sources of income for the monks.

This service ended in the 16th century with the dissolution of the monasteries, and the ferry rights were sold. Such rights were prized possessions; others assigned in medieval times included those at Eastham Ferry and at the village of Ince on the southern shores of the estuary. The Ince service continued until the 1890s, when the construction of the Manchester Ship Canal cut access to the pier, while that at Eastham Ferry continued until the 1930s. Perhaps the earliest charter of all was that granted to the canons at Norton Priory in the 12th century to operate a ferry across the Runcorn Gap. Remarkably, the original vellum document still remains and is on display in the priory museum (see Chapter 3).

In the early days, crossings were by rowing boat and then mainly under sail from the 16th century. Journey times were unpredictable due to the risks posed by the winds and the tides, and scheduled services only became a realistic proposition with the advent of steam power at the beginning of the 19th century, first with paddle steamers and then steamships. This resulted in a flurry of pier building and by the end of the century boarding points on the Cheshire and Wirral shorelines included Runcorn, Ince, Ellesmere Port, Woodside, Seacombe, Egremont and New Brighton plus a string of locations with the word 'ferry' in the name: Eastham Ferry, New Ferry, Rock Ferry, Monks Ferry.

At 850ft, one of the longest piers was that at New Ferry, while the grandest was at New Brighton, where a wider structure alongside had a pavilion theatre at the end. Another refinement from the mid-1800s was the floating landing stage designed to rise and fall with the tides. The first of these, Prince's Landing Stage at Pier Head, was so successful that by the 1890s it had been extended to be almost half a mile long, at the time the longest floating structure in the world. Others included those at New Brighton, Eastham and Woodside.

Business was good, with additional income generated by using ferries as luggage boats to carry goods and vehicles, and occasionally diverting ships for tugboat duties. However, by the beginning of the 20th century, several

The Mersey Ferries' *Royal Iris of the Mersey* berthed at Seacombe Ferry Terminal ▼

factors had contributed to a decline in the number of ferry services, including changing patterns of employment, the opening of road and rail tunnels, and sand and mud deposits affecting boat access to some piers. The height of the closures was around 1930 and the last was at New Brighton in 1972, leaving the three terminals that remain today.

Nowadays Mersey Ferries operates a commuter service between Pier Head, Seacombe and Woodside and the hugely popular River Explorer Cruises at other times. Two vessels are used – the *Snowdrop* and the *Royal Iris of the Mersey* – typically with one on duty and the other held in reserve or operating special cruises such as those on summer evenings or along the Manchester Ship Canal (www.merseyferries.co.uk).

In recent years the *Snowdrop* has been painted in a bold psychedelic scheme to commemorate the Dazzle Ships of World War 1. These unusual designs were intended to make it more difficult for enemy commanders to work out the range, speed and direction of targets. The artwork was by Sir Peter Blake, whose other credits include co-designing the cover of the Beatles' Sgt. Pepper's Lonely Hearts Club Band album.

Around the estuary, some signs remain of earlier stopping points, such as the abutments of the now-dismantled piers at Monks Ferry, New Ferry, Egremont and Eastham Ferry: all fine viewpoints. The visitor centre at Eastham Country Park also houses an exhibition on the Eastham Ferry.

The Mersey Ferries' *Snowdrop* approaching Seacombe Ferry Terminal ▼

Port Sunlight

South of the Cammell Laird shipyard the next waterside access is at Rock Ferry and **New Ferry**. As the names suggest, these were also calling points for ferries, and the remnants of the pier at New Ferry make another fine viewpoint. Here, an interpretation panel shows landmarks on the shores opposite and describes the maritime history of the area.

In the winter months, the large areas of mudflats exposed at low tide are important feeding grounds for wading birds. To the south, they are backed by the low cliffs and grassland of **Shorefields Nature Park** with, just beyond, **Port Sunlight River Park** extending out from the shoreline.

The river park can be reached by road from the A41 or by a footpath from Shorefields. Its highest point is known as the Summit, with panoramic views of Liverpool, Birkenhead and the estuary. Other features include a lake and a waterside promenade with, at the far end, a picnic area, overlooking a quay where ships sometimes berth. The park was reclaimed from a landfill area on the site of Bromborough Dock. A heritage centre includes a cafe and education centre, and

> **WIRRAL MARITIME HERITAGE TRAIL**
> When walking or cycling along the promenades beside the Mersey it is worth looking out for the elegant information boards associated with the Wirral Maritime Heritage Trail, which are typically in engraved metal and mounted on plinths. The trail extends from Eastham Country Park to New Brighton. At each location, the boards give insights into local maritime history. Places with plaques include the promenades near Seacombe and Woodside ferry terminals, and the former pier at Eastham Country Park. See www.visitwirral.com for more information.

display boards and interpretation panels describe the history of the park and its wildlife (www.thelandtrust.org.uk).

The dock was once one of the busiest around the estuary, handling raw material and finished goods for the nearby factory at **Port Sunlight**, including consignments of the world-famous Sunlight soap. These were transported along the River Dibbin, whose estuary was filled in during construction of the docks. Today its outfall, now just a narrow channel, can be seen beside the picnic area at the river park.

Telephoto view of the waterfront in Liverpool and Birkenhead from Port Sunlight River Park ▼

▲ Gardens at Port Sunlight village

The factory in Port Sunlight was founded in the late 1800s by the industrialist William Hesketh Lever who had the imaginative idea of creating a garden village for workers at the plant. Designs were commissioned from over thirty leading architects and more than 900 houses were built in a range of architectural styles, set among leafy boulevards, parks and gardens. Nowadays most are privately owned and the village is a major tourist destination, where highlights include **Port Sunlight Museum**, which describes the history of the village, and the **Lady Lever Art Gallery**, home to the family's extensive collection of paintings, furniture and pottery (www. liverpoolmuseums.org.uk). The website of the Port Sunlight Village Trust gives more information on the village and museum (www.portsunlightvillage.com).

▲ **Upper to Lower:** Wading birds at Shorefields Nature Park / Houses at Port Sunlight village / A lone curlew feeding on the mudflats, next to Port Sunlight River Park

The Mersey Ferry Snowdrop departs from Woodside Ferry Terminal, as viewed by telephoto lens from Port Sunlight River Park

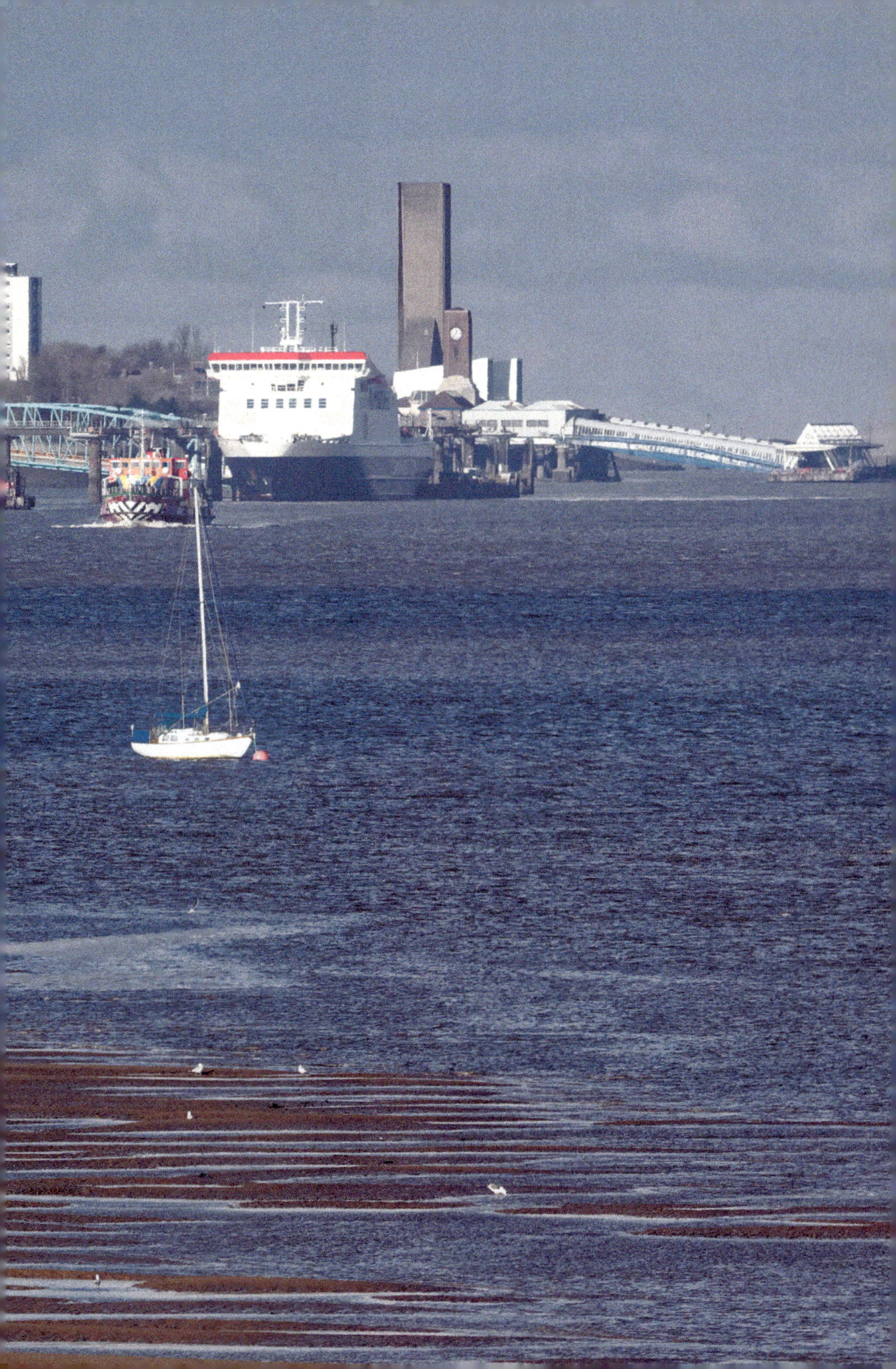

Eastham Country Park to Frodsham

Heading upstream, the next public access to the waterside is around **Eastham Country Park** (www.wirral.com). As at Shorefields, the park lies above the low sandstone cliffs that fringe this part of the Mersey. In addition to woodland and waterside walks, the visitor centre has displays on the wildlife and history of the park, including Eastham Pleasure Gardens. Once popular with day-trippers arriving by paddle steamer from Liverpool, the gardens were closed in the 1930s.

The remains of the ferry pier provide good views of the estuary and toward the entrance locks to the Manchester Ship Canal. Ships sometimes pass surprisingly close by en route to and from the locks. The brick-built kiosk that housed the ticket office is now home to a café, and other eating places nearby include the Eastham Ferry hotel, the Tap pub, and some delightful tea gardens next to the ranger's office.

The park is about a mile from the village of Eastham and lies on the Wirral Circular Trail, a 37-mile cycle route around the peninsula, which is followed in part by **Cycle Routes #3** and **#4**. Heading upstream, the former docks in Ellesmere Port are the next place with waterside views – an area now redeveloped for apartment blocks, a restaurant and hotel. The Ship Canal passes along the shoreline and is followed by a promenade for half a mile, ending at the port

> **EASTHAM PLEASURE GARDENS**
> A day out to the gardens involved quite an entertainment 'package'. For your 3d entrance fee you had for your amusement a boating lake, cafes, zoo, bandstand, open air stage and 'pierrot' performers, a dancing platform, entertainers stalls, shooting range, roller coaster and water chute ride and a 'Victorian Palace' (a ballroom). An advert in the Echo notes this ballroom provided "sitting accommodation for 3000 or 4000 people, and may be used for concerts and theatrical representations, or for dancing when the weather is wet." Unfortunately it burnt down in the 1950s.
> *From an information leaflet published by Wirral Council*

entrance and a good viewpoint for the former lighthouse, just beyond. A plaque at the opposite end indicates points of interest across the Mersey.

However, the main visitor attraction at Ellesmere Port is the **National Waterways Museum**. Housed in buildings around the former docks, it is dedicated to the history of canal building in the UK. Here can be seen working examples of industrial machinery, boats at various stages of restoration – including barges, narrowboats and tugs – and one of the most popular exhibits, Porters Row, where four cottages illustrate living

Twilight view of Helsby Hill from a viewpoint on the Sandstone Trail, near Frodsham ▼

conditions for dock workers and their families from the early 1800s through to the 1950s.

Throughout the museum there is a wealth of information on how life must have been for those working on the canals, along with the complex feeding and stabling arrangements for the horses that towed the barges. During the tourist season, the museum also operates narrowboat rides along the Shropshire Union Canal, which was built in the 18th century to provide a link to Chester and beyond. Check the museum webpages for opening hours and visitor information (www.canalrivertrust.org.uk).

Other attractions in Ellesmere Port include the huge Cheshire Oaks Designer Outlet shopping complex and the Blue Planet Aquarium (www.blueplanetaquarium.com).

From the museum, the Manchester Ship Canal follows the shoreline around to the Runcorn Gap, with no public access again until Runcorn. However, there are fine views of this part of the estuary from hills to the south, as described in **Walk #6**, which begins in the historic market town of **Frodsham**, itself a popular tourist destination (www.visitcheshire.com). The highest point on the walk is the war memorial on Overton Hill, which for guests at the nearby Forest Hills hotel can be reached via a wheelchair-accessible path that starts at the hotel (www.foresthillshotel.com). Visitors are also welcome for meals and afternoon tea.

Another way to see this part of the estuary is on the cruises operated along the Ship Canal during the tourist season by Mersey Ferries. The trips take about six hours and depart from Pier Head in Liverpool or Salford, and the return journey is by coach. See Chapter 5, Maritime Connections, for more information. Boat trips are also operated from Frodsham along the River Weaver on board a restored steam ship, the *Danny* (www.thedanny.co.uk).

Upper to Lower: The remains of the ferry pier at Eastham Country Park, with Liverpool waterfront in the distance / Remains of an Iron Age hill fort at Woodhouses Hill on the Sandstone Trail to the west of Overton Hill, near Frodsham / Seventeenth-century thatched cottages in Frodsham next to the Old Hall Hotel ▼

Port Sunlight

The starting point for this ride is the railway station **(A)** in Port Sunlight (www.merseyrail.org). Turn right at the main exit and then right again to reach the car park behind the Gladstone Theatre, following a cycleway sign for Eastham Country Park.

At the far end of car park, a narrow path runs alongside the security fence for the Unilever factory, but soon widens, reaching a ramp up to Stadium Road **(B)** after about a mile. Turn left at the top of the ramp and – still following signs for Eastham Country Park – left again at Commercial Road, dismounting as indicated to cross to the other side. On reaching Riverview Road **(C)**, turn right and, just before a mini roundabout, head left **(D)** along a narrow

▲ An approaching ship seen from the former ferry pier near Eastham Country Park

path through trees, now following a sign for the Wirral Circular Trail.

The Mersey soon comes into view and the cycleway leads to a car park for Eastham Country Park and then the access road to the main entrance **(E)**. The park has a visitor centre and tea garden, whilst other attractions near the entrance include a pub, hotel and café, as well as waterside views from the remains of a former pier.

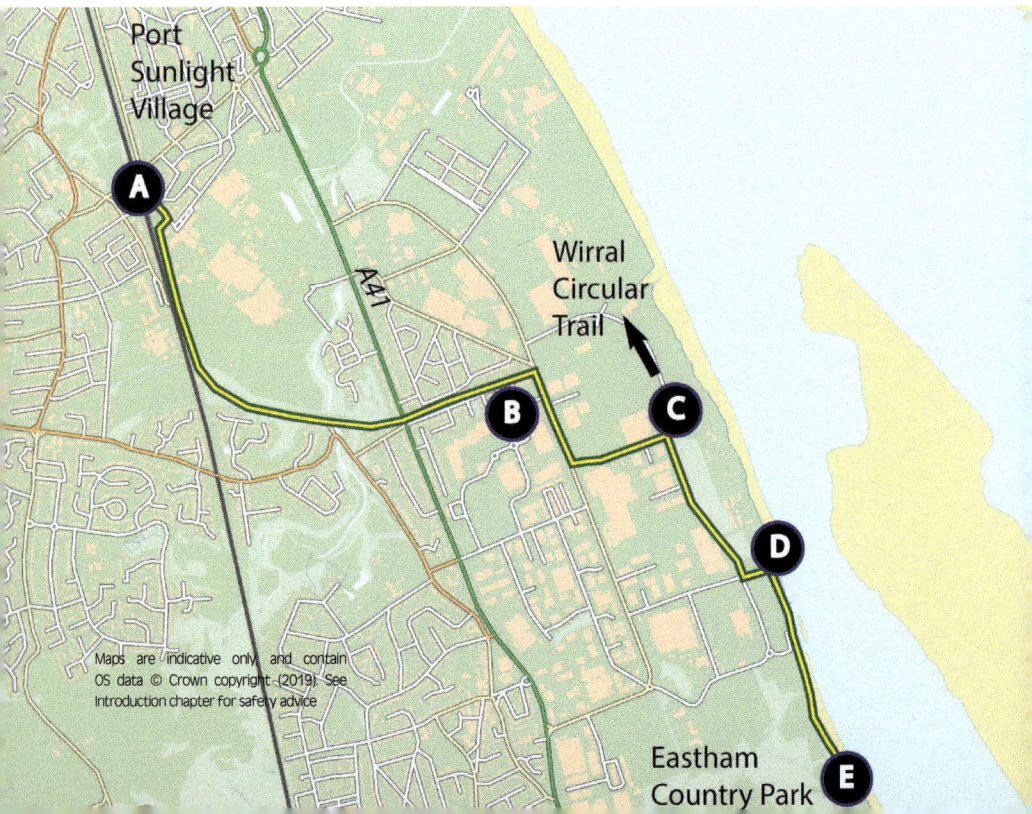

Port Sunlight Village

Wirral Circular Trail

Maps are indicative only and contain OS data © Crown copyright (2019). See Introduction chapter for safety advice

Eastham Country Park

For the return journey, retrace the route to Port Sunlight where a pleasant way to see the different architectural styles is to meander through the streets at will; popular stopping-off points are the museum (www.portsunlightvillage.com) and Lady Lever Art Gallery (www.liverpoolmuseums.org.uk). There is a self-guided trail in the village and maps can be purchased from the museum; there is also a street map in the entrance hall to the station.

For a longer ride, the tour of the village could be made first and then a detour made to Woodside Ferry Terminal on the way back from Eastham Country Park. The terminal is about 5-6 miles away and to reach it follow the Wirral Circular Trail signs northwards from Commercial Road. Although this part of the trail runs mainly inland, there are spectacular views across the water to Liverpool once at Woodside.

From Woodside, either cycle back to Port Sunlight or return by train from nearby Hamilton Square Station. Other options include continuing along the trail to New Brighton or taking the ferry to Liverpool. The descriptions for Cycle Route #3 and Walk #4 give more details. Again, some excellent cycle maps for the Wirral are available from the Visit Wirral website (www.visitwirral.com).

CYCLE ROUTE 4 🚲

Distance: 6-7 miles, plus 1-2 miles in Port Sunlight
Start/end: Port Sunlight station
Key features: Cycling is a fine way to explore Port Sunlight and the surrounding area, and this trip begins with an out-and-return visit by cycleway to Eastham Country Park on the shores of the Mersey, followed by a tour of the village.

Upper to Lower: A sign at an entrance to Eastham Country Park / A canopy of trees along the cycleway from Port Sunlight ▼

Gladstone Theatre in Port Sunlight ▼

Frodsham Heights

This route follows the Sandstone Trail as far as the top of **Overton Hill** and then returns to Frodsham. The height gain is 300–400 feet and, although initially along pavements and well-graded paths, there are some potentially slippery rocky and muddy sections higher up, so appropriate footwear is essential.

The starting point is Frodsham railway station **(A)**. The entrance road leads down to Church Street – a short way from the start of the Sandstone Trail at the Bears Paw Hotel to the right. For this walk, turn left on reaching Church Street and continue uphill, within half a mile reaching a flight of steps to the right **(B)**, a sign for the trail indicating the way. The steps lead to a path that climbs gently uphill and, once past St Laurence's Church, crosses a road to reach Bellemonte Road. Then, soon after passing the Bulls Head pub, where the road veers left, turn right into Middle Walk **(C)** to reach a narrow path into the woods, signs for the trail still indicating the way.

The climbing now begins in earnest and – after a few steep sections – the trail reaches the top of Overton Hill **(D)** and its impressive war memorial. A plaque indicates landmarks in an arc from Chester around to Warrington. This marks the end of the outward route and for the return trip retrace the route to the station.

For a longer walk, you could continue along the trail, although the terrain now becomes more difficult in places with some steep rocky steps to negotiate, unfenced sandstone edges, and paths that are sometimes waterlogged. Sandstone Trail signs again indicate the way.

The next high point is Woodhouses Hill, about a mile from Overton Hill. Here an interpretation panel describes the geological background to the formation of the estuary. A short distance beyond, a detour leads into the Woodhouses Hill Extension, an area of woods and grassland with the remains of an Iron Age fort. There is another fine viewpoint nearby.

This could be a suitable place to start the return journey as the trail now heads away from the edges to pass through woodland. A more ambitious alternative would be to continue on to Helsby Hill – another sandstone outcrop with estuary views – and then to the station in Helsby for trains back to Frodsham. This would be a nice one-way walk of 7 to 8 miles.

Looking towards the estuary, Wirral and south Liverpool from Overton Hill ▼

▲ A plaque at the top of Overton Hill shows distances to local landmarks

However, as Helsby Hill is not on the trail, it requires good navigation skills and a suitable map. In outline, the route involves leaving the trail by turning right at the first road reached and then following a zigzag route along roads and footpaths to the top of the hill. A choice of trails then heads down through woods past sandstone cliffs and outcrops to reach the outskirts of the town and hence roads to the station.

WALK 6

Distance: About 3 miles and a height gain of 300-400 feet
Start/end: Frodsham station
Key features: Frodsham lies on the banks of the River Weaver to the south of the estuary and is at the foot of a sandstone ridge that runs roughly parallel to the shoreline here, with great views towards Liverpool and the Wirral Peninsula. The ridge is part of the 34-mile long Sandstone Trail, which begins in the town and ends at Whitchurch in Shropshire (www.sandstonetrail.co.uk).

▲ A sign for the Sandstone Trail in the woods below Overton Hill

The war memorial at the top of Overton Hill ▼

Maps are indicative only and contain OS data © Crown copyright (2019). See introduction chapter for safety advice

Fort Perch Rock and New Brighton Lighthouse

Further reading

To learn more about the history, culture and sights around this part of the estuary, the following guides and reviews provide a fine introduction:

Making the most of the Mersey: a Leisure Guide to your Estuary, (Mersey Basin Campaign, 2007)

Merseyside and Wirral, Jarrold Short Walks for all the Family, Tony Marsh, (Jarrold, 2002)

Merseyside Meanders: Country Walks & Town Trails around Wirral, Liverpool and Southport, Michael Smout, (Sigma Leisure, 2002)

New Brighton: Our Days Out Remembered, (Trinity Mirror Media, 2011)

On the Waterfront, Peter de Figueiredo, in Mersey the river that changed the world, Ian Wray (ed.), photography by Colin McPherson, (The Bluecoat Press, 2007)

Riverside Rambles along the Mersey, Ron Freethy, (Sigma Leisure, 2004)

Walk & Cycle about Wirral Peninsula: A Merseytravel Guide to Wirral Peninsula Walks and Cycling routes, www.merseytravel.gov.uk, (Merseytravel, 2009)

Wallasey through Time, Ian Collard, (Amberley Publishing, 2009)

Wirral: the Official Visitor Guide, Wirral Council, www.visitwirral.com

Wirral Waterfront: the Jewel in the Crown of England's Northwest, Guy Woodland, (Cities500 International Publishers, 2005)

The Further Reading sections in Chapters 4 to 6 have additional sources of information on the environment, maritime heritage and wildlife of the region. For more background on the history of the ferries across the estuary, see the Mersey Ferries and Merseyside Maritime Museum websites (www.merseyferries.co.uk; www.liverpoolmuseums.org.uk).

Winter colours at Widnes Warth

chapter 3

UPPER ESTUARY

Between Runcorn and Widnes, sandstone formations force the Mersey through the Runcorn Gap, site of the Silver Jubilee Bridge.

Sights nearby include Norton Priory, the Catalyst Science Discovery Centre and the waterside nature reserves at Spike Island and Wigg Island.

Further upstream there are miles of canal and riverside walks in Warrington and many reminders of the town's seafaring past.

The tidal influence ends in the town and a scenic spot with a weir and woodland marks the head of the estuary.

VISIT IDEAS

See the following chapters for more sights
in the Upper Estuary on different themes:

Chapter 4 – Rivers and Tides

- Headwaters of the Mersey, Peak District
- Source of the Mersey, Stockport
- Sandstone geology, various locations
- Mersey Tidal Bore, various locations

Chapter 5 – Maritime Connections

- Roman artefacts, Warrington
- Replica of Liverpool Castle, Chorley
- Manchester Ship Canal cruises

Chapter 6 – Wildlife

- Seal, sturgeon and wading bird exhibits,
  Warrington
- Birdwatching, Warrington

M57

LIVERPOOL

WIDNES

Spike I
Cataly

Pickerings
Pasture

The Runcorn Gap

M53

Nortor
Haltor

Liverpool John
Lennon Airport

Hale
Head

Runcorn
Hill

RUN

UPPER ESTUARY

The Upper Estuary extends from Warrington to the Runcorn Gap where sandstone formations force the Mersey through a narrow constriction. This is a natural crossing point between Runcorn and Widnes and the arches of the Silver Jubilee and Mersey Gateway bridges are visible for miles around.

In Runcorn, places to visit include Wigg Island Community Park, the ruins of medieval Halton Castle and Norton Priory, and Runcorn Hill Park with views towards Liverpool and the Wirral. On the opposite shoreline in Widnes, the Catalyst Science Discovery Science centre and Spike Island Nature Reserve are other attractions.

Further upstream, the Mersey meanders past woods and meadows and Moore Nature Reserve, one of the largest in the region. The tidal influence ends in Warrington, and the Mersey is perhaps at its most accessible here with a wide choice of walking and cycling routes across floodplain meadows and alongside the various canals through the town.

M62

Risley
Moss

WARRINGTON

Paddington
Meadows

Woolston
New Weir

Sankey
Bridges

Howley Weir

Fiddlers
Ferry

Moore Nature
Reserve

Widnes
Warth

Wigg
Island

M56

M6

0   5   10km

Runcorn and Widnes

Runcorn lies on the southern shores of the Mersey. The sandstone quarries at **Runcorn Hill Park**, one of the highest places in the town, once supplied stone around the world, including for the Anglican cathedrals in Liverpool and Chester and parts of New York Harbour. **Walk #7** passes through the park, with fine views of the estuary and south Liverpool from the sandstone edges (www.runcornhillpark.co.uk).

To the east, the ruins of **Halton Castle** are on another sandstone outcrop with views towards Widnes, Warrington and beyond. The first defences were probably built in the 11th century although the present-day remains are from a later period. The inner grounds are normally closed to the public but a scenic path runs around its walls. An impressive building at the entrance was once an 18th century courthouse and now houses the Castle Hotel, which includes a popular pub. Local bus services from Runcorn stop nearby.

There is a display on the castle at nearby **Norton Priory**, which dates

▲ The Silver Jubilee Bridge from Wigg Island showing the sea wall between the estuary and the Manchester Ship Canal

from the 12th century and lies in a leafy valley formed by a minor tributary of the Mersey, now largely dried up due to drainage works. The priory remained a place of worship until the dissolution of the monasteries in the 16th century and a Georgian mansion was built in the grounds in later years.

An impressive museum describes the history of the priory while further downhill lies a restored 18th century walled garden, open seasonally. Perhaps the first ever charter for a ferry across the

St Mary's Church in Widnes seen from a Mersey Ferries cruise along the Manchester Ship Canal ▼

Mersey is on display in the museum, as described in Chapter 2. Another highlight is a twice life-size 14th century statue of St Christopher, the patron saint of travellers, depicting the saint carrying a child across a river, and carved from the local red sandstone. There is a restaurant and gift shop on site, tearooms at the walled gardens and an active programme of events; check the website for opening times (www.nortonpriory.org). Bus services from the town centre, about two miles away, stop nearby.

Two canals pass through Runcorn: the 18th century Bridgewater Canal, and the Manchester Ship Canal, which was opened in the 1890s. Nowadays the Bridgewater Canal is used for leisure boating and its towpath provides a pleasant way to reach some of the sights in the town on foot or by bike. These include the Brindley Theatre near the town centre, and Norton Priory, about half a mile along a path to the north of the canal.

The Ship Canal is still used by ocean-going vessels and is perhaps best seen from a waterside promenade that passes beneath the Silver Jubilee Bridge. Within the town, it was created by building a sea wall along the shores of the Mersey so access to the estuary is limited, but the waterside can be reached at **Wigg Island Community Park**, where a swing bridge crosses the canal.

The park is about a mile from the town centre and was created on a former industrial site. It has waterside walks, woodland trails and several bird hides overlooking the mudflats (www.friendsofwiggisland.co.uk). The area near the swing bridge is a good viewpoint for the Mersey Tidal Bore as described in Chapter 4, Rivers and Tides. For cyclists and walkers, the busy main roads that lead to the park can be largely avoided by following side streets from the town centre.

On the opposite shores of the Mersey in **Widnes**, **Spike Island Nature Reserve** is another reclaimed area (www.visithalton.me). The Sankey Canal begins here, built to transport coal to Widnes from St Helens, and the first industrial canal in England (www.sankeycanal.co.uk). Walk #8 describes the reserve in more detail.

The walls of Halton Castle ▼

Nearby is the multi-storey **Catalyst Science Discovery Centre** (www.catalyst. org.uk). It features exhibits on local industrial history, chemistry and the chemical industry. There is a café on the ground floor, and an unusual glass-sided lift runs up the side of the building to a top-floor observation gallery with good views of the estuary and the Mersey Gateway Bridge road crossing: one of the largest civil engineering projects in the region in recent years.

Also worth a visit is nearby Victoria Promenade, which is on the route of the coast-to-coast Trans Pennine Trail, which also passes through Spike Island. **Cycle Route #5** follows this part of the way. The promenade is another good vantage point for the Mersey Tidal Bore; see Chapter 4.

The Visit Halton website (www. visithalton.me) includes information on these and other tourist sites in the area, and Halton Borough Council publishes some excellent free walking and cycling maps (www.halton.gov.uk).

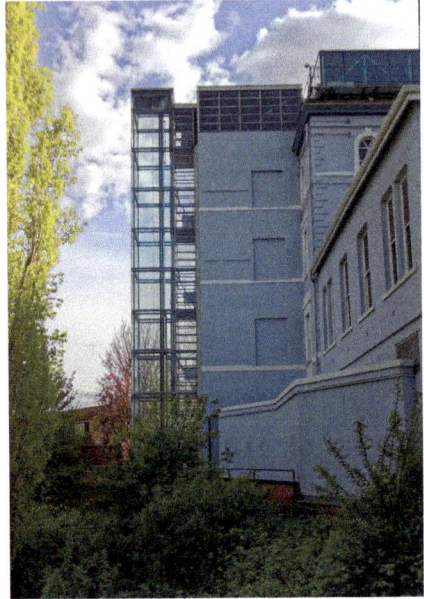

▲ The glass-walled elevator at Catalyst Science Discovery Centre

The Bridgewater Canal near Runcorn town centre ▼

MARITIME MANCHESTER

Although the tidal influence in the Mersey ends in Warrington, there is a strong maritime connection with Manchester via the Manchester Ship Canal, which begins near Ellesmere Port, passes through Runcorn, and ends a couple of miles from the city centre.

The canal was built in the 1890s primarily to allow ocean-going ships to reach Manchester. It is nearly as long as the Panama Canal and when opened was regarded as one of the engineering wonders of the world. Between Manchester and Irlam it follows the course of the River Irwell, and then the Mersey for much of the way downstream.

For the first few decades, the Port of Manchester was a huge success, with the freight handled reaching a peak in the 1950s, but it was eventually closed in the 1980s. However, the canal still thrives, serving industrial works to the west of the city and the logistics hub of Port Salford, as well as many destinations further downstream. including the Port of Runcorn.

▲ IWM North at Salford Quays

MediaCityUK at Salford Quays ▲

The former docks in Manchester have been largely converted to residential and commercial use, including one of the region's top visitor attractions, The Quays, part of Salford Quays. This is home to the Imperial War Museum North (IWM North) and The Lowry art gallery and theatre, as well as pubs and restaurants. See www.thequays.org.uk and www.visitsalford.info for more information and a programme of events.

The Quays can be reached by tram or bus from the city centre, but perhaps the most stylish way to arrive or depart is on one of the special cruises along the Ship Canal. These are operated by Mersey Ferries during the tourist season (www.merseyferries.co.uk) from both Liverpool and a dock in Salford close to the Quays. There is an informative commentary on the history of the canal, with time to explore after the cruise before returning by coach. There are of course many other visitor attractions in the city and the Visit Manchester website gives more information (www.visitmanchester.com), while Chapter 5, Maritime Connections, gives more background on the history of the canal.

▲ A Mersey Ferry on the Ship Canal in Warrington

Runcorn Hill

This out-and-return trip is mainly along roads and well-graded paths, although with a few steeper, potentially muddy sections, requiring appropriate footwear. There are also some steep unfenced edges within the park which require care.

The starting point is the main railway station in Runcorn (**A**). From the entrance, turn right along Shaw Street and, at the end, right again at the traffic lights onto Greenway Road. After half a mile, opposite the **war memorial (B)**, is an information board describing an extraordinary act of bravery during World War 1 by a local soldier whose statue appears here: Thomas Alfred Jones. Not far beyond, turn left along Highlands Road. A right turn soon after leads to the main car park for **Runcorn Hill Park (C)**, where a display board includes a useful map of the main trails.

The cenotaph at the war memorial ▶

View towards Liverpool and the Mersey Estuary from Runcorn Hill Park ▼

▲ Esposito's Deli at Runcorn Hill Park'

The first sandstone edge (**D**) is nearby and worth a visit. It is reached via a gate next to a warning sign. Having made this short detour, leave the car park at the far end to enter the reserve, and carry straight on at the first junction. This is now part of the Mersey Valley Timberland Trail: a 22-mile walk that meanders through the sandstone hills south of the Mersey to the village of Lymm, east of Warrington.

After passing an electricity pylon, steps descend to a footbridge. Then, as the path veers left, turn right along a smaller path at a 'Run the Hill' sign, soon reaching a grassy area with a bench – another fine viewpoint (**E**). This marks the end of the route.

For the return journey, go back to the main path, turn right and descend steps to reach a wider tarmac path. Turn right here and, keeping left at junctions, follow the path to reach the more formal part of the park, continuing past a bandstand and bowling greens to reach stairs that lead back to the car park (C).

WALK 7

Distance: 3 miles with a height gain of 200-300 feet
Start/end: Runcorn station
Key features: Runcorn Hill Park is just over a mile from the town centre with good views across the estuary towards Liverpool and the Wirral from the sandstone edges near the top (www.runcornhillpark.co.uk).

An interesting extension, of less than a mile, is to turn right at the bowling greens and then right again to reach a café – Esposito's Deli – with a model boating lake a short way beyond (**F**). Some impressive outdoor sculptures are passed on the way and a wall-sized display board in the café describes the history of the quarries at Runcorn Hill.

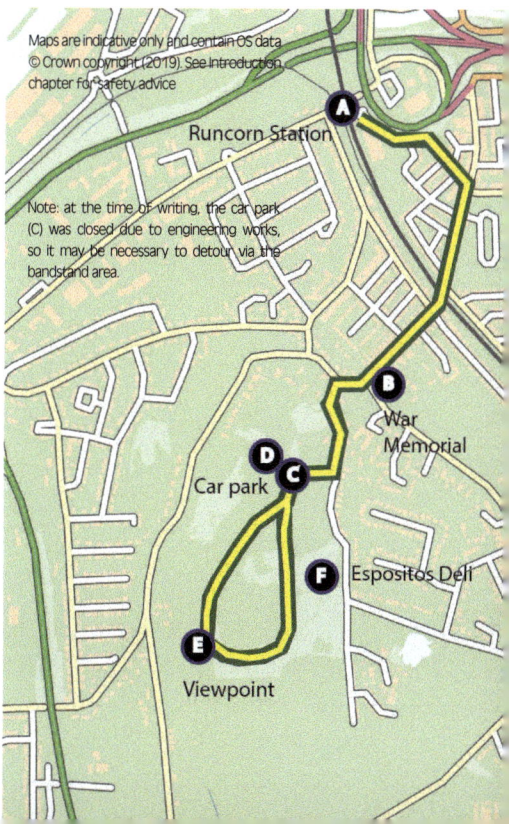

Maps are indicative only and contain OS data © Crown copyright (2019). See Introduction chapter for safety advice

Runcorn Station

Note: at the time of writing, the car park (C) was closed due to engineering works, so it may be necessary to detour via the bandstand area.

A

B

War Memorial

D C

Car park

F Espositos Deli

E

Viewpoint

Widnes Promenade

This walk is mainly along flat tarmac paths, although with a few short climbs and descents to negotiate.

The starting point is the **Catalyst Science Discovery Centre (A)** about a mile from Widnes town centre and a worthwhile destination in its own right; see www.catalyst.org.uk for information on what to see and how to get there by bus.

From the main entrance to the centre, walk down to the locks at the entrance to the Sankey Canal and follow it past the marina, crossing over to Spike Island via a footbridge. A waterside path then runs alongside the Mersey.

Several interpretation panels describe the industrial and maritime history of the area, including the Mersey Flats, a type of sailing barge that once plied the estuary. The timbers of one abandoned here in the mid-20th century are visible at low tide **(B)**. Nearby, a large pool is all that remains of Widnes Dock **(C)**, built to load and unload barges travelling along the canal.

Once back at the canal, cross the footbridge over the entrance locks and head

▲ The Sankey Canal at Spike Island; there is a large resident population of ducks and geese here

Runcorn and the estuary from Victoria Promenade ▼

▲ A park alongside Victoria Promenade

Distance: About 2 miles
Start/end: Catalyst Science Discovery Centre
Key features: In Widnes there are fine views of the estuary from Spike Island Nature Reserve and Victoria Promenade. This walk follows the Sankey Canal through the reserve, visits the promenade and ends at the site of a former transporter bridge.

left up a low hill to reach a road. Follow this to a ramp, indicated by a sign for the Trans Pennine Trail. This leads down to **Victoria Promenade (D)**; at the far end, climb another ramp to the remains of a pier. This was part of a transporter bridge that once stood here and a fine viewpoint for the estuary, as is the beer garden of the Mersey Hotel alongside **(E)**. This marks the end of the outward section of the route and it is then just a short walk back to the discovery centre.

For a longer walk, a pleasant detour could be to continue along the Trans Pennine Trail beneath the Silver Jubilee bridge to **Pickerings Pasture Local Nature Reserve (F)**, with its waterside views and woodland walks – a good place for birdwatching. The round-trip distance from the transporter bridge pier to the far end of the reserve is 4 to 5 miles. Cycle Route #5 describes the route.

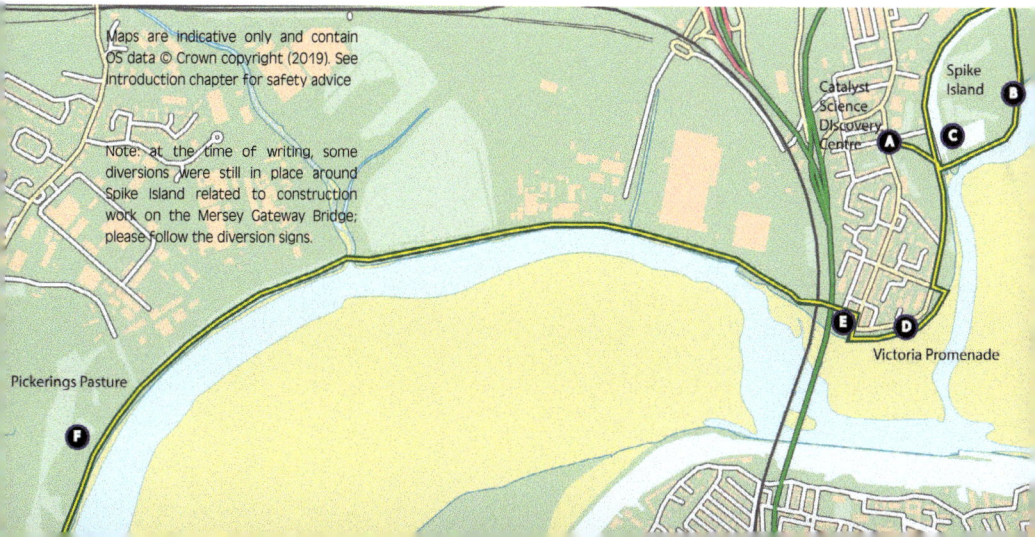

Maps are indicative only and contain OS data © Crown copyright (2019). See Introduction chapter for safety advice

Note: at the time of writing, some diversions were still in place around Spike Island related to construction work on the Mersey Gateway Bridge; please follow the diversion signs.

Telephoto view of Fiddler's Ferry and Warrington from Halton Castle

The Runcorn Gap to Warrington

Upstream from Widnes and Runcorn towards Warrington, the character of the Mersey changes as it meanders past woods, farmland and meadows. However, the tidal influence is still evident in the mudflats exposed at low tide and the rush of incoming water with the rising tide.

In this reach, there is limited access to the southern shores due to the Manchester Ship Canal, but there are several good viewpoints on the northern side. These are reached via short detours from the Trans Pennine Trail, which runs alongside the Sankey Canal to the outskirts of Warrington.

Heading east from Spike Island, the first landmark is **Widnes Warth** where a raised walkway passes over reed beds and marshes at the waterside. Halton Castle is just visible on an outcrop on the horizon with Wigg Island and the Mersey Gateway and Silver Jubilee bridges off to the right. An interpretation panel explains that 'warth' is an Old English word meaning either a 'look-out point' or a 'bend in the river'; other panels describe the birdlife and maritime history of the area. There are several bird hides nearby.

As it continues towards Warrington, the trail cuts across a wide bend in the Mersey beside a security fence for Fiddler's Ferry Power Station, a major landmark in this area. **Fiddler's Ferry** itself lies about a mile beyond and is home to a boat maintenance yard, sailing club and a popular waterside pub. Lock gates provide access from the Sankey Canal to the Mersey, and there are many yachts, dinghies and motor vessels stored on dry land or moored in the canal.

As the name suggests, Fiddler's Ferry was once an important crossing point for the Mersey. A ferry operated here for several hundred years, and the Ferry Tavern offered accommodation to travellers. An interpretation panel provides more information. This part of the estuary is another possible viewpoint for the Mersey Tidal Bore; see Chapter 4, Rivers and Tides, for details.

Future Flower, a 14-metre-tall artwork with wind-powered lights at Widnes Warth designed by architects Tonkin Liu ▼

▲ The Sankey Canal at Fiddler's Ferry

On the opposite shoreline, the trees in the distance are part of the extensive **Moore Nature Reserve**, an area of woodland, wetlands, lakes and meadows. This is a great place for wildlife watching with a network of trails and several bird hides. The car park is reached from Moore village, and an information board there shows the walking routes available; see www.fccenvironment. co.uk and the reserve's Facebook page for more details. If cycling along the Trans Pennine Trail, another way to reach the reserve is to follow the trail to the railway bridge over the Mersey near Moore where a path branches off to the southwest and leads to a minor road which passes the entrance.

The paths of the Mersey and the Sankey Canal diverge to the west of Warrington

▲ **Upper to Lower:** Bird hide at Widnes Warth / The Mersey at Fiddler's Ferry / View from a lakeside hide at Moore Nature Reserve

in an area called Sankey Bridges, with the canal heading north and the Mersey looping around floodplain meadows towards the town centre. Until the mid-20th century, much of the waterfront through the town was lined with wharfs and warehouses, and **Cycle Route #6** and **Walk #9** explore some of this maritime past.

Several maritime exhibits can also be found in **Warrington Museum & Art Gallery**, among its more general displays on geology, natural history and culture (www.culturewarrington.org). These relate to the role of shipbuilding and river transport in the development of the town, and to an ancient Roman port at modern-day Wilderspool to the south, including examples of pots and tools excavated at the site, and a Roman actor's mask (see Chapter 5).

There is also a display on Warrington Friary, once situated next to the medieval bridge across the Mersey close to present-day Bridgefoot. Established in the 13th century, it was closed during the dissolution of the monasteries, as were Norton Priory and Birkenhead Priory further downstream. Several archaeological finds are on display and a small part of the excavations has been preserved beneath a glass panel in the floor of the Friar Penketh pub nearby.

Other destinations in the town with a Mersey connection include **Risley Moss Local Nature Reserve** and **Warrington Transporter Bridge** (see later). The reserve includes some of the last remaining examples of the wet woodland and peat bogs that once lined the river valley floor to Manchester. It is about two miles east of the town and highlights include a visitor centre and miles of woodland walks (www.warrington.gov.uk). It is open all year except on Fridays and some Bank Holidays (www.warrington.gov.uk); see Chapter 6, Wildlife, for more details.

In recent years, access to the Mersey in Warrington has greatly improved with the opening of a major flood defence scheme to help protect the town from tidal flooding. **Cycle Route #6** follows these defences for part of the way and then the **New Cut Heritage and Ecology Trail** to the top of the estuary on the eastern side of the town (www.newcuttrail.com). The waterside walks of **Paddington Meadows** lie to the south.

Other tourist destinations in the town include Grappenhall Heys Walled Garden, Gulliver's World Theme Park and Walton Hall and Gardens; see www.warrington.gov.uk and www.visitcheshire.com for more information and ideas on other places to visit. There is a tourist information desk in Warrington Market.

For getting around, there are frequent bus and train connections to places around the estuary, such as Widnes, Runcorn and Liverpool. For cyclists, a comprehensive route map for the town is available from the council website (www.warrington.gov.uk).

The Mersay at Paddington Meadows in Warrington ▼

Maritime Warrington

For visitors to Warrington it is sometimes a surprise to learn that the town once had docks, wharfs and an active shipbuilding industry. The centre of activity was at Bank Quay near the town centre where there were shipyards, warehouses and factories. Nowadays, the town's main railway station, Warrington Bank Quay, bears its name.

During the 18th century, the town supplied around half the sailcloth required by the Royal Navy. In later years, local shipyards built vessels such as schooners and paddle steamers as well as the Mersey Flat barges once common around the estuary. Smaller yards at Sankey Bridges to the west also built barges and the occasional sailing ship and steamship. One claim to fame for a foundry at Bank Quay was that it was the source of the ironwork for the Britannia Bridge across the Menai Straits at Anglesey.

Perhaps the most famous locally built ship of all was the ill-fated clipper *RMS Tayleur*, hailed as the largest iron merchant vessel of the time. Launched from Bank Quay in 1853 and towed down the Mersey to Liverpool for outfitting, the ship sank the following year on its maiden voyage after running aground off the coast of Ireland. A display

▲ Bishops Wharf in Warrington in the 1950s, courtesy of Warrington Museum & Art Gallery (Culture Warrington)

in **Warrington Museum & Art Gallery** refers to this as 'Warrington's Titanic' and notes that it was operated by the same shipping line, the White Star Line.

Other quays near the town centre included Bishops Wharf, which was situated alongside the present-day Riverside Retail Park, and Howley Quay a short way upstream. These remained in use until the mid-20th century and can be seen on **Cycle Route #6** along with several other reminders of the town's maritime past, such as Black Bear Park, Warrington Dock and the New Cut Canal; see the route description later in this chapter. However, the only commercial shipping in the town nowadays consists of vessels passing along the Manchester Ship Canal.

SCHOONER PORT

...the sailing flats continued to use the old Mersey river to Warrington. In 1830 it was estimated that the sailing barges made 7000 passages through the difficult channels between Runcorn and Warrington. At the time it was accepted that 40 tons was the limit for vessels reaching Warrington by this route but vessels of 100 to 120 tons and drawing 7½ to 8 feet could reach Bank Quay at Warrington on spring tides. In 1836 some 60,000 tons of toll free traffic came to Warrington by the river although most craft proceeding to Bank Quay required two tides as they were usually grounded when short of their destination.

From Schooner Port: two centuries of upper Mersey sail, H.F. Starkey

▼ The Silver Jubilee bridge at night, looking upstream towards Runcorn

TRANSPORTER BRIDGES

An interesting and perhaps not widely known sight in Warrington is a transporter bridge about a mile from the town centre.

This was built in 1916 to transport railway wagons and, in later years, road vehicles too, within an industrial site spread across the banks of the Mersey. These were carried in a gondola suspended by cables from an overhead gantry, which would be traversed back-and-forth across the water. Its history is described on the website of the Friends of Warrington Transporter Bridge, along with ways to reach the bridge on foot, and the campaign to see it restored (www.warringtontransporterbridge.co.uk).

The bridge was used until the 1960s and is one of eight remaining worldwide, and the only rail transporter bridge. Remarkably, for about fifty years there were three of these unusual bridges across the Mersey: a second slightly to the north of the existing bridge and an altogether larger structure at the Runcorn Gap, which were both built in 1905 and dismantled in the 1960s.

The design of the Widnes–Runcorn Transporter Bridge was slightly different in that the gondola was an open platform controlled by a driver sitting in a cabin above. Up to 300 passengers and several vehicles could be carried at a time, and the bridge's opening led to the demise of the ferry service which had operated since the Middle Ages.

The transporter bridge's fate in turn was sealed by the opening of the Runcorn–Widnes road bridge in 1961. Of a similar design to the Sydney Harbour Bridge in Australia, it was renamed the Silver Jubilee Bridge in 1977 in honour of the Queen's 25 years on the throne.

On the Runcorn side few signs remain of the transporter bridge, but in Widnes the access ramp has been preserved and is a good viewpoint for the estuary. This includes the building that housed the waiting rooms and ticket office, and plaques to commemorate the opening of the bridge and a later ceremony in 1913. **Walk #8** visits this area.

▲ Warrington Transporter Bridge

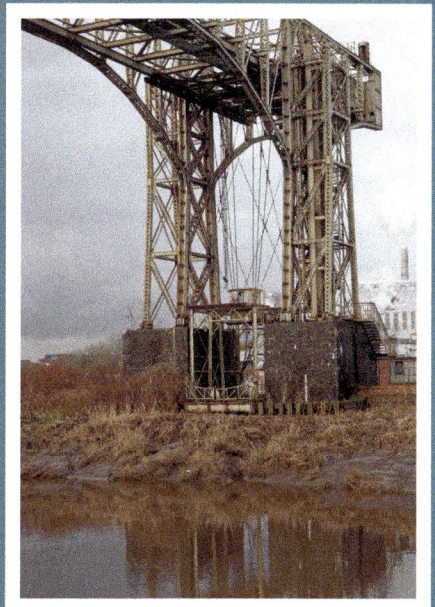

Close up view of the gondola used to transport goods and vehicles ▶

Warrington Waterways

The starting point for this walk is the *Well of Light* artwork (**A**) at Market Gate in Warrington town centre, about half a mile from the main bus and railway stations. The route is mainly along well-graded paths and tarmac, although an unmade section can be muddy at times.

Begin by heading downhill along Bridge Street, soon passing a water sculpture, part of the *River of Life* feature created by artist Steven Broadbent and inspired by the course of the Mersey through the town. Cross Academy Way and then, on reaching a busy roundabout, follow the road left, crossing at the traffic lights (**B**) to reach Riverside Retail Park. At the next lights, just before a traffic island, cross over to Wharf Street and the banks of the Mersey (**C**). This area – Bishops Wharf – was once lined with warehouses and wharfs to handle goods transported along the Mersey. The Mersey Tidal Bore is sometimes seen here, as described in Chapter 4, Rivers and Tides.

▲ Water sculptures in the *River of Life* feature in Warrington

Continue to follow the road and, where it reaches a low incline, turn right along a waterside path beside flood defences. Due to the influence of the tides, water levels can change by several metres in a day in this area. At times of high tides and/or heavy rainfall it is therefore worth checking the Environment Agency's website to see if any flood warnings are in force (www.gov.uk).

Soon after passing a viewing platform jutting into the Mersey, the path reaches **Howley Weir (D)**. This is normally the tidal limit of the estuary, although it is sometimes overtopped on the highest tides. A small channel to the side is a disused lock, Howley Lock, its upstream gates still intact. No longer operational, it was used until the 1950s by barges travelling along the Mersey. Chapter 5, Maritime Connections, discusses its role.

The weir is at a bend in the Mersey and the path turns left here to pass beneath Howley suspension footbridge, an elegant black and white painted structure. On reaching a road (Howley Lane), turn right and follow this to its end, where a track leads to **Kingsway Bridge (E)**, shortly beyond the headquarters of Warrington Rowing Club.

▲ Artwork on the flood defences near Wharf Street showing that the route here is part of the Mersey Way, a long-distance footpath from Warrington to Liverpool (see Chapter 1)

▲ The viewing platform and path near Howley Weir partly covered by water during an unusually high tide

Distance: About 3-4 miles
Start/end: Warrington town centre
Key features: The Mersey passes close to the centre of Warrington and this walk gives a flavour of the many miles of waterside paths in the town. It follows the banks of the Mersey for about a mile, returning along the opposite side.

Cross the bridge by following the path beneath it and using the sloping ramps on the far side. Then turn right along the towpath toward Victoria Park, a sign indicating the way. This leads to Black Bear Park, a linear park that runs alongside Victoria Park. Its unusual name derives from Black Bear Canal, which once provided a link to the Manchester Ship Canal. The canal was last used in the 1960s by barges carrying hides for tanneries alongside the Mersey but was then filled in for safety reasons. A grassy depression nearby is all that remains of the entrance lock, known as Manor or Latchford Lock. Boats waiting to enter would berth at nearby Howley Quay, on the far side of the river.

On reaching the waterside again, a narrow and occasionally muddy path heads back to the footbridge (**F**). From there, retrace the route back to the start of the walk in the town centre.

For a longer walk, before crossing Kingsway Bridge continue alongside the Mersey until after about half a mile the path joins the New Cut Heritage and Ecology Trail. This then heads east through woods for just over two miles to end close to Woolston New Weir at the head of the estuary, as described in **Cycle Route #6**. To avoid the walk back, there are occasional bus services to the town centre along the A57 Manchester Road, less than half a mile to the north. Several paths and roads branch off in this direction; however, be sure to check bus timetables when planning the route (www.networkwarrington.co.uk).

An early morning view across the Mersey towards the 281-foot-high spire of St Elphin's parish church in Warrington, along the route of Walk #9

Mersey Route 62

This route is mainly along side streets and well-graded tracks, and generally flat, although with some busy roads to negotiate in Warrington and around Hale. Be sure to check train times for the return journey before setting off (www.nationalrail.co.uk).

Highlights include Sankey Valley Park, Fiddler's Ferry, Widnes Warth, Spike Island, Pickerings Pasture Local Nature Reserve, and the many interpretation panels describing the wildlife and maritime history of the estuary. Sankey Valley Park is an attractive linear park beside the Sankey Canal and Sankey Brook, a tributary of the Mersey (www.warrington.gov.uk), while Pickerings Pasture is an area of woodlands, meadows and waterside walks described in Chapter 1.

The starting point is **Warrington Central Station (A)** from where a right turn leads to a set of traffic lights. Turn left along Tanners Lane, a busy road that may be safer to follow on foot. At the next traffic lights turn right along Bewsey Road and then at the next lights continue straight along Lodge Lane to reach a roundabout, from where an access road leads straight on into **Sankey Valley Park (B)**. After crossing the brook and canal, turn left onto a path that follows the canal. After about a mile, a bridge leads over a dual carriageway and, soon after, a footbridge crosses back over the canal. A right turn then leads to Liverpool Road (**C**), a busy main road.

Cross both this and the level crossing beyond as indicated by signs, then follow a narrower path alongside the canal to a little-used road. This area is called Sankey Bridges and was once bustling with a dock and shipbuilding yards. Lock gates provided access for barges to and from Sankey Brook, and hence the Mersey.

Now on the Trans Pennine Trail, continue right alongside the canal to **Spike Island** in Widnes. The route is well signposted from here – sometimes using the abbreviations TPT or (62). Sights along the way include **Fiddler's Ferry (D)** and **Widnes Warth**, as described earlier in this chapter. On reaching Spike Island, the next destination is Victoria Promenade in Widnes, an area described in **Walk #8**.

The trail now detours briefly along side streets before passing beneath the Silver Jubilee Bridge to rejoin the waterfront. A gentle climb leads past industrial works to a low hill which is a fine viewpoint for this part of the estuary. **Pickerings Pasture Local Nature Reserve (E)** is just beyond and reached via a wooden stairway down to a footbridge across Ditton Brook, another tributary of the Mersey.

In the reserve, the trail initially follows the waterfront before passing through woodland to reach Hale Road. This is another busy road to follow with care, although traffic slows temporarily through the village of **Hale (F)**. Here, a pleasant detour is to walk to Hale Head Lighthouse, as described in **Walk #3**, again in Chapter 1.

After another busy stretch of road, the trail doubles back on itself soon after the start of the perimeter fence for Liverpool John Lennon Airport **(G)**. Still following Trans Pennine Trail signs, turn right into Eastern Avenue then right again onto Alderfield Drive to ride around the outskirts of Speke. After about a mile, a signed path on the right leads to an underpass and steps beneath Speke Boulevard, which is followed for a short time before passing through an industrial estate to reach the grassy expanse of **Halewood Doorstep Green (H)**. Cycleway signs then show the way across the Green to Blackburne Drive and Higher Road.

From Higher Road, there is the choice of returning to Warrington from Hunts Cross or Halewood stations. Hunts Cross Station **(I)** is nearest and reached by turning left along Higher Road and then right on reaching Speke Road. Both are busy roads so again take care.

A longer and more scenic alternative is to head for Halewood Station **(J)**. To reach this, cross Higher Road into Halewood Triangle Park and then, immediately after a bridge over a railway line, leave the trail by turning right at a sign for the

CYCLE ROUTE 5

Distance: 19-20 miles returning by train
Start/end: Warrington/Hunts Cross or Halewood
Key features: The Trans Pennine Trail – National Cycle Route 62 – provides a fine way to see much of the Upper Estuary. This route follows it from the outskirts of Warrington to Hale, then continues to Hunts Cross or Halewood in south Liverpool, with the return journey by train. There are two flights of steps to negotiate.

unusually named Ducky Pond. An interpretation panel at the pond describes its history and includes a useful map showing routes through the park. The path then continues to a junction where a right turn at a sign for the Environment Centre leads to a pyramid-shaped rock set in the path, just before a road. A right turn here onto an unsigned path leads across Rainbow Drive and through woodland to Hollies Road. The station is a short way to the right.

Alternatively, see the next page for ideas for extending this route, including some websites for free cycle maps relevant to the trip.

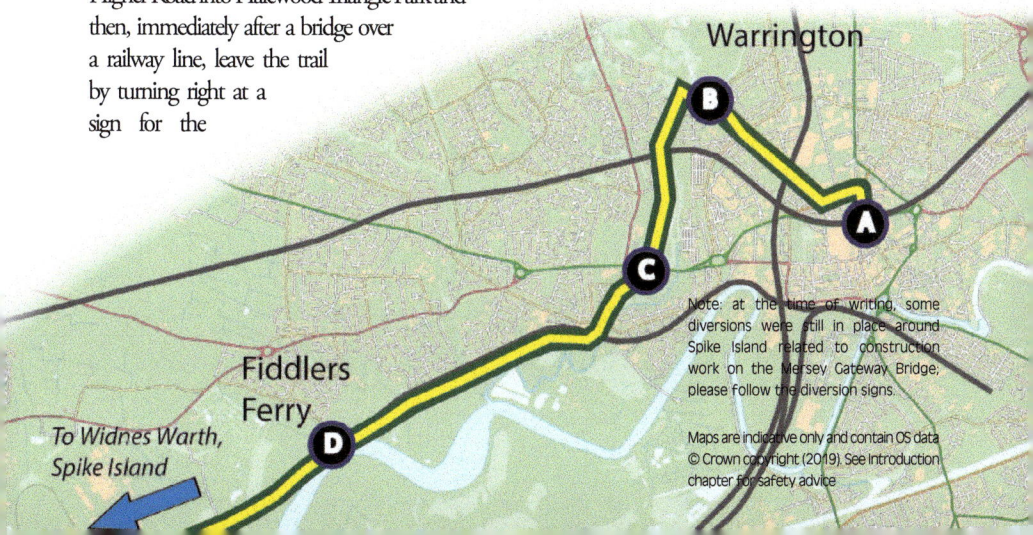

Warrington

Fiddlers Ferry

To Widnes Warth, Spike Island

Note: at the time of writing, some diversions were still in place around Spike Island related to construction work on the Mersey Gateway Bridge; please follow the diversion signs.

Maps are indicative only and contain OS data © Crown copyright (2019). See introduction chapter for safety advice

IDEAS FOR EXTENDING CYCLE ROUTE #5

From Higher Road, instead of heading for Halewood Station, another option is to continue along the Trans Pennine Trail past the turn towards Ducky Pond.

The trail is known as the Liverpool Loop Line in this area and follows a disused railway line. After about three miles, National Cycle Route 56 branches off to the left to Sefton Park, about 3 to 4 miles away, and one of the most scenic in Liverpool. It is then about a mile via side streets to reach the waterfront in Liverpool, which leads north to Albert Dock and Pier Head, from where the fastest train services back to Warrington are from Liverpool Lime Street Station.

Cycle Route #2 describes the route from Sefton Park to Pier Head (see Chapter 1) while more information is available from www.transpenninetrail.org.uk. Several free cycle maps relevant to both Cycle Routes #2 and #5 are available from the websites of Warrington Borough Council (www.warrington.gov.uk), Halton Borough Council (www.halton.gov.uk) and Merseyrail (www.merseyrail.org).

The Sankey Canal near Sankey Bridges on Cycle Route #5; the train is carrying coal to Fiddler's Ferry Power Station, just visible in the distance

The Mersey viewed from the Trans Pennine Trail above Pickerings Pasture on Cycle Route #5 ▶

Warrington Navigation

This route is mainly along tarmac and graded paths with little change in elevation.

The starting point is **Riverside Retail Park (A)**, which is within a mile of the town centre and the two main railway stations: Warrington Central and Warrington Bank Quay. The first part of the route is described in **Walk #9** but in summary initially follows Wharf Street before turning right at a slight incline to follow a path alongside the Mersey past Howley Weir to **Kingsway Bridge (B)**.

Once past the bridge, continue following the Mersey to the start of the New Cut Heritage and Ecology Trail (www.newcuttrail. com). This takes its name from the New Cut Canal, which was built to provide a shortcut for barges heading to and from Manchester along a route known as the Mersey and Irwell Navigation. The now-blocked entrance locks are a short way beyond with the distinctive roof of the former lock-keeper's cottage – now privately owned – visible above a wall nearby. Interpretation panels describe the history of this part of the navigation, and Chapter 5, Maritime Connections, gives more details.

From here, the trail leaves the banks of the Mersey to follow the canal, whose overgrown channel is visible in woods to the right. After just over two miles, the end is reached at a gate onto a wider track **(C)**. Interpretation panels here provide more information on the history of the canal.

Before heading back, a scenic detour is to park the bike securely and walk along the track to the river. Here an impressive Victorian structure stretches across the channel; built to trap debris before it reached a flow regulation weir downstream, that was replaced by Woolston New Weir in the 1990s, which now marks the top of the estuary. There are good views of this area from a low hill on the opposite side of the river, accessed via a footbridge alongside the debris control structure.

For the next stage of the ride, once back at Kingsway Bridge cross to the other side where a sign indicates the way to the next destination: **Victoria Park (D)**. A wide tarmac path then runs through Black Bear Park, following the route of the former Black Bear Canal; the remains of the access lock (Manor Lock) still visible nearby. See Walk #9 for more information on the canal.

After about a mile, the path reaches National Cycle Route 62 – the Trans Pennine Trail – near to a swing bridge across the Manchester Ship

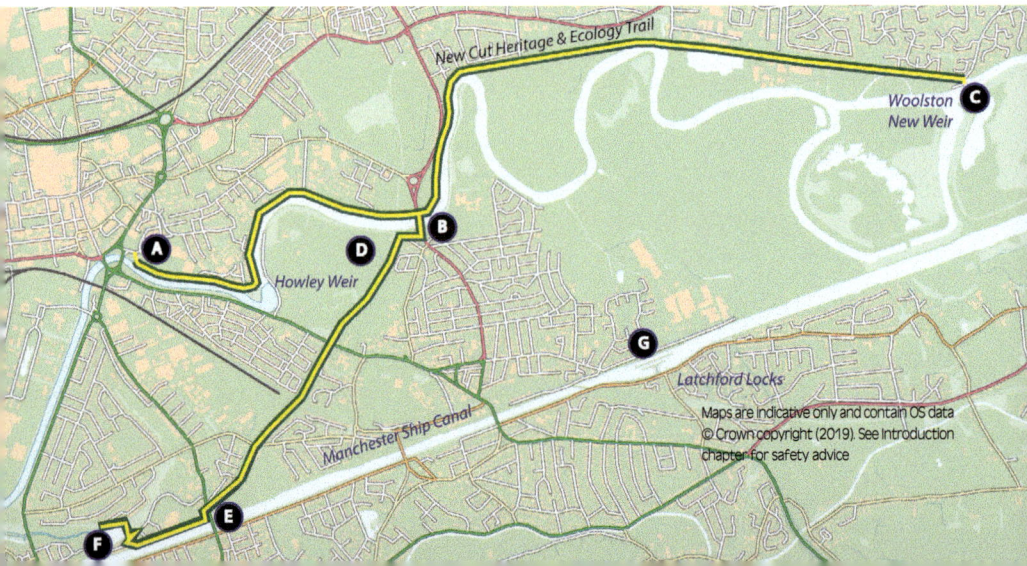

Canal. Wilderspool Causeway, the busy main road across the bridge, is most safely crossed at the traffic lights (**E**). The trail now briefly follows the canal, a (62) sign showing the way. The remains of the other entrance lock to Black Bear Canal – 20 Steps Lock – are visible almost directly beneath the bridge.

The trail then turns right to meet a side street, and right and left turns lead to a path around an area of open water overlooked by apartment blocks. This is the remains of **Warrington Dock** (**F**), which used to lie alongside a wide loop of the Mersey until the channel was diverted along a straighter section to the west.

Access to the dock was via the now-derelict Walton Lock at the western end of the basin, and the original channel is visible just beyond, now a wide tree-lined valley. In the opposite direction, the remainder of the loop was filled in to create a pleasant linear park, which leads almost as far as Bridgefoot near the town centre. The dock marks the end of this part of the route.

To return to the start, head back to the town centre via Kingsway Bridge and Wharf Street. For a longer ride, perhaps consider an out-and-return detour from Wilderspool Causeway to **Latchford Locks** (**G**), one of the largest and most impressive structures on the Ship Canal. This is a round-trip of about three miles, and follows the canal along the Trans Pennine Trail.

Another possibility would be to continue west along the Trans Pennine Trail from Warrington Dock to Sankey Bridges to join Cycle Route #5 about two miles away. The trail passes the Mersey and another disused canal en route. Once at Sankey Bridges, either retrace Route #5 to the town centre via Sankey Valley Park, a distance of about three miles, or, more ambitiously, continue the 16 to 17 miles to Hunts Cross or Halewood stations for trains back to Warrington. Returning from Widnes is another option, although the station is about two miles from the trail along busy roads.

CYCLE ROUTE 6 🚲

Distance: About 11 miles
Start/end: Riverside Retail Park, Warrington
Key features: Warrington has a rich maritime history and this route explores both the Mersey and some of the canals which cross the town, including the Manchester Ship Canal.

▲ **Upper to Lower**: A sign to mark the start of New Cut Heritage and Ecology Trail / Warrington Dock

Entrance lock for boat access between the Mersey and the marina on the Sankey Canal at Fiddler's Ferry

Further reading

To learn more about the history, culture and sights around this part of the estuary, the following guides and reviews provide a fine introduction:

A Hundred Years of the Manchester Ship Canal, Ted Gray, (Aurora Publishing, 1993)

A Pictorial History of the Mersey and Irwell Navigation, John Corbridge, (E.J. Morten, 1979)

Making the most of the Mersey: a Leisure Guide to your Estuary, Mersey Basin Campaign, (2007)

On the Waterfront, Peter de Figueiredo, in Mersey the river that changed the world, Ian Wray (ed.), photography by Colin McPherson, (The Bluecoat Press, 2007)

Railways and Waterways to Warrington, Peter A. Norton, (Cheshire Libraries, 1984)

Riverside Rambles along the Mersey, Ron Freethy, (Sigma Leisure, 2004)

Schooner Port: two centuries of upper Mersey sail, H.F. Starkey, (G.W. & A. Hesketh, 1983)

The River Mersey, Ron Freethy, (Terence Dalton Ltd., 1985)

The Sinking of RMS Tayleur: The Lost Story of the Victorian Titanic, Gill Hoffs, (Pen & Sword Books Ltd., 2014)

Walk & Cycle about Heart of the Estuary: A Merseytravel Guide to the Heart of the Estuary walks and cycling routes, Mersey Basin Campaign, (2008)

Warrington through Time, Janice Hays, (Amberley Publishing, 2010)

The website of Warrington Museum & Art Gallery (www.culturewarrington.org) also has much useful background. Chapters 4 to 6 suggest additional books and websites on the environment, maritime heritage and wildlife of the region.

Low tide at the waterfront in Liverpool

part two

ESTUARY THEMES

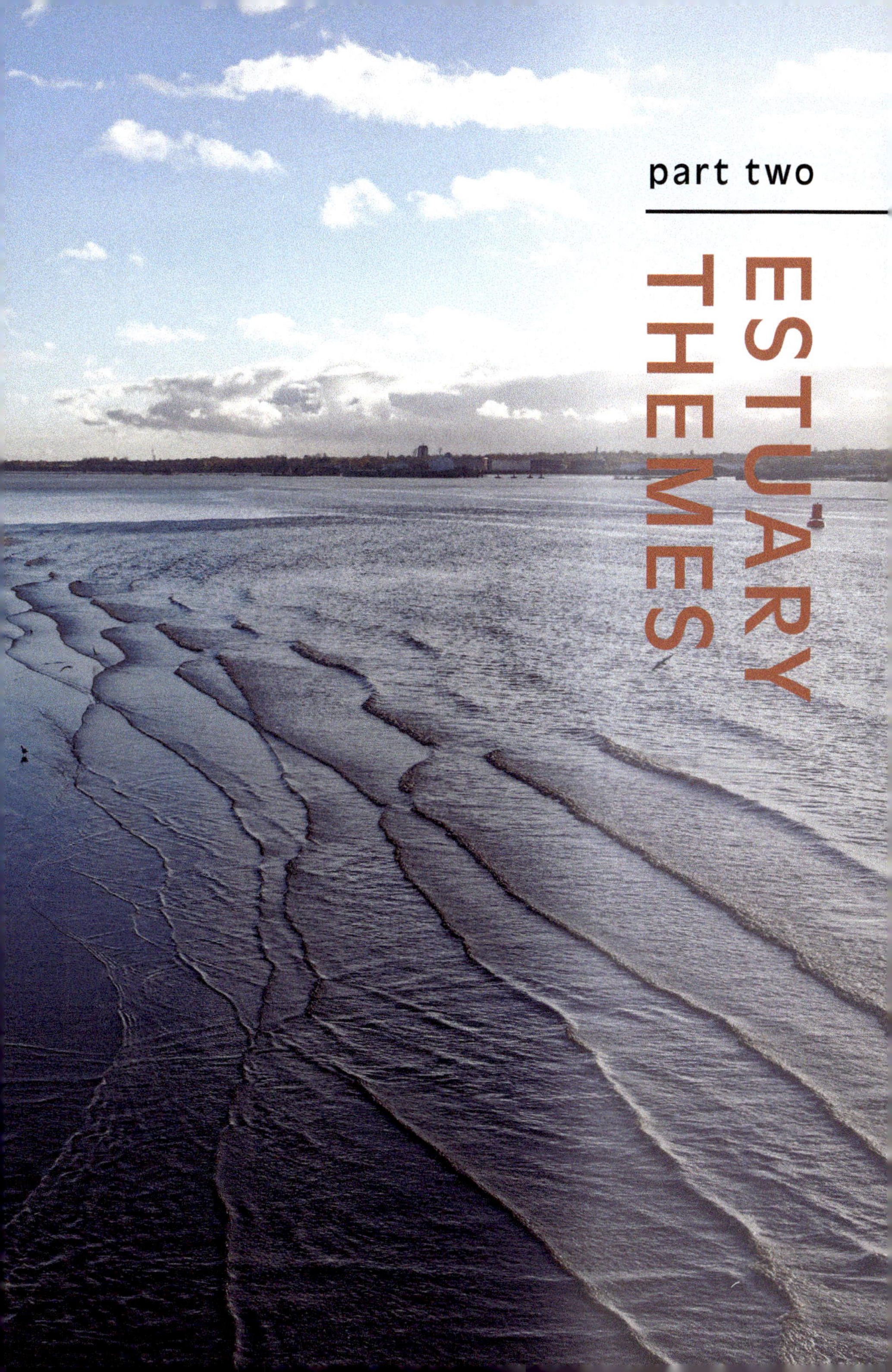

The Mersey Tidal Bore approaching Wigg Island in Runcorn, having passed beneath the Silver Jubilee Bridge

chapter 4

RIVERS AND TIDES

The Mersey begins in Manchester fed by tributaries flowing down from the Peak District and Pennines.

During the Industrial Revolution water quality deteriorated greatly, but the improvements in recent decades have been a major success story.

The tidal influence begins in Warrington and affects shipping and wildlife in the estuary, with a tidal bore forming on the highest tides.

Indeed, our understanding of the tides owes much to the pioneering work of scientists from Liverpool and the Wirral.

VISIT IDEAS

Liverpool Bay

See the following chapters for more information on places to visit within the different areas:

Chapter 1 – Lower Estuary (Liverpool)

- The Alt Estuary
- Crosby Marine Lake
- Panoramic 34, Liverpool
- Old Dock tours, Liverpool
- Sefton Park, Liverpool
- Otterspool Promenade, Liverpool
- Hale Head
- Pickerings Pasture Local Nature Reserve

Some of these places are passed on Cycle Routes #1 and #2 and Walks #1 and #3

Chapter 2 – Lower Estuary (Wirral, Cheshire)

- Entrance gate to Birkenhead Docks
- Birkenhead Priory
- Bidston Observatory
- Bidston Lighthouse
- Port Sunlight River Park
- Eastham Country Park
- Frodsham and Helsby

Some of these places are passed on Cycle Routes #3 and #4 and Walks #4, #5 and #6

Chapter 3 –Upper Estuary

- Runcorn Hill
- Halton Castle
- Spike Island, Widnes
- Transporter bridge plaque, Widnes
- Sankey Valley Park, Warrington
- Fiddler's Ferry
- Howley Weir, Warrington
- Woolston New Weir, Warrington
- Manchester Ship Canal

Some of these places are passed on Cycle Routes #5 and #6 and Walks #7, #8 and #9

Alt Estuary

Crosby Marine Lake

NEW BRIGHTON

Leasowe

The Birket

Bidston Hill

Birkenhead Docks

BIRKENHEAD

WIRRAL

The Narrows

Pier Head

LIVERPOOL

Otterspool Promenade

Port Sunlight River Park

River Dibbin

Garston

Sp Ga Co Re

Eastham Country Park

ELLESMERE PORT

RIVERS AND TIDES

The Mersey begins in Stockport, to the south of Manchester. The transition from river to estuary is in Warrington and by Widnes and Runcorn the channel is considerably wider, although sandstone outcrops then force it through the Runcorn Gap.

Freed from these constraints, the estuary forms a wide inland sea at high tide, larger than any lake or reservoir in England, while the mudflats exposed as the tide goes out are a prime feeding ground for wintering birds.

Sandstone formations then cause another constriction and, by Liverpool, the channel is little more than half a mile wide. Here the flood tide speeds along at several miles per hour and the change in water levels between low and high tide can exceed 10 metres.

An understanding of the tides is important for shipping and the region has long been at the forefront of tidal prediction. The first systematic observations of tide levels began in Liverpool and many port authorities worldwide once relied on estimates from Bidston Observatory on the Wirral.

Another consequence of the high tidal range is that, on the highest tides, a tidal bore sometimes forms near Hale Head and travels as far upstream as Warrington.

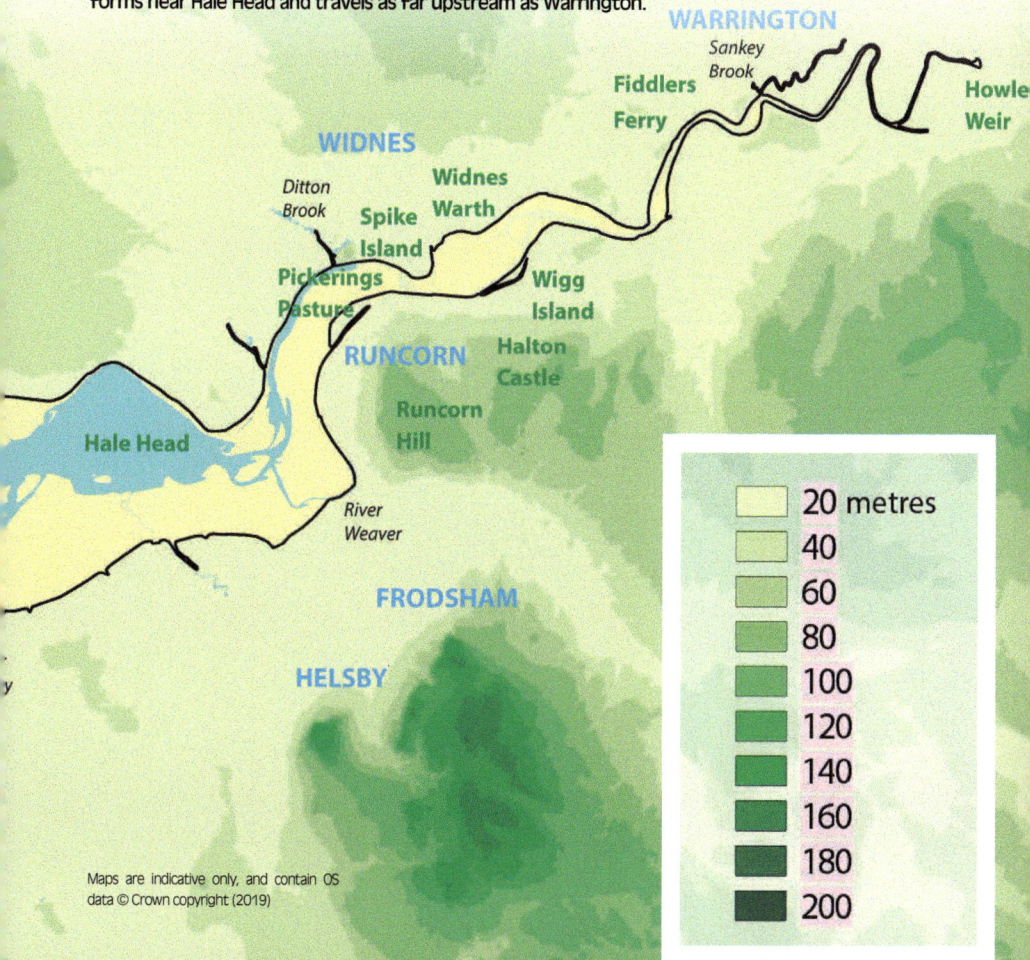

WARRINGTON

Sankey Brook

Fiddlers Ferry

Howle Weir

WIDNES

Ditton Brook

Widnes Warth

Spike Island

Pickerings Pasture

Wigg Island

RUNCORN

Halton Castle

Runcorn Hill

Hale Head

River Weaver

FRODSHAM

HELSBY

	20 metres
	40
	60
	80
	100
	120
	140
	160
	180
	200

Maps are indicative only, and contain OS data © Crown copyright (2019)

A brief tour of the basin

Upstream from the estuary

The Mersey Basin drains an area of almost 2000 square miles and includes parts of the Peak District and the Pennines. Several million people live in the basin, with perhaps a million in the main settlements around the estuary shores.

Often, a river is considered to start in its headwaters but the Mersey begins lower down, in Stockport to the south of Manchester. Here two main tributaries meet – the Goyt and the Tame – of which the Goyt is the larger and rises in the Goyt Valley, an area of forests, reservoirs and moorland in the Peak District where the highest point is Shining Tor, almost 600m above sea level. The meeting place with the Tame occasionally attracts sightseers and is close to the eastern end of the Merseyway shopping centre in Stockport alongside a footpath beneath the M60 motorway.

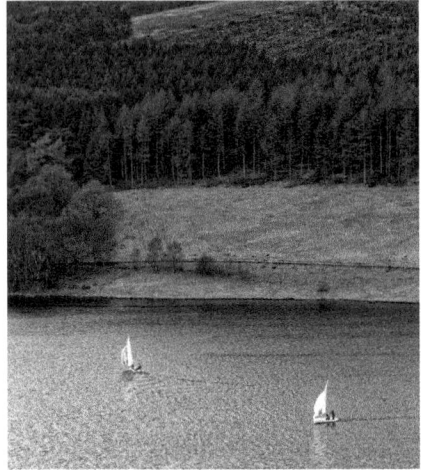

▲ The Goyt Valley lies between Buxton and Macclesfield and is popular with walkers, cyclists and sailing enthusiasts (www.goytvalley.co.uk)

This sign in Stockport celebrates the start of the Mersey; the full inscription reads *Water is Life & Heaven's Gift. Here Rivers Goyt & Tame become Mersey Flowing Clear from Stockport to the Sea* ▼

The river network in the Mersey Basin; the catchment of the River Alt lies to the north of Liverpool

Maps are indicative only, and contain OS data © Crown copyright (2019)

The next major tributary is the River Irwell, which rises in the Pennines north of Manchester and meets the Mersey west of the city. Its channel was widened, deepened and straightened between the confluence and Manchester when the Manchester Ship Canal was built in the 1890s, as was that of the Mersey to Warrington. The canal was built primarily to provide a link to the Port of Manchester, which thrived for several decades, until it was closed in the 1980s. However, it continues to serve sites between Warrington and Manchester as well as locations further downstream.

Chapter 5, Maritime Connections, describes the history of the port and canal in more detail.

There are two smaller tributaries in the reach between the Irwell confluence and Warrington: Glaze Brook and the River Bollin. The river and canal then part company just east of the town and the tidal influence begins a short way downstream at Woolston New Weir, which was built in the 1990s to replace an older structure associated with the Ship Canal. Cycle Route #6 explores this picturesque area.

The upper Goyt Valley
viewed from near Buxton

The northern and eastern shores

Woolston New Weir marks the start of the estuary and is about 30 miles from the sea. On the northern side of the Mersey, the next major tributary is Sankey Brook, which rises near St Helens and meets the estuary on the western outskirts of Warrington. Along with the Sankey Canal, the brook is the centrepiece of an attractive linear park – Sankey Valley Park; the lowermost mile or so is tidally influenced, presenting a flood risk on the highest tides. Cycle Route #5 visits the park and canal.

Before the coast, the only other significant tributary is Ditton Brook. This rises on a low sandstone ridge in south Liverpool and, where it meets the Mersey, forms the eastern boundary of Pickerings Pasture Local Nature Reserve. One of the highlights here is a great view of the estuary from a low hill alongside the brook, again visited on Cycle Route #5.

In Liverpool, several rivers once flowed into the Mersey, but these have largely disappeared due to the engineering works described later and are often called the 'lost rivers of Liverpool'. One remains though – the River Alt – which rises in northeast Liverpool in the general area of Aintree Racecourse and meets the sea just south of Formby Point. Owing to coastal erosion, the

▲ The Mersey in Warrington

▲ Ditton Brook where it meets the Mersey

course of its estuary has changed many times and, because of the flatness of the terrain, pumping is used in the lower reaches to help with flood control: a common arrangement in East Anglia but rare in northwest England.

▼ The Mersey near Hale Head

WHERE DOES THE ESTUARY BEGIN AND END?

The start of an estuary is usually taken to be the Normal Tidal Limit, marked on the Ordnance Survey's 1:25000 scale maps as 'NTL'.

This is the furthest point upstream that normally has a tidal influence, and for the Mersey is at Howley Weir near the centre of Warrington. However, on the highest tides the weir is submerged as the flood tide passes over it and a noticeable upstream flow develops, sometimes with ducks hitching a free ride among the debris brought in by the incoming tide. On rare occasions, seals have swum over the weir while chasing fish upstream; Chapter 6, Wildlife, describes some of these sightings.

▲ Looking towards Woolston New Weir from upstream

▲ Sand dunes and beach at Formby Point

The flow can persist for an hour or more and moves along at quite a pace. Further upstream, the effect becomes weaker as the tide fights against the downstream flow and eventually the river seems to stop in its tracks, with little movement visible on the water surface.

Where this happens depends on river flows and tide levels on the day but sometimes extends to Paddington Meadows, a mile downstream from Woolston New Weir. The risks from an extreme tidal and surge event were factored into design of the weir, so there is a good case to consider it the highest tidally influenced point in the Mersey. This would therefore make it the top or head of the estuary, although many books and reports consider it to be at Howley Weir.

As for where the estuary ends, the westernmost limit is normally taken to be New Brighton, as it is in this guide. However, sometimes it is considered to be Dove Point near Meols on the north Wirral coastline. On the opposite shoreline, suggestions for the end-point range from Royal Seaforth Dock, across the water from New Brighton, to Southport many miles north. A maritime definition is also widely used whereby the end of the estuary as a whole is assumed to be at the entrance to the dredged channel that ships follow to port, for which the closest land is Formby Point. That is the approach used here.

There is another difference of opinion regarding how to describe the upper and lower parts of the estuary. Usually the Runcorn Gap is taken as the dividing line and the term Inner Estuary used for the widest part immediately downstream. However, some studies call this the Middle Estuary while others use that term for the Upper and Inner estuaries combined. Most though call the part beyond the Narrows the Outer Estuary. The map in the Introductory chapter shows the boundaries used in this guide.

The southern shores

On the southern shores of the estuary, the Manchester Ship Canal cuts across the path of the rivers that once flowed into the Mersey from Warrington to its entrance, about three miles beyond Ellesmere Port. Between Warrington and Wigg Island in Runcorn, the canal was excavated across land to the south of the Mersey. For the remainder of its course it then crosses marshlands and mudflats, protected on the seaward side by a sea wall. Viewed from the promenade in Widnes, this can sometimes lead to the unusual sight of ships seeming to float high above the estuary as they pass along the canal.

The largest tributary to meet this part of the Mersey is the River Weaver, which flows down from hills beyond Crewe and Nantwich and then through the outskirts of Frodsham. It once joined at a wide tidal inlet but now enters the canal directly, with sluices on the sea wall to help regulate levels. The term 'tidal inlet' is another name for a river delta or estuary and is widely used in descriptions of the Mersey.

The Weaver remains navigable for some distance upstream and one popular tourist destination is the remarkable Anderton Boat Lift near Winsford, built in the 19th century to raise boats the 50 feet or so from the River Weaver Navigation to the Trent & Mersey Canal. The watertight tanks in the lift can hold two narrowboats or a single barge at a time (www.canalrivertrust.org.uk).

The next tributary to meet the Mersey is the River Gowy, about five miles downstream of the Weaver. This smaller river rises southeast of Chester and in its lower reaches is the centrepiece of Gowy Meadows Nature Reserve (www.cheshirewildlifetrust.org.uk). It then passes through the grounds of the huge Stanlow Oil Refinery to enter the estuary via an inverted siphon beneath the Ship Canal. During the 12th century, Stanlow Abbey was built on a small promontory next to the inlet, but was relocated after about a century, partly due to the risk from storms and flooding. The site was then used as a monastic grange or farm. The ruins are now a scheduled monument, although normally not accessible to the public.

Looking towards the former tidal inlet of the River Weaver from Overton Hill near Frodsham; see Walk #6 ▼

The Wirral shores

Heading downstream from the oil refinery, the Ship Canal passes the former docks at Ellesmere Port. After another mile it enters a picturesque cutting bounded on the seaward side by a low hill called Mount Manisty, created from material excavated during construction of the canal. The hill was named in honour of the engineer who oversaw works in this area.

The entrance to the Ship Canal is at Eastham Locks, just south of Eastham Country Park. Low sandstone cliffs extend most of the way from here to Tranmere, just south of Birkenhead. The only significant tributary in this reach is the River Dibbin whose source is in a low line of hills running roughly parallel to the shore along the Wirral. This meets the Mersey alongside Port Sunlight River Park and once had a much larger inlet, but this was enclosed with the construction of Bromborough Dock.

Following a major expansion in the 1930s, the main role of the dock was to serve the Lever Brothers' factory at Port Sunlight about a mile upstream, with raw materials and goods transported to and from the factory along the river. It was closed in the 1980s and initially used as a landfill site before being landscaped to create Port Sunlight River Park, a popular waterside destination. Further inland, the River Dibbin follows a more natural course and forms the centrepiece of Brotherton Park and Dibbinsdale Nature Reserve (www.dibbinsdale.co.uk), a short walk from Bromborough Rake Station.

The only other major tributary before the coast is the Birket, which drains much of the north of the peninsula. At nearly a mile across, its tidal inlet, which was known as Wallasey Pool, would once have been a distinctive feature of the coastline. It extended so far inland that the northeast tip of the Wirral was almost an island, isolated by the tides and marshy floodplains. However, in the 19th century it was enclosed during development of Birkenhead Docks. The original watercourse – heavily modified – is still visible in places, including near Leasowe Lighthouse and alongside the community park of Bidston Moss.

About a mile to the south was another inlet, Tranmere Pool. The area in-between formed a headland that until the 19th century was covered with woods and meadows; indeed, the name Birkenhead may derive from the Old English word for birch tree. This inlet too was enclosed – in this case during construction of the Cammell Laird shipyard – and the forests cleared to make way for houses and factories. However, some of the earliest buildings on the headland remain in the form of 12th century Birkenhead Priory, which has an interesting museum describing the history of the area.

The outfall from the River Dibbin alongside Port Sunlight River Park ▼

A low embankment alongside the Birket near Leasowe Lighthouse ▼

Liverpool

In Liverpool, several rivers once flowed down to the Mersey from the low sandstone hills that run roughly parallel to the shore through the city. Nowadays, though, few traces remain, due to dock building and drainage works.

The largest and most southerly was Garston River, which had several water mills along its lower reaches, and a fishing community and salt works at its tidal inlet. However, in the 19th century the inlet was enclosed when Garston Docks were built, originally to handle coal brought by rail from Spike Island in Widnes.

About a mile downstream, the smaller Jordan River had an inlet known as Otters Pool. The river's two main tributaries now supply the ornamental lakes in Sefton Park, one of the largest and most scenic parks in the city. The outflow from the lower lake disappears into a culvert, although the original route of the watercourse is still visible in the form of a wide tree-lined valley on the opposite side of Aigburth Road. This is the centrepiece of Otterspool Park, which provides a fine walking route to its namesake alongside the Mersey, Otterspool Promenade. See Cycle Route #2 for a description of the promenade in this area.

The most historically significant tributary of all was simply called the Pool and flowed into the Mersey about two miles downstream of Otters Pool. Its source was in the Edge Hill area of the city and it passed close to modern-day Liverpool Lime Street Station before following the routes of what are now Whitechapel and Paradise Street. The tidal inlet of the river was a natural choice for a harbour due to its sheltered waters and the defensive potential offered by a low sandstone ridge immediately to the north. Its status was formalised in 1207 when a Royal Charter was issued by King John to encourage people to settle in the newly established borough or township of 'Liuerpul'.

The port developed slowly over the following centuries until in 1715 the inlet was enclosed to create the first commercial wet dock in the world: the Old Dock. This was an immediate success prompting demand for more berths, although – due to a lack of suitable sites – most new docks were created by building sea walls out into the estuary and backfilling the enclosed areas to accommodate roads, quays and warehouses.

One consequence of this major feat of land reclamation is that for several miles the channel of the Mersey is narrower than it would otherwise be, in some places by more than half a mile. As a result, several notable buildings once on the shoreline are now inland, such as St Nicholas' Church near Pier Head in Liverpool, while new features have been created such as Crosby Marine Lake (see Walk #1), plus of course Pier Head itself. Chapter 5, Maritime Connections, discusses the history of the port further.

▼ One of the ornamental lakes in Sefton Park

The Palm House ▼

In these views south from the Panoramic 34 restaurant (above) and north from the Royal Liver Building (below), it is easy to imagine the path of the natural shoreline of the Mersey, before the docks were built. Chapter 1 describes these popular destinations.

THE MERSEY WATERFRONT

The Mersey waterfront is a product of the industrial revolution. Over the past 300 years, the riverside scene has been transformed. For the early 18th century traveller journeying down the River Mersey, the impression would have been largely rural. Some buildings would have been glimpsed, perhaps a scattering of cottages and farms, the odd medieval church or timber-framed manor house. In the small towns of Stockport and Warrington, workshops and dwellings huddled together on the river banks, whilst at Liverpool, still a modest port, warehouses, hostelries and lodging houses clustered around the pool. Apart from the ruined castle at Halton and the remains of the priory at Birkenhead, there was no architecture of any great ambition. 100 years later, industrialisation had taken hold, and over the following century urban expansion occurred on an unprecedented scale.

From 'On the Waterfront', Peter de Figueiredo

The sandbanks of the Inner Estuary at low tide, viewed from Liverpool Cathedral

FACTS AND FOLKLORE

'The Mersey drains an area of 4,680 square km, from the Irish Sea to the Pennines, taking in all of Merseyside and Greater Manchester, most of Cheshire and parts of Lancashire and the High Peak District.'

'The Mersey was the ancient boundary between the Saxon kingdoms of Mercia and Northumbria – the name Mersey originates from the Old English "maere", meaning "boundary".'

'The River Mersey is roughly 110 km long (70 miles). The combined length of the Mersey and all its tributaries is around 1,700 km (1,056 miles).'

'Today, the Mersey officially starts beneath the Merseyway shopping centre right in the middle of Stockport, where the Rivers Goyt and the Tame meet. But according to folklore it used to start upstream in Marple. At some point a careless mapmaker mislabelled the local rivers, and ever since the Mersey has started in Stockport.'

Selected quotations from Who Saved the Mersey ... and Who Killed it in the First Place?, Matthew Sutcliffe

What lies beneath?

One unusual aspect of the Mersey Estuary is that it does not have the classic funnel shape of many estuaries, but instead has two constrictions due to the underlying geology: the Runcorn Gap between Widnes and Runcorn, and the Narrows between Liverpool and Birkenhead.

At the Runcorn Gap, the channel is forced between sandstone outcrops less than half a mile apart. This has long been a natural crossing point, and one of the first regulated ferry services in the estuary began here in the 12th century. Two centuries before, there may have been a Mercian fort on the southern shores, although the ruins and the promontory on which it stood (Castle Rock) were removed during construction of the railway bridge in the 1860s and the Manchester Ship Canal in the 1890s. A transporter bridge was built here in 1905 but replaced in the 1960s by what is now known as the Silver Jubilee Bridge. The Mersey Gateway road crossing a short way upstream was opened in 2017. Chapter 3 describes the transporter bridge in more detail.

▲ Sandstone outcrops alongside Bidston Windmill on Bidston Hill on the Wirral

Exposed sandstone rock at the Old Dock in Liverpool ▼

In contrast, at the Narrows the underlying bedrock causes the channel to narrow over several miles before expanding again, a shape sometimes likened to an hourglass. At its narrowest point, it is little more than half a mile wide and this bottleneck results in strong currents that help prevent sediment settling. This natural scouring combined with a depth in places of more than 20 metres contributed to the growth of Liverpool as a port, albeit with some ship-handling challenges as discussed in Chapter 5, Maritime Connections. The two road tunnels beneath the Mersey are sited in this area.

The dominant rock type is again sandstone and extends beneath much of Liverpool, the Wirral and the southern shores. Lower lying areas are largely covered by drift material from glacial, river and marine deposits, but the underlying rock is exposed in places, such as the low cliffs along the northern shores of the Inner Estuary and the southern parts of the Wirral coastline. Sandstone outcrops are also a feature in the hills above Frodsham (Walk #6), at Runcorn Hill and Halton Castle in Runcorn, and at Bidston Hill on the Wirral (Walk #5).

Sandstone is prized as a building material and the local Sherwood sandstone has a distinctive red-brown colour, sometimes interspersed with lighter-coloured layers such as yellows and whites. The largest quarries were in the Runcorn area and supplied stone worldwide, including for Liverpool Cathedral and Fort Perch Rock at New Brighton.

Walk #7 visits this area, and other opportunities to see the local geology include the Sandstone Trail above Frodsham (Walk #6), and the low cliffs alongside Hale Head (Walk #3) and Eastham Country Park (Cycle Route #4). The bedrock is also evident at the Old Dock in Liverpool, where entertaining tours are offered by experts from Merseyside Maritime Museum.

Twilight view towards the sandstone edges at Helsby Hill from near Frodsham (see Walk #6) ▼

The rhythm of the tides

The tides are caused primarily by a combination of the gravitational pulls of the sun and moon, and are often called the astronomical tides. In the Mersey, as in most places around the UK, this results in two high tides a day with the peaks just over twelve hours apart, advancing by about fifty minutes each day.

These effects are strongest when the sun, moon and Earth are aligned, resulting in unusually high tides called spring tides. These occur roughly every two weeks, as do the so-called neap tides in-between, which have a particularly low range. The origin of the term 'spring tide' is unclear but bears no relationship to the season.

The influence of the sun on tide levels is about half that of the moon and other factors include orbital variations plus local effects due to the topography of the sea floor and coastline. For example, the time taken from low to high tide at the Narrows is roughly the same as on ebb tides, whereas at Fiddler's Ferry near Warrington the rate of change is markedly faster on the flood tide.

Spring tides occur around the time of the full and new moons and are typically highest around the equinoxes in March and October, when the sun is almost over the equator. This is often a good time to see the Mersey Tidal Bore and some viewing points are described later in this chapter. Longer-term variations also occur such as an 18.6-year pattern that last reached a peak in 2015, resulting in unusually high tides that year. Many other variations occur with different phases and magnitudes, known as harmonics by tidal experts.

The speed and power of the incoming tide can be most impressive to see. In the UK, the tidal range at Liverpool is only exceeded in the Severn Estuary, which itself has one of the largest ranges in the world. On the highest tides, the rise in levels exceeds 10 metres at Liverpool and is still several metres at some locations upstream, such as Fiddler's Ferry and near Warrington town centre.

Waves overtopping the promenade at Pier Head on a high spring tide ▼

▲ A tide stone behind the Old Hall Hotel on Main Street in Frodsham marking the maximum water level reached in 1862, in an area once affected by tidal flooding; the hotel is a pleasant place to stay or stop for a meal or refreshments (www.oldhallhotelfrodsham.co.uk)

▲ Artwork on flood defences near Warrington town centre

Another factor to consider is the short-lived increase in water levels that can occur due to atmospheric effects. Called 'surge', this effect is most significant during strong winds and low pressure over the oceans and is most likely in stormy conditions. Surge heights of 1 to 2 metres have been observed in Liverpool Bay. When coinciding with the peak of a spring tide, surge can lead to unusually high water levels. It is at times like these that coastal flood alerts and warnings are most likely to be issued by the Environment Agency (www.gov.uk).

During stormy weather, another risk is from wave action, especially around the mouth of the estuary and along the coast. The dangers arise not just from flooding, but because stones and other debris may become projectiles capable of shattering glass and injuring people. For safety, access to the waterfront is therefore sometimes restricted in places such as New Brighton.

The tidal flood risk extends a surprisingly long way inland and Warrington in particular was once ranked one of the locations most at risk from flooding in the UK. However, in recent years there have been major improvements to the flood defences in the town, which as a side benefit have created some great walking and cycling opportunities, such as those described in Walk #9 and Cycle Route #6.

Much of the shoreline of the estuary is protected by sea defences. The Manchester Ship Canal also acts as a barrier in areas once affected by tidal flooding, such as Frodsham Marsh and the lower reaches of the rivers Weaver and Gowy. Further upstream, the canal acts as a diversion channel for flood flows that might otherwise affect Warrington, thereby reducing the risks from river-related (fluvial) flooding in the town.

THREE TIDAL SEQUENCES
This page – Howley Weir in Warrington before and after being overtopped by an unusually high tide; the images were taken about 23 minutes apart

Facing page (left) – a sudden rise in levels at Bishops Wharf near Warrington town centre following arrival of the Mersey Tidal Bore; the images were taken over a period of 54 minutes, with the first two about 4 minutes apart

Facing page (right) – the entrance to Canning Half Tide Dock at Pier Head in Liverpool on a falling tide; the images were taken over about 5 hours with the first three at roughly hourly intervals

Tidal observations and predictions

Given how many factors affect the tides, it is perhaps surprising that astronomical tide predictions can be made for months to years ahead. These are essential for shipping operators, port authorities and leisure activities such as sailing, angling, beachcombing, metal detecting and coastal walks.

An easy way to check predictions is from the small tide table booklets usually found on sale at seaside resorts in RNLI shops, tourist offices, newsagents, and fishing tackle shops, and available directly from publishers such as Laver Publishing.

Online estimates are another useful source, such as those published on the websites of the BBC, the UK Hydrographic Office (www.admiralty.co.uk) and the National Tidal and Sea Level Facility (www.ntslf.org). The NTSLF website also includes current observations of levels at Gladstone Dock in the northern dock system in Liverpool, which is a key gauge in the national network of tide gauges operated by the Environment Agency.

The Agency also operates several automated gauges in the Upper Estuary to help with flood warning operations in Warrington, with values again published to a website (search for 'River and Sea Levels' on www.gov.uk). There are also many traditional manually read gauges around the estuary, which consist of graduated scales painted or engraved onto sea

▲ Laver's Liverpool & Irish Sea Tide Table Booklet has been published annually for more than half a century (www.laverpublishing.com)

walls, or attached to them. One of the tide level sequences shown earlier includes an example.

Tidal predictions are made by solving complex mathematical equations and until the late 19th century these had to be solved laboriously by hand. Both the speed and accuracy of the calculations then improved with invention of the Tide Prediction Machine, a type of analogue computer. The basis of the approach was to use an intricate array of pulley wheels of different sizes to represent the influences of the sun, moon and other factors,

Part of the Roberts-Légé tide prediction machine at the National Oceanography Centre in Liverpool ▼

▼ Bidston Obervatory on Bidston Hill, Wirral

▲ The instrumentation kiosk for the Liverpool tide gauge at Gladstone Dock in the northern dock system; readings are received here from two submerged bubbler pressure sensors near the dock entrance (source: National Tidal and Sea Level Facility)

▲ This exhibit at the National Oceanography Centre (right) illustrates just how large the tidal range is at Liverpool; the scale only covers the top five metres of the change in levels on a high spring tide. The glass case on the left houses the Doodson-Légé tide prediction machine (www.tide-and-time.uk)

with the responses combined by a wire or tape threading its way through the machine. The results were then plotted on a chart or displayed on a dial for operators to interpret.

Bidston Observatory on the Wirral (www.bidstonobservatory.org.uk) was a leading centre for designing and operating these machines. From the 1920s to the early 1960s its scientists provided tidal predictions for perhaps two thirds of the world's port authorities, before computer-based approaches took over. Owing to the expense and complexity, only about thirty machines were ever made, including two landmark designs built for use at Bidston: the Roberts-Légé machine manufactured in 1906 and the second largest of all, the Doodson-Légé machine, delivered in 1950, which weighed 1.8 tons.

Scientific work continued at the observatory until 2004 when operations were transferred to the campus of the University of Liverpool. This is now performed at the National Tidal and Sea Level Facility, which from 2010 has been part of the National

Oceanography Centre. Here, work continues on the pioneering tidal research started more than a century ago on the Wirral.

In recent years, the Roberts-Légé and Doodson-Légé machines have been restored in collaboration with National Museums Liverpool and are on display at the centre's Tide and Time exhibition (www.tide-and-time.uk). This is open to the public on one afternoon each month. Visits usually include a demonstration of one of the machines in action and a presentation on the history of the centre and current research.

Bidston Obervatory is now privately owned but is sometimes open to the public on Heritage Open Days in September (www.heritageopendays.org.uk), and private tours are held occasionally at other times.

The early days of tidal prediction

Some of the earliest contributions to understanding the tides were from William Hutchinson, the dock master at the Old Dock in Liverpool from 1759 to 1793, who for 29 years made the first systematic tidal observations in the UK.

The resulting record of the timing and height of peak levels has proved invaluable for research. One of the first applications was by Richard and George Holden who in 1770 published the first publicly available tide tables for Liverpool, which for many years were the standard for port operations. Hutchinson (1715 to 1801) was also instrumental in setting up the Liverpool pilot service and the first lifeboat station around the Mersey, at Formby. He also invented the first parabolic reflector suitable for use in a lighthouse, which was installed at Bidston Hill.

An imaginative memorial to his life appears in a pedestrianised area in the Liverpool ONE retail complex at Thomas Steers Way close to Albert Dock. Fountains set into the pavement rise and fall to mimic the cycle of the tides and phases of the moon, while paving tiles show stylised representations of his handwritten observations and the approximate routes of the Old Dock and former shoreline. An interpretation panel notes some of his other accomplishments, which included being 'a privateer captain, ship-owner, boat builder, commercial trader, inventor, philanthropist' as well as 'the Dock-Master of the Old Dock'.

The display also acknowledges the earlier work of Jeremiah Horrocks. Born in Liverpool in about 1619, he made the first successful prediction of a transit of Venus across the sun, providing insights into the planet's size and orbit. He also made important contributions to calculating the orbit of the moon and understanding its influence on the tides. Although he died in his twenties, his achievements were widely acknowledged, including by Isaac Newton later that century.

Fountains and pavement inscriptions to commemorate William Hutchinson on Thomas Steers Way in Liverpool ▼

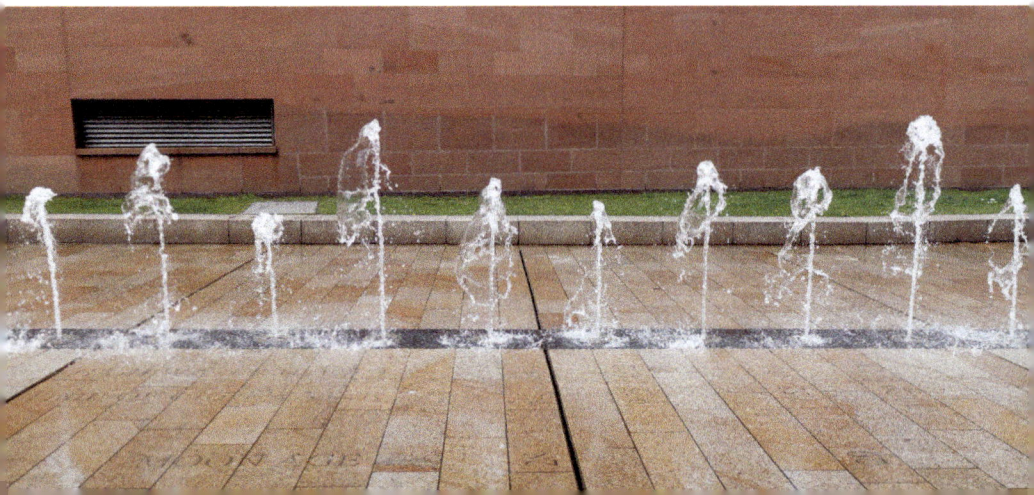

INTERPRETING TIDAL PREDICTIONS

Tidal predictions are usually straightforward to interpret, but there are some things to watch out for, particularly if it is important to know the time of peak levels, such as when viewing the Mersey Tidal Bore, monitoring flood warnings, or watching wading birds.

Perhaps the first check to make is on the locations for which estimates are provided. With online sources, if there is no obvious choice of site, an approximate value can be estimated from comparisons with nearby locations. In contrast, to use tide tables, look for the high water times and heights at the closest location you can find; after which, at a beach, for example, more of the sand with be exposed as the tide goes out. Near the front of the book there will be an adjustment for other places in the same area. For example, average high-water times at Widnes are about 45 minutes later than at Gladstone Dock in Liverpool. This information is not always available from online sources but will be included in printed booklets.

Another consideration is whether the predicted times of high and low water are in local time or Greenwich Mean Time (GMT). During winter, these are the same, but British Summer Time is one hour ahead, only returning to GMT when the clocks go back in autumn. Sometimes this correction is already included, but more usually a prominent warning shows that this adjustment is required; forgetting to apply it is a common reason for missing the tidal bore!

For engineering design studies, such as for flood defences or quays, it is often important to know the heights of water levels above the UK national datum. This is because most other infrastructure is built to this datum. Historical tide gauge readings are an important source of information for these types of study, but for operational reasons a small correction factor often needs to be applied if they are to be expressed relative to datum values. The factors to apply for the UK National Tide Gauge Network are published on the NTSLF website (www.ntslf.org).

Surge forecasts are also published on the NTSLF website, and the values that appear can be added to the astronomical tide predictions to estimate the overall water level at a site. On the graphs on the website, these are called the *surge model residual forecasts*. However, given the many interactions between river flows, currents and wave action, the resulting estimates for peak levels in the estuary are only approximate and actual values may be different on the day. Perhaps surprisingly, negative values of surge can also occur, such as during periods of unusually high atmospheric pressure over the Irish Sea, resulting in lower levels than expected.

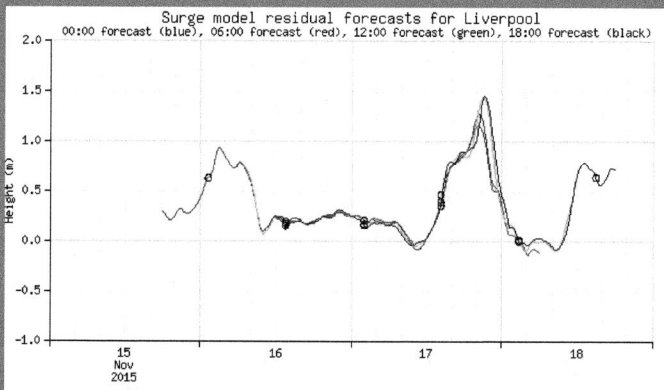

This graph from 15 November 2015 shows a surge forecast for Liverpool of almost 1.5 metres on the 17th, and was downloaded from the website of the National Tidal and Sea Level Facility; the black circles indicate the times of high tide (www.ntslf.org)

A dynamic estuary

As well as affecting currents and water levels, the tides influence the quality of water in the estuary. Twice a day they bring in sediment and nutrients from the sea and flush pollutants from the lowermost reaches. Between mean low and high tide, the volume of water increases by a factor of about five to reach nearly three times that of Windermere, England's largest natural lake.

At high tide, the area of water enclosed within the estuary is about 35 square miles, but this is more than halved as mudflats and sandbanks are exposed at low tide. Tidal currents also move these deposits around, especially in the Inner Estuary where the main low water channel has migrated from bank to bank several times since records began. In Liverpool Bay, many changes to the sandbanks have also been seen over the years, such as along the north Wirral coastline and around Formby Point. Dredging is therefore required in parts of the shipping lanes, as discussed in Chapter 5, Maritime Connections.

As sediment settles, the larger particles are deposited as mud or sand while the finer silt remains in suspension. The silt gives the water a muddy, grey-brown colour, perhaps seen most dramatically in Warrington on the incoming tide when there is often a marked contrast with the clearer river water flowing downstream. However, despite its appearance, water quality is much improved from a few decades ago and one sign is the increasing number of salmon (see Chapter 6, Wildlife). Indeed, historical accounts suggest that the

estuary once teemed with fish and supported several fishing settlements along its shores as far upstream as Warrington.

All this changed in the early years of the industrial revolution due to pollution from processes such as dyeing, tanning and bleaching, with chemical industries adding to the problem in later years. As towns and cities grew, the volume of untreated sewage entering the water also increased, leading to a toxic mix of raw sewage, heavy metals, solvents and solid waste. Water quality probably reached a low point in the 1960s and 1970s but since then the improvements have been remarkable and have rightfully attracted recognition, including the award of the International Thiess Riverprize in 1999, for which the citation stated:

A combination of massive investment in the water infrastructure by a privatized water company, tough environmental legislation, and major sewage upgrades made the difference. The remarkable transformation was made possible by the work of many organisations and individuals

working together. The Mersey Basin Campaign was a pioneer in partnership. Today the Mersey and its tributaries are cleaner than at any time since the end of the industrial revolution. Water quality has improved and fish have returned to formerly polluted stretches of the river. For the first time in living memory, juvenile salmon have been found in the upper reaches of the river near Stockport. (www.riverfoundation.org.au)

The Mersey Basin Campaign was established in 1985 and perhaps uniquely at the time – at least in the UK – was a true partnership between national government, local authorities, businesses, and community, school and voluntary organisations. One influential figure was the then Secretary of State for the Environment, Michael Heseltine, who highlighted the potential links between cleaning up the Mersey and waterside investment and economic regeneration. The three key aims identified were:

- to improve river quality across the Mersey Basin to at least a 'fair' standard by 2010 so that all rivers and streams are clean enough to support fish;
- to stimulate attractive waterside developments for business, recreation, housing, tourism and heritage; and,
- to encourage people living and working in the Mersey Basin to value and cherish their watercourses and waterfront environments.

The campaign also built on existing initiatives, such as those by North West Water – predecessor to United Utilities – to reduce the amount of raw sewage entering the river and

> **RIVER CONDITIONS IN THE PAST**
> Everyone living on Merseyside was well aware of the dreadful conditions in the river – indeed, local folklore insisted that it was impossible to drown in the Mersey as one would be poisoned first.
> *From Water Quality and Fisheries in the Mersey Estuary, England: A historical perspective by P.D. Jones*

estuary. This included a major project to build a network of interceptor sewers and tunnels on the eastern shores of the estuary, from Speke in the south to Crosby in the north. These trap waste before it enters the Mersey, and it is then processed at an associated treatment works at Sandon Dock in the northern dock system.

Community involvement was another important factor and more than twenty Action Partnerships worked on projects at a local level. Some of the waterside parks and promenades that now dot the shores of the estuary arose from these types of initiatives, such as the Speke and Garston Coastal Reserve.

In 2010, the campaign ended as planned after 25 years, a major achievement as many such initiatives fizzle out in just a few years. It finished on a high note with many objectives achieved, and its work is continued by the original partners and newer organisations such as the Mersey Rivers Trust (www.merseyriverstrust.org.uk). A legacy website describes the history and achievements of the campaign (www.merseybasin.org.uk) as does Ian Wray's superb book *Mersey; the River that Changed the World.*

◀ **From left to right:** sandbanks and/or mudflats viewed from Widnes Warth in the Upper Estuary and at Hale Head and Otterspool Promenade further downstream

The Mersey Tidal Bore

People are often surprised to learn that a tidal bore sometimes forms on the Mersey. Admittedly, it is on a much smaller scale than some better-known examples, such as the Severn Bore in southwest England, but is still a great example of this natural phenomenon and one of only about twenty in the UK.

Tidal bores form when water levels in an estuary rise so quickly that a wave appears at the front of the incoming tide. This then travels upstream against the flow, sometimes for great distances inland. On the Mersey, the bore starts near Hale Head to the west of Widnes and makes its way nearly 10 miles upstream to Warrington, where it reaches a sudden end on hitting Howley Weir near the town centre.

The height of the wave depends on many factors, including the river flow, tides, and wind speed and direction, and may reach 30-60cm or more. However, it sometimes disappoints, so a good attitude is to assume it will not occur but be pleased if it does.

On the best days and at the best locations, expect to see a line of surf across much of the channel followed by a series of smaller waves known as whelps. Sometimes the first signs of its approach are the sound of rushing water in the distance and wading birds startled into flight, providing great birdwatching opportunities.

The tidal bore racing past flood defences opposite Wharf Street in Warrington ▼

> **OBSERVING TIDAL BORES**
> The website of the National Tidal and Sea Level Facility (www.ntslf.org) gives the following 'Tips for observers':
> - *It is better to arrive half an hour too early than a minute too late – rainfall, wind and other factors affect the time of arrival of the bore; its appearance cannot be predicted with certainty.*
> - *Bores can disappoint, because of various factors, even if the predicted tide is very high.*
> - *If you can go a number of times you will have a better chance of seeing something quite awe inspiring.*
> The website also describes the causes of tidal bores, with examples of several others around the world.

In contrast, on a disappointing day, all that occurs is a change in flow direction with little or no discernible wave. However, there are still compensations, such as the waterside views and admiring the power of the incoming tide.

In its early stages around Hale Head, the beginnings of the bore are modest, perhaps with little more to see than a small wave or tidal front moving upstream in the channel closest to the shore. The estuary is so wide here that it takes time for the various channels to fill, so other fronts may form in the distance, sometimes turning downstream and causing a satisfying splash if they meet others travelling in the opposite direction.

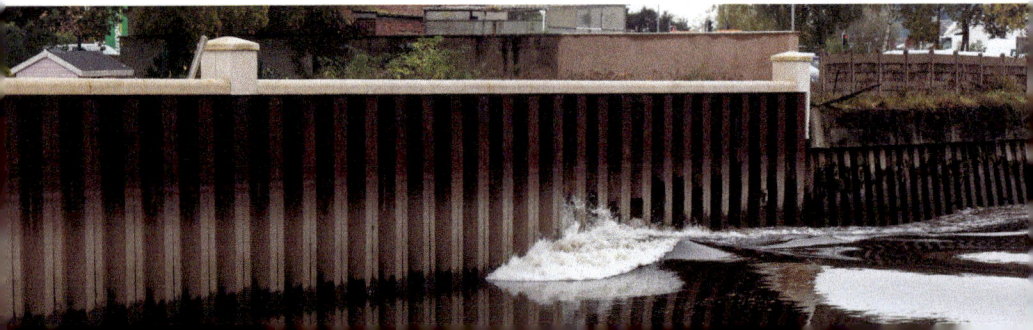

Heading upstream, there is quite a delay as the wave makes its way the 1 to 2 miles to the next place with waterside views: Pickerings Pasture. Here the main channel becomes more distinct so a fully formed wave may have already developed, gaining strength as it continues to the Runcorn Gap, sometimes merging with a second wave arriving from the other side.

Immediately beyond, separate channels follow the Runcorn and Widnes shorelines. The bore travels along both but is often stronger on the Runcorn side; the title page to this chapter shows an example. Possible vantage points include Victoria Promenade in Widnes and the waterfront at Wigg Island Community Park in Runcorn. As at Hale Head, smaller tidal fronts may snake across the sandbanks ahead of the incoming tide.

The channels merge before the Mersey Gateway crossing and the bore then heads off into the distance, slowing markedly again before gaining strength as it approaches Fiddler's Ferry, occasionally with a low line of surf across part of the channel. It then becomes more fully developed as it approaches Warrington, and viewpoints include the Forrest Way Bridge in Sankey Bridges, Centre Park Bridge near the town centre, and Wharf Street, next to Riverside Retail Park.

In this final stretch, the bore speeds up noticeably as it passes between flood defence walls before slowing again for the last half mile or so to Howley Weir. It then dissipates rapidly as it enters the stilling pool beneath the weir, although sometimes a much smaller reflected wave can be seen heading downstream a few minutes later from locations such as Wharf Street and Centre Park Bridge.

▲ **Upper to Lower:** The early stages of the tidal bore are just visible as it approaches the lighthouse at Hale Head / A weak tidal bore approaching Fiddler's Ferry / The tidal bore viewed from Forrest Way Bridge in Warrington with the whelps (following waves) evident

Gulls take to the air ahead of a weak tidal front

The Mersey Tidal Bore approaching
Wigg Island in Runcorn

Tidal bore prediction

As with all natural phenomena, estimating when the bore will occur is not an exact science, but some conditions that help include:

A high tide of 10 metres or more at Liverpool (Gladstone Dock)

Low river flows in the Mersey, such as after a dry spell

Little or no wave action, such as when winds are light.

Another advantage of a calm day is that the bore should stand out more clearly against the surrounding water. Tidal surge may also have an effect, although, as noted earlier, the impact is difficult to predict due to the complex flow patterns within the estuary, affecting the timing and size of the bore, or even breaking it up.

The best viewing times are during the highest spring tides, which usually occur from February to April and from August to October. However, videos of the bore on websites suggest that – in the past, at least – it has occurred in most months of the year, although with March and September perhaps best represented. If levels are high enough, conditions are sometimes suitable for a day or two either side of the highest tides of the month, and it sometimes forms when tides are less than 10 metres at Liverpool.

The section on tidal prediction earlier in this chapter suggests some ways to find out tide times and heights, although be sure to check whether the times are listed in GMT or local time. Typically, the bore starts to form around Hale Head around three hours before high water in Liverpool and arrives in Warrington within 15 to 20 minutes of high tide, but sometimes a few minutes after.

Intermediate times at Widnes/Runcorn, Fiddler's Ferry, and Forrest Way in Warrington are **approximately** 1¼ to 1¾ hours, 35-50 minutes, and 10 to 30 minutes before high water.

As in any activity near water, it is important to choose a safe viewing location. Always watch the bore from a safe place and never venture out on the sands or mudflats; remember also that once the tidal bore has passed the river will keep rising, by several metres in some places.

Some excellent water safety advice from the Royal National Lifeboat Institution (RNLI) is reproduced in the introduction to this guide and on the day it is advisable to check the website of the Environment Agency for any flood alerts or warnings in force (www.gov.uk).

On arriving at the waterside, it is usually clear whether the bore has passed; if it has, there will be a vigorous flow upstream meaning that the opportunity has been missed. However, on days with windblown waves this may not be obvious so try watching rocks or other objects on the shoreline to see if they are being submerged by the tide, which occurs rapidly if so.

If all is well, photographers in particular should get ready, since at some locations, such as central Warrington, the bore passes by at several miles per hour.

◀ The tidal bore in its final stages as it approaches Howley Weir in Warrington

Further reading

There are many publications on the environment and natural history of the Mersey Basin and the following reports, papers and websites provide useful insights:

A Hundred Years of the Manchester Ship Canal, Edward Gray, (Aurora Publishing, 1993)

Both sides of the river: Merseyside in poetry and prose, Gladys Mary Coles (ed.), (Headland, 1993)

From Astronomy to Oceanography – a brief history of Bidston Observatory, J. Eric Jones, (downloaded from www.noc.ac.uk)

Britannia (1586), William Camden, in Both sides of the river: Merseyside in poetry and prose, Gladys Mary Coles (ed.), (Headland, 1993)

Garston's River, Archive Leaflet C8, Garston & District Historical Society, www.garstonhistoricalsociety.org.uk, (Garston History Society, 1999)

Liverpool: a landscape history, Martin Greaney, (The History Press, 2013)

Liverpool's Drainage History: Seventeenth Century to MEPAS, G.N. Olsen, (Proceedings of the Institution of Civil Engineers, 1997)

Mersey the river that changed the World, Ian Wray (ed.), photography by Colin McPherson, (The Bluecoat Press, 2007)

On the Waterfront, Peter de Figueiredo, in Mersey the river that changed the world, Ian Wray (ed.), photography by Colin McPherson, (The Bluecoat Press, 2007)

The Mersey Estuary – Back from the Dead? Solving a 150-Year Old Problem, P.D. Jones, (Journal of the Chartered Institute of Water and Environmental Managers, 2000)

Thirteen from Twenty-Five, Walter Menzies, Mersey Basin Campaign, www.merseybasin.org.uk, (SourceNW, 2009)

Three Georges and one Richard Holden: The Liverpool tide table makers, P.L. Woodworth, (Transactions of the Historic Society of Lancashire and Cheshire, 2002)

Water Quality and Fisheries in the Mersey Estuary, England: A historical perspective, P.D. Jones, (Marine Pollution Bulletin, 2006)

Who Saved the Mersey...and Who Killed it in the First Place? Words: Matthew Sutcliffe; Interviews: Kate Fox; Photographs: Dan Kenyon, Tony Hall, Matthew Sutcliffe, Mersey Basin Campaign, www.merseybasin.org.uk, (SourceNW, 2009)

www.allertonOak.net The Allerton Oak website has fascinating insights into both local history and the environment. It includes a series of suggested walks and a section on the lost rivers of Liverpool.

www.historicengland.org.uk The Historic England website gives information on the location and history of scheduled monuments and other items of historical interest, such as the former abbey at Stanlow Point.

www.thefriendsofpickeringspasture.org.uk The Friends of Pickerings Pasture website has many interesting articles on the wildlife and environment of the Mersey, including one from 2016 called 'The Tidal Bore on the River Mersey'.

www.merseybasin.org.uk The legacy website of the Mersey Basin Campaign is a treasure-trove of information on the history, wildlife and environment of the Mersey, and the history and achievements of the campaign. See www.merseyriverstrust.org.uk also.

www.roydenhistory.co.uk Local historian Mike Royden has published a wealth of information on his website on the history of Liverpool, Merseyside, southwest Lancashire and Cheshire.

www.tide-and-time.uk Tide and Time is an informative site from the National Oceanography Centre describing the history of tidal science in Liverpool.

Telephoto view of Leasowe Lighthouse from near New Brighton

MARITIME CONNECTIONS

The Mersey Estuary had a key role in the development of the region with docks, fisheries and shipbuilding yards as far upstream as Warrington.

A network of canals provided onward links, including the Manchester Ship Canal, which carries ocean-going ships to this day.

Milestones in Liverpool include the opening of the world's first commercial wet dock and innovations in navigation and maritime safety.

Nowadays increasing numbers of cruise ships visit the city and the port can handle some of the largest container vessels in the world.

VISIT IDEAS

See the following chapters for more information on places to visit within the different areas:

Chapter 1 – Lower Estuary (Liverpool)

- Leeds & Liverpool Canal
- Another Place artwork, Crosby
- World Museum, Liverpool
- Three Graces, Liverpool
- Old Dock tours, Liverpool
- Albert Dock, Liverpool
- Merseyside Maritime Museum, Liverpool
- International Slavery Museum, Liverpool
- Hale Head Lighthouse

Some of these places are passed on Cycle Routes #1 and #2 and Walks #1, #2 and #3

Chapter 2 – Lower Estuary (Wirral, Cheshire)

- Hilbre Island
- One O'Clock Gun, Birkenhead
- Former lighthouses: Leasowe, Bidston Hill, New Brighton
- Former ferry piers: Egremont, Monks Ferry, New Ferry, Eastham Ferry
- National Waterways Museum, Ellesmere Port

Some of these places are passed on Cycle Routes #3 and #4 and Walks #4 and #5

Chapter 3 –Upper Estuary

- Bridgewater Canal
- Spike Island, Widnes
- Sankey Canal
- Fiddler's Ferry
- Howley Weir, Warrington
- Warrington Museum & Art Gallery
- Manchester Ship Canal
- Salford Quays

Some of these places are passed on Cycle Routes #5 and #6 and Walks #8 and #9

Maps are indicative only, and contain OS data © Crown copyright (2019)

MARITIME CONNECTIONS

The Mersey Estuary has a rich maritime history whose modern-day foundations were laid in the 18th century with the opening of the first commercial wet dock in the world: the Old Dock in Liverpool.

This was so successful that others soon followed and the Port of Liverpool became one of the busiest in the country with links to most major towns and cities via a network of canals, including Manchester along the Manchester Ship Canal.

To help manage the increasing traffic, key developments included establishing the Liverpool Pilotage Service and introducing semaphore and electrical telegraph systems, forerunners of today's radio- and satellite-based communications.

Nowadays the Port of Liverpool handles more freight than ever and a new deep-water container terminal accommodates some of the world's largest vessels; however, many reminders of the days of steamships and sail remain.

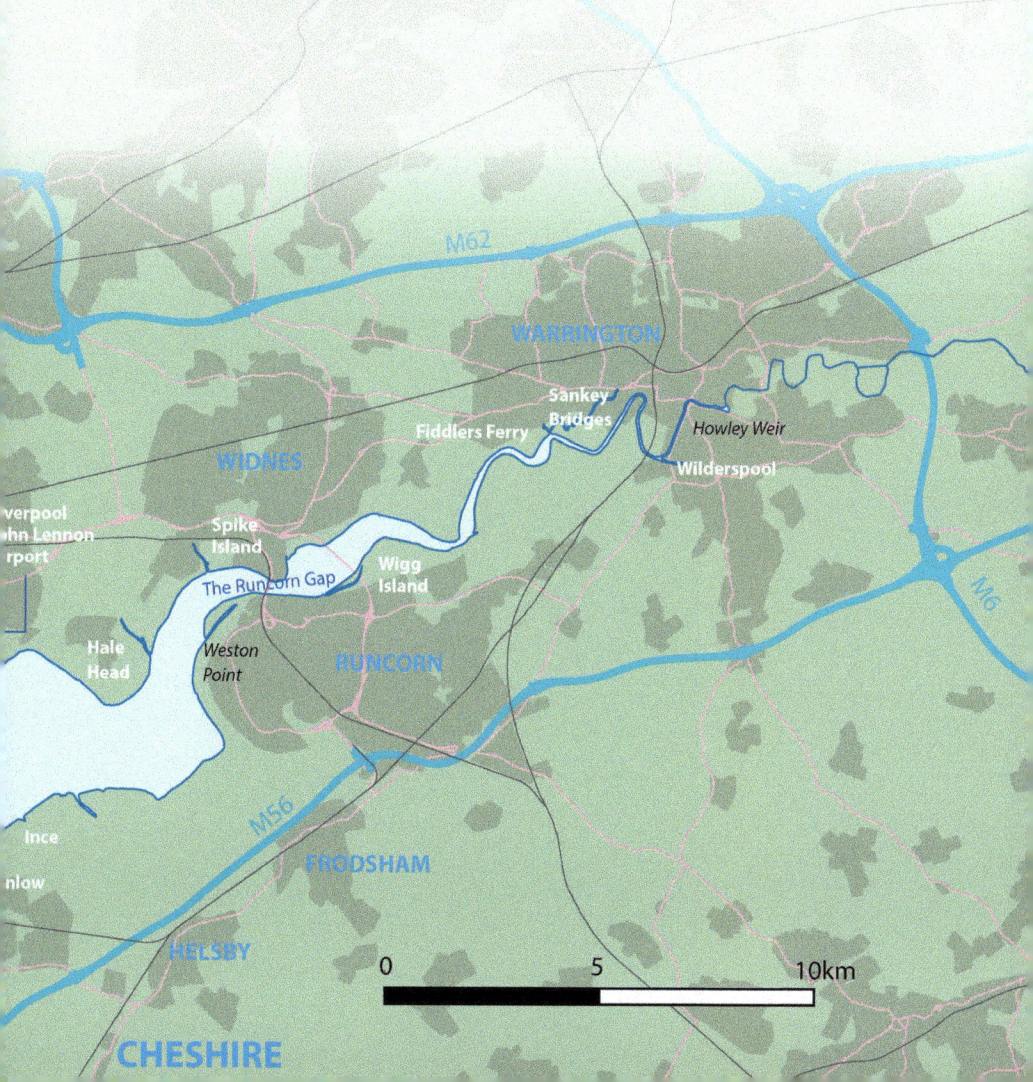

M62

WARRINGTON

Sankey
Bridges

Fiddlers Ferry

Howley Weir

WIDNES

Wilderspool

verpool
hn Lennon
rport

Spike
Island

Wigg
Island

The Runcorn Gap

M6

Hale
Head

Weston
Point

RUNCORN

Ince

M56

nlow

FRODSHAM

HELSBY

0   5   10km

CHESHIRE

The Port of Liverpool

Early developments in the region

In northwest England, one of the first known ports was at Meols on the north Wirral coastline, established in the Iron Age at a natural harbour formed by a sandbank. From about 200 BC trade extended to the Mediterranean and the port remained in use through Roman, Anglo-Saxon and Viking times. However, by the 15th century activity had all but ceased due to the shifting sands, a feature of this stretch of coastline.

Within the estuary itself, the earliest port was at Wilderspool to the south of Warrington and served a Roman settlement: an industrial centre for pottery, glass, iron, bronze and lead goods. The Mersey was known as Seteia by the Romans and the settlement was thought to be called Veranitum. A display at Warrington Museum & Art Gallery features several archaeological finds including a Roman actor's clay mask, one of only three found in the UK. Viking logboats found during the construction of the Manchester Ship Canal are evidence that centuries later these Norse invaders reached Warrington and the Manchester area.

▲ The Roman actor's clay mask on display at Warrington Museum & Art Gallery, courtesy of Warrington Museum & Art Gallery (Culture Warrington)

During the 1800s, huge numbers of sailing ships were often in port as shown in this glass lantern slide of George's Dock and Goree Warehouses, one of the earliest images available of the Port of Liverpool (Courtesy National Museums Liverpool) ▶

Map of Liverpool showing how it appeared in 1650 (© Liverpool Record Office, Liverpool Libraries)
From The Stranger in Liverpool, published by Thomas Kaye, 1829 ▶

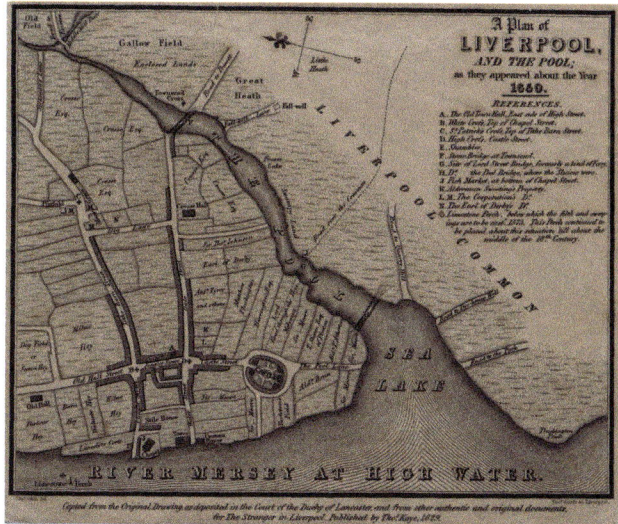

Development of the port

The growth of Liverpool as a port began with the granting of a Royal Charter by King John in 1207. This 'Letters Patent' – an open letter or proclamation – offered land and tax incentives to settle at what until then had been just a small farming and fishing village. A particular attraction was the sheltered, easily defended anchorage at a tidal inlet called the Pool, in part afforded by a low ridge to the north that became the site of Liverpool Castle.

The castle was demolished in the 1700s but a plaque on the Queen Victoria Monument at Derby Square commemorates its location. There is also a model of it at the Museum of Liverpool and a part-completed scale replica at Lever Park near Chorley, commissioned by William Hesketh Lever, the founder of Port Sunlight Garden Village (www.historicengland. org.uk)

A coastal trade soon developed but growth was slow until the 17th century and the start of transatlantic crossings. Some notable firsts included the arrival of the *Friendship* carrying tobacco from North America in 1648 and the voyage of the *Antelope* to Barbados in 1666 to trade linen cloth for sugar cane. By the end of the century the population had reached several thousand and overtaken that of Warrington, until then the largest town around the estuary.

However, the size of the harbour was increasingly becoming a constraint with larger vessels having to be unloaded offshore or while run aground onto mudflats, both time-consuming operations that placed cargoes at risk from the wind and the tides. These concerns led to the novel idea of building an enclosed dock in the Pool in which water levels were controlled by gates: the first commercial wet dock in the world. Called the Old Dock, it was opened in 1715 and soon led to a lively trade in tobacco, cotton, grain and sugar, with salt, coal and manufactured goods offered in return.

More docks were soon commissioned, but a new construction technique was required due to the lack of suitable sites – building sea walls out from the shoreline and backfilling the enclosed areas. Chapter 4, Rivers and Tides, discusses this feat of land reclamation in more detail.

However, an ignominious side to all this activity was the slave trade, which reached a peak in the second half of the 18th century before it was abolished in 1807. The International Slavery Museum at Albert Dock provides a poignant reminder and hosts the annual Slavery Remembrance Day, including a lecture and walk of remembrance.

By the end of the 18th century, the docks stretched for more than six miles along the Mersey to form one of the largest interconnected systems in the world. This connectivity allowed part loads to be collected and unloaded at different warehouses within the shelter of the dock system. Other innovations included hydraulic power systems to operate gates, cranes and lifts and an overhead railway running the length of the docks.

Allied to the growth in trade was a massive increase in passenger travel, particularly for transatlantic crossings and emigration to the USA, Canada, Australia, New Zealand and South Africa. The idea of pleasure cruises also caught on with the advent of steamships. For instance, it now took one to two weeks to cross the Atlantic, compared to a month or more under sail.

Cruise destinations soon spanned the world, including South America, the Caribbean, India and China. Built in the early 20th century, the Three Graces at Pier Head were one symbol of this success, as

▲ A container vessel passing the cranes of Liverpool2, whose maximum extended height is similar to that of the Royal Liver Building at Pier Head

headquarters for the Royal Liver Friendly Society, the Cunard Steamship Company, and the Mersey Docks and Harbour Board.

By the 1950s, cargo and passenger ship movements reached a peak, but several factors then conspired to start a gradual decline, including competition from air travel and the introduction of container ships. As vessel sizes increased, the focus of activity also began moving towards the deeper waters near the mouth of the estuary. For example, one key development was the opening of the container terminal at Royal Seaforth Dock in 1971.

These various changes led to many of the older docks being closed and much has been written on the social upheavals this caused (see Further Reading). However, the port has continued to adapt, with recent developments including the opening of a new cruise terminal in 2007 and the deep-water Liverpool2 container terminal in 2017, which is able to handle some of the largest container ships in the world. As a result, in terms of tonnage, more freight is handled than ever before, and Liverpool is now a top destination for cruise ships.

LIVERPOOL OVERHEAD RAILWAY

As the Port of Liverpool expanded, better ways of moving people around were required and this led to the novel idea of building the first overhead electric railway in the world, running the length of the dock system.

This was opened in 1893, initially stretching from Alexandra Dock in the north to the former Herculaneum Dock in the south, and later extended to Seaforth Sands near Crosby and Dingle near Sefton Park, a round trip of about 13 miles. It was widely known as the 'Dockers Umbrella', as the overhead tracks gave somewhere to shelter from the rain. To give an idea of how revolutionary it was, horses and carts were still in use in the docks as late as World War 2.

At its peak, nearly twenty million passengers were carried a year, including tourists visiting to see the port, which was considered one of the engineering wonders of the world. However, by the 1950s increasing maintenance costs and falling revenue led to the line being closed and demolished. Some signs remain, such as at the entrance to the old tunnel to Dingle Station and a plaque on Georges Dock Building at Pier Head. The Museum of Liverpool also has a display on the history of the line, which features a restored motor coach open for visitors to explore.

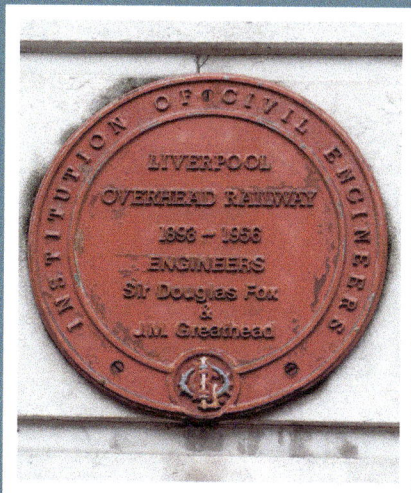

▲ Plaque commemorating the overhead railway on Georges Dock Building

Looking towards the now-closed tunnel to Dingle Station from Sefton Street near Brunswick railway station ▼

The Three Graces viewed from
Canning Half Tide Dock

Albert Dock

Albert Dock, opened in 1846, was one of the first in the world to site warehouses alongside the quays, thereby reducing the time required to load and unload vessels. Innovative fireproofing and security measures reduced the risks from fire and theft, two problems that plagued the shipping industry at the time. This gave ship owners the confidence to store high-value goods, such as tobacco, wines and silk. As a result, bonded status was granted, allowing customs duty to be paid on removing goods from storage rather than at the quayside: a more flexible approach.

The dock thrived for many years but size constraints eventually led to its decline. The last commercial use was in the early 1970s and the area was abandoned with the gates left open, causing the basin to silt up. However, after a few bleak years, the site was earmarked for redevelopment and the first phase was completed in 1984 in time for two landmark events that year: the International Garden Festival and the start of the Cutty Sark Tall Ships Race.

▲ Albert Dock viewed from afloat

The dock continues to flourish in this new role and is nowadays a major tourist attraction, with many shops and restaurants and a year-round programme of events, of which the highlight is the Summer on the Dock festival (www.albertdock.com). Visitors also flock to Tate Liverpool, the Beatles Story exhibition and the Merseyside Maritime Museum. Following a ceremony in 2018, it was renamed Royal Albert Dock Liverpool, in recognition of its contribution to regenerating the waterfront. Chapter 1 gives more information on the main attractions.

Albert Dock viewed from the Royal Liver Building ▼

VISITING THE OLD DOCK

Opened in 1715, the Old Dock in Liverpool remained in use for more than 100 years. It laid the foundations for the growth of the port, but was eventually closed when it could no longer handle the largest ships. A Custom House was then built on the site, itself demolished in 1948.

However, the dock was not forgotten and was partly excavated during construction of the huge Liverpool ONE retail and leisure complex. A small section of the remains can be seen through a glass window in the pavement next to the John Lewis store, while, for a closer look, experts from Merseyside Maritime Museum lead entertaining tours on some weekdays; see Chapter 1 for more information.

The site is reached by descending a flight of stairs beneath a car park. Archaeological finds on display include examples of coins and pottery dropped from ships or quaysides. The original brick and mortar walls remain intact in places, although this was not a particularly waterproof method of construction so sandstone blocks were normally used in later docks.

Nearby, the Thomas Steers Way pedestrianised area – named after the dock's designer – and the Lyver Pool, a water feature, celebrate the origins of the port. On the pavement, lines of grey tiles show the paths of the northern quayside and original shoreline. Fountains and interpretation panels also celebrate the life of a former dock master – William Hutchinson – whose many contributions to maritime safety are summarised in Chapter 4, Rivers and Tides. The Old Dock is the uppermost dock in the 1765 map below.

John Eyes' map of Liverpool (1765) (© Liverpool Record Office, Liverpool Libraries) ▼

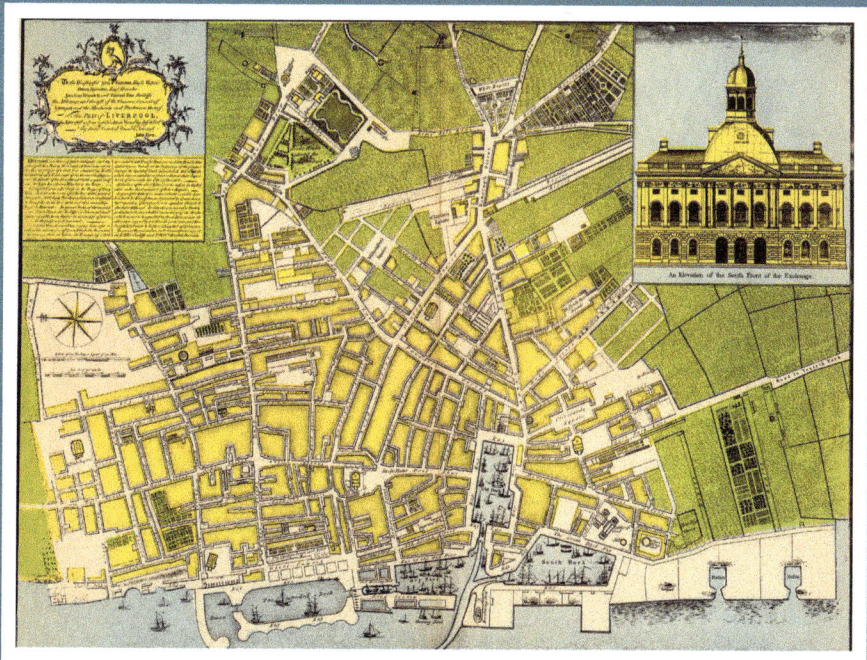

Sailing ships in Canning Dock, with the warehouses of Albert Dock and the former port pumphouse (now a pub) in the background

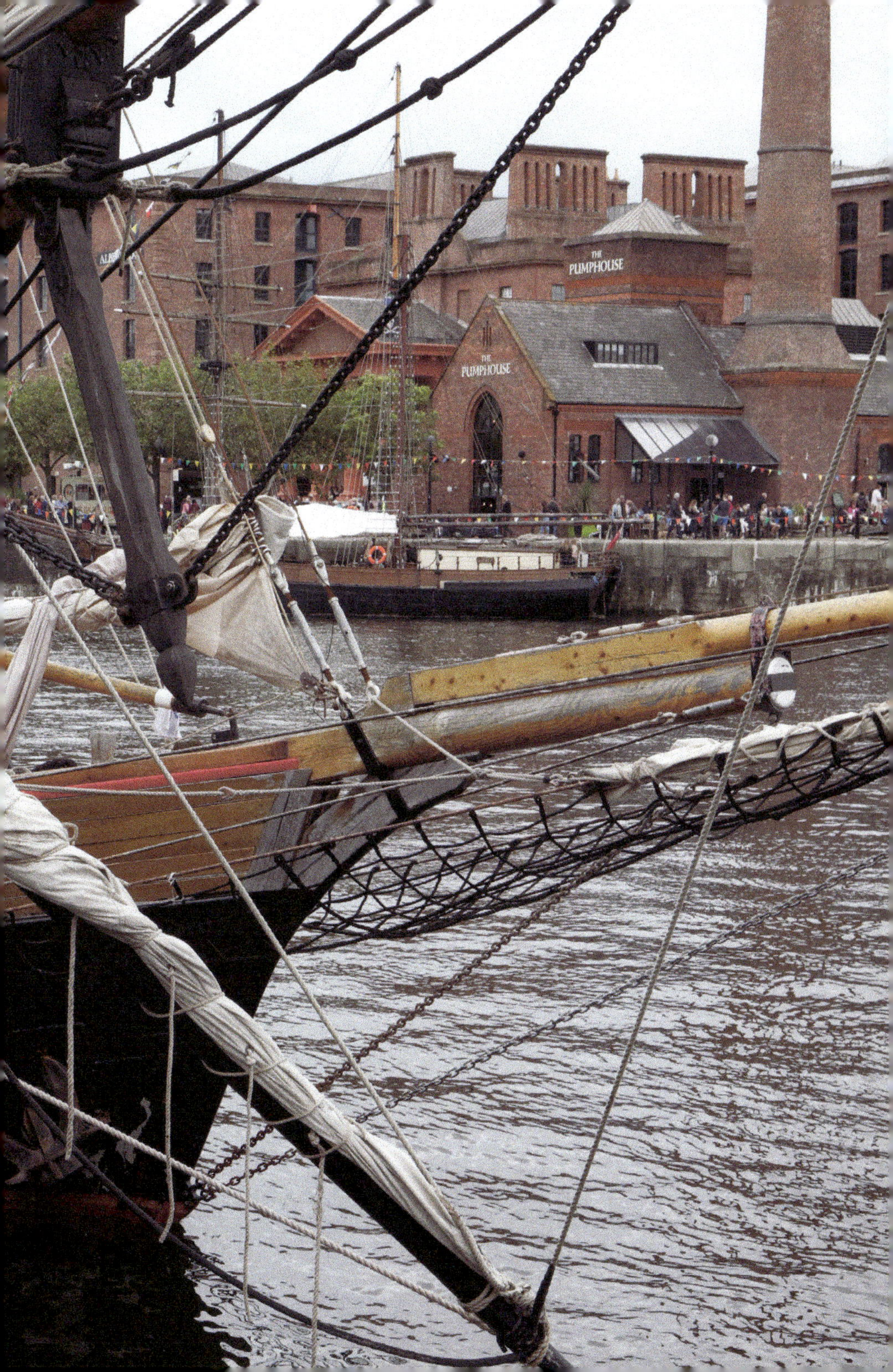
THE PUMPHOUSE
THE PUMPHOUSE

The cruise ship renaissance

During the 19th century, several shipping companies were founded to cater for the demand for long-distance passenger travel. Perhaps the most famous were the White Star Line – owners of the ill-fated Titanic – and the Cunard Line, which grew out of the more prosaically named British and North American Royal Mail Steam Packet Company.

The first scheduled transatlantic service from Liverpool was in 1840 to Halifax and Boston on board the wooden paddle steamer *Britannia*, operated by Cunard. Other lines started and before long destinations included Japan, West Africa and New Zealand, and even trips along the Amazon. To cater for the demand, the Cunard Building at Pier Head was opened in 1917 to serve as a passenger terminal and headquarters, while the White Star Line had a similarly grand building nearby on James Street.

The peak of Liverpool traffic was in the 1950s before a gradual decline began. However, recent years have seen a renaissance, and Liverpool is now a top cruise destination with ships from many lines visiting the city. In large part this turnaround was due to the opening of a new waterfront cruise terminal in 2007; a replacement terminal with even better facilities is under construction near the present site.

▲ A cruise ship berthed at Liverpool Cruise Terminal

In addition to tours of the city, popular day-trip destinations for passengers include Port Sunlight, Chester and North Wales. Indeed, ship arrivals and departures have become part of the spectacle, and visit dates appear on the cruise terminal website (www.cruise-liverpool.com). Some interesting ways to see ships in port include the promenade walks described in Walks #2 and #4 or a trip on the Mersey Ferry (www.merseyferries.co.uk).

As one of the Three Graces, the Cunard Building of course remains a highlight of the waterfront. Nowadays it is used for office accommodation and is home to the British Music Experience (see Chapter 1). The White Star Line building has been converted to a luxury maritime-themed hotel.

Liverpool waterfront, from the cruise terminal to the Museum of Liverpool ▼

Shipping in the estuary

Viewed from the waterfront in Liverpool, there sometimes seems to be a constant procession of ships going by, especially around high tide when access to the docks is easiest.

Most cargo ships are heading to or from the Port of Garston in the south of Liverpool or the entrance locks for the Manchester Ship Canal. Across the water, Stena Line ferries for Belfast are often berthed at the 12 Quays Terminal in Birkenhead, while less frequent visitors include vessels entering or leaving Birkenhead Docks and the huge tankers that offload crude oil at Tranmere Oil Terminal.

At the waterfront, cruise ships berth at the landing stage alongside the cruise terminal. Mersey Ferries also operates a year-round service, as does the Isle of Man Steam Packet Company. Towards the coast, container ships are normally heading to Royal Seaforth Dock; other traffic for the northern docks includes bulk cargo ships and P&O Ferries from Dublin.

On a smaller scale, the launches operated by Liverpool Pilotage Service are a common sight, as are twin-hulled vessels ferrying crews to and from the offshore windfarms in Liverpool Bay. In fine weather, leisure craft include yachts and dinghies associated with the various sailing clubs around the estuary and boats heading to and from Liverpool Marina.

Although the tonnage of freight carried far exceeds that of a century or two ago, the trend to larger ships means that fewer vessels visit the port compared to the hundreds under sail or steam that might once have been berthed at quays or moored offshore.

The Inner Estuary would also once have been bustling with traffic, with Mersey Flats a common sight – a type of flat-bottomed barge designed to navigate the canals and shallow tidal waters. Paddle steamer and then steamship ferries served Runcorn, Ellesmere Port and several other destinations around the estuary, including New Brighton, and Runcorn was a centre for shipbuilding, including schooners and steamships.

Beyond Runcorn, the Mersey and Irwell Navigation provided a route to Warrington and Manchester along the Mersey and the River Irwell, one of its main tributaries. The plans for the scheme were published in 1712 by Thomas Steers, designer of the Old Dock in Liverpool, and took account of earlier channel works commissioned in the late 17th century by Thomas Patten, a leading industrialist in Warrington.

The scheme was completed in the 1730s. In addition to channel works, it included several short lengths of canal to bypass meandering sections, and eight weirs with locks alongside to allow barges to pass. The lowermost weir was Howley Weir in Warrington at the end of a cut across a particularly tortuous bend known locally as the Hell Hole, and this became the normal limit for tidal influences in the estuary. This scenic spot is visited on Walk #9 and Cycle Route #6.

The navigation was used for transporting goods such as timber, coal, cotton and slate, and for about twenty years had no competition, but this changed with opening of the Sankey and Bridgewater canals. When the Manchester Ship Canal was opened in 1894, this also affected traffic in the Inner Estuary. Nevertheless, commercial shipping to Warrington continued until the 1950s and Chapter 3 discusses this little known maritime aspect of the town.

▲ **Left to right:** Howley Lock in Warrington was used until the 1950s by boats travelling towards Manchester along the Mersey and Irwell Navigation; some of the the upstream gates are still in place / A support vessel at one of the windfarms in Liverpool Bay

New Brighton Pier and Marine Promenade, New Brighton, 1920 (© Historic England). During the 1900s there were several ferry piers around the estuary. The last to close (in 1972) was that at New Brighton, here pictured in 1920 along with the former pleasure tower in the town, already in the process of being dismantled. Chapter 2 gives more information on the history of ferry services on the Mersey ▼

▲ A twilight view of Birkenhead Docks from Liverpool Cathedral; the entrance to the docks is to the right of the image, with Albert Dock in the foreground

Brunswick Dock is at the southern end of the docks and part of Liverpool Marina; as well as yachts and motor cruisers other users include patrol vessels and support ships for the offshore windfarm industry ▼

DOCKS AROUND THE ESTUARY

NAME	DATE	KEY FEATURES	CURRENT STATUS	WHERE TO FIND MORE INFORMATION
Birkenhead Docks	1847 to present	Built along the course of Wallasey Pool	Cargo handling, part of the Port of Liverpool	Chapters 2 and 4; Cycle Route #3
Cammell Laird Shipyard, Birkenhead	1820s to present	Founded at Wallasey Pool then relocated to Tranmere Pool; more than 1,000 ships built, including some of the first iron steamships	Shipbuilding, marine and engineering services	Chapter 4
12 Quays Terminal	2002 to present	Built on land reclaimed from disused areas in Birkenhead Docks	Terminal for Stena Line ferries to Belfast	Cycle Route #3
Tranmere North and South	1960 to present	Two jetties in Tranmere near Birkenhead serving Tranmere Oil Terminal	Crude oil is pumped to Stanlow Oil Refinery	
Mersey Wharf	To present	Two cargo berths in the Mersey, alongside Port Sunlight River Park	Serves a storage and logistics facility	Chapter 2
Bromborough Dock	1895 to 1986	Built in the tidal inlet of the River Dibbin; extended in 1931 primarily to serve the Lever Brothers factory at Port Sunlight	Now infilled and the site of Port Sunlight River Park	Chapter 2
Port of Garston	1850s to present	Built in the tidal inlet of Garston River; originally built to handle coal transported by rail from Spike Island in Widnes	Now handles both containerised and bulk cargo	

The Mersey Ferry Snowdrop *approaches Pier Head*

NAME	DATE	KEY FEATURES	CURRENT STATUS	WHERE TO FIND MORE INFORMATION
Ellesmere Port	1795 to 1950s	At the entrance to the Shropshire Union Canal; built to handle canal freight, then from the 1890s a port on the Manchester Ship Canal	Now the site of the National Waterways Museum	Chapter 2
Runcorn Docks	1770s to present	Originally built at the entrance to the Bridgewater Canal, and Runcorn and Latchford Canal, with a link to the Weaver Navigation via the Runcorn and Weston Canal	Since the 1890s a port on the Manchester Ship Canal	
Widnes Dock West Bank Dock	1833 to 1900s (Widnes Dock)	At the entrance to the Sankey Canal; built to handle coal transported along the Sankey Canal, and later also serving local chemical industries. Also West Bank Dock just downstream of the Runcorn Gap	The remains of Widnes Dock can be seen at Spike Island Nature Reserve; some signs of West Bank Dock remain downstream of the Silver Jubilee Bridge	Chapter 3; Walk #8 and Cycle Route #5
Warrington (various sites)	1730s to 1960s	Several quays on the Mersey and Irwell Navigation including Bank Quay and Bishop's Wharf	Disused; some signs remain in the town	Chapter 3; Walk #9 and Cycle Route #6

See the main text for information on the Port of Liverpool

MERSEY FLATS

From the 18th to the early 20th century, Mersey Flats – a type of barge – were a common sight in the estuary. With strong, flat hulls, they were designed to carry cargo along canals and in shallow tidal waters. If necessary, they could be beached on mudflats or sandbanks at low tide. Larger vessels were also used in coastal waters.

For canal use, the maximum size was dictated by the size of the locks, and the largest were about 20 metres long with a fully laden weight of 80 tons or more. In the early days, Flats travelled under sail in open water and were horse-drawn or manhandled along canals, but steam and then diesel power took over, with any unpowered vessels towed behind known as dumb barges or butties.

Several shipyards around the estuary built Mersey Flats, including at Fiddler's Ferry, Runcorn, Widnes, and Sankey Bridges in Warrington. Some remained in use until the 1960s but remarkably few remain, despite the huge numbers made. Perhaps the best preserved example is the Mossdale at the National Waterways Museum in Ellesmere Port, while the remains of a sunken craft appear at low tide alongside Spike Island in Widnes, its history described on an interpretation panel nearby (see Walk #8). There is also a scale model of a Mersey Flat at the Museum of Liverpool.

The remains of a Mersey Flat at Spike Island, Widnes, with the Mersey Gateway bridge in the background ▶

The *Santa Rosa* barge being launched at the old shipyard at Fiddler's Ferry. Courtesy of Warrington Museum & Art Gallery (Culture Warrington) ▼

"SANTA ROSA" BEING LAUNCHED

The canal network

The growth of ports around the estuary gave rise to a flurry of canal building to provide connections to towns and cities in the region and bypass the tides and shifting sands.

The first was the Sankey Canal, which was the first in England. Built to transport coal from mines around St Helens, it was opened in 1757. The original entrance locks were in Warrington on Sankey Brook, a tributary of the Mersey, but the canal was soon extended towards the deeper waters at Fiddler's Ferry and Spike Island in Widnes, again with locks at both sites. Cycle Route #5 follows the section from Warrington to Widnes.

Within twenty years, a competitor was opened on the opposite side of the Mersey: the Bridgewater Canal, which extended from northwest Manchester to Runcorn via south Warrington. It too was built to transport coal – in this case from mines owned by the Duke of Bridgewater – and was the first in the country to follow the lie of the land rather than an existing watercourse. Consequently, no locks were required other than in Runcorn where a spectacular flight descended to the level of the estuary, with a second set added in

▲ Narrowboats on the Bridgewater Canal in Runcorn

later years to meet demand. To the east of Runcorn, a tunnel nearly three quarters of a mile long provided a link to the Trent & Mersey Canal, and is nowadays an interesting challenge for leisure boaters.

Passengers could also travel by packet boat from Manchester or Warrington to Runcorn in a few hours to connect with ferries to Liverpool, a far more comfortable journey than by horse and carriage. The estuary crossings were originally under sail, but faster and more reliable paddle steamers later became the norm. In an effort to compete, the Mersey and Irwell Navigation was upgraded in the early 19th century by adding a canal section between

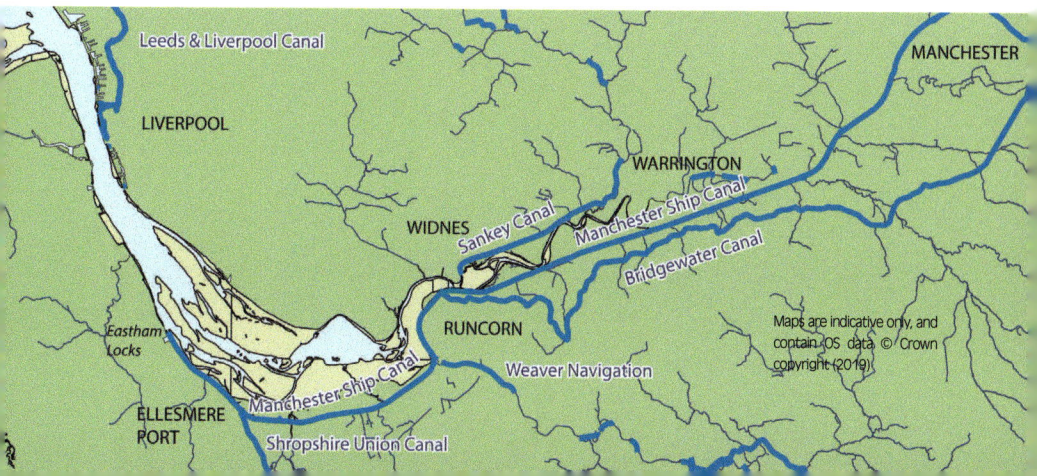

Runcorn and Warrington to bypass the tidal waters of the Upper Estuary. Named the Runcorn and Latchford Canal, it carried both freight and passengers.

However, despite all this activity, ships still had to negotiate the at-times treacherous waters of the Inner Estuary downstream of the Runcorn Gap, and this was one of the main reasons for building the Manchester Ship Canal. Larger than any existing canal, the entrance locks from the Mersey were in deeper waters beyond Ellesmere Port, allowing ocean-going ships to bypass both the Inner and Upper estuaries.

Opened in 1894, the Ship Canal immediately affected trade on the Bridgewater and Sankey canals, although both continued to be used commercially for several decades. In recent years, the Bridgewater Canal has become popular for leisure boating, but most of the Sankey Canal is now closed except for marinas at Fiddler's Ferry and Spike Island. There are active campaigns to see the Sankey Canal reopened (www.sankeycanal.co.uk) and to restore one of the flights of locks in Runcorn on the Bridgewater Canal (www.unlockruncorn.org). In contrast, the Runcorn and Latchford Canal was largely built over during the construction of the

▲ **Upper to Lower:** Disused warehouse on the Leeds & Liverpool Canal (see Cycle Route #1) / The entrance to the northern end of Preston Brook Tunnel on the Trent & Mersey Canal. The canal was opened in 1777 and the tunnel re-opened to navigation in 1984 following extensive repairs

The two entrance locks to the Sankey Canal with Widnes Dock just beyond (see Walk #8) ▼

Ship Canal, although the final section in Warrington was used until the 1960s to provide a link to the Mersey; this area is visited on Cycle Route #6.

Further downstream in the estuary, three other waterways provided access to areas inland, and again these remained in commercial use into the 20th century. The longest was the Leeds & Liverpool Canal, built to provide a route to Leeds over the Pennines through the coalfields of Lancashire, with a link to the northern docks in Liverpool via a flight of locks called Stanley Locks. Cycle Route #1 visits this area and then follows the canal for a few miles. Now popular for leisure boating, a tunnel section was opened in 2009 beneath Pier Head to provide narrowboat access to berths in Salthouse Dock adjacent to Albert Dock, with the visiting boats a colourful addition to the docks.

On the opposite shoreline, the Shropshire Union Canal heads from Ellesmere Port to Chester and beyond. However, access to the port was cut in the 1890s with the construction of the Ship Canal, removing direct access to the Mersey. Instead, it became a canal port, with its lighthouse gaining the unusual claim to fame of being the only one on a canal in the UK.

The docks at Ellesmere Port were finally closed in the 1950s due to declining traffic and are now home to the National Waterways Museum. The museum is dedicated to the history of the canal network in the UK, with narrowboat trips operated along the Shropshire Union Canal during the tourist season; see Chapter 2 for more details.

The only other waterway downstream from the Runcorn Gap is the Weaver Navigation, originally created to transport salt from mines around Winsford to and from Runcorn Docks. This largely follows the course of the River Weaver apart from a short canal section to bypass the tidal section of the river. There is also a link to the Trent & Mersey Canal via the spectacular Anderton Boat Lift, built to raise narrowboats and barges the fifty or so feet into the canal.

When the Ship Canal was built, Runcorn became a canal port, and remains in use as such to this day. A scenic way to see the Navigation is on board the *Danny*, a restored steam ship that offers cruises throughout the tourist season (www.thedanny.co.uk); for more information see the Introduction to this guide.

Boats moored on the Sankey Canal at Fiddler's Ferry ▼

CANALS AROUND THE ESTUARY

NAME(S)	ROUTE	YEAR(S) OPENED	CURRENT STATUS	WHERE TO FIND MORE INFORMATION
Bridgewater Canal	Worsley to Runcorn	1761 to Manchester, extended to Runcorn in 1776	Navigable to Runcorn Old Town	Chapter 3 www.bridgewatercanal.co.uk
Shropshire Union Canal (Ellesemere Canal)	Ellesmere Port to Chester	Progressively opened, reaching Ellesmere Port in 1795	Navigable to the National Waterways Museum	Chapter 2 www.canalrivertrust.org.uk
Leeds & Liverpool Canal	Leeds to Liverpool	Progressively opened from 1773 to 1846	Navigable with access to Salthouse Dock in Liverpool	Chapter 1 Cycle Route #1 www.llcs.org.uk
Runcorn and Latchford Canal (Old Quay Canal)	Runcorn to Warrington	1804 to 1890s	Largely built over in the 1890s by the Manchester Ship Canal	Chapter 3 Cycle Route #6
Runcorn and Weston Canal	A link between Runcorn Docks and the Weaver Navigation	Weston Canal 1859	Still in water but not used	
Sankey Canal (St Helens Canal)	St Helens to Widnes	1757 to Sankey Bridges, 1762 to Fiddler's Ferry, 1830s to Widnes	No longer navigable but marinas at Fiddler's Ferry and Spike Island	Chapter 3 Cycle Route #5 www.sankeycanal.co.uk

See the main text for information on the Manchester Ship Canal

A tug at Eastham Locks, the entrance to the Manchester Ship Canal, with Liverpool in the distance

The Manchester Ship Canal

The idea for a new canal to Manchester from the Mersey was championed by local industrialist Daniel Adamson. This would be much wider and deeper than any existing route and start in deeper water, thereby avoiding problems with the tides and shifting channels in the Inner and Upper estuaries.

The canal was opened in 1894 by Queen Victoria and at 36 miles long is only 12 miles shorter than the Panama Canal. Its construction was a huge engineering achievement involving more than 10,000 people at times, including the famed navigators – often called navvies – who could excavate prodigious amounts of material in a day, all by hand.

The entrance from the Mersey is at Eastham Locks a few miles downstream from Ellesmere Port. From there to Runcorn it follows the shoreline and then heads across country to Warrington, from where it follows the Mersey and River Irwell to Manchester.

The total height gained is nearly 20 metres and there are four sets of locks in addition to those at Eastham, all most

▲ An ocean-going ship leaving Latchford Locks in Warrington with the Thelwall Viaduct on the M6 in the distance

impressive structures due to the size of the vessels they serve. Similarly, the bridges across the canal need to allow ocean-going ships to pass; as well as fixed structures, there are several swing bridges, two vertical-lift bridges and, perhaps uniquely, a swing aqueduct, built to carry the Bridgewater Canal (the Barton Swing Aqueduct).

Once the canal was opened, the Port of Manchester grew rapidly and soon became the third busiest in the UK, reaching a peak annual tonnage in the

A tug and ship approaching Eastham Locks, viewed from the remains of Eastham Ferry pier ▼

1950s. However, a rapid decline then ensued for various reasons including competition from road and air transport and limitations on the size of vessels that could be handled. The docks were eventually closed in the 1980s, but the canal continues to thrive, serving locations such as industrial works in Manchester and Irlam, the Port Salford logistics hub, Runcorn Docks, and the various chemical works between Runcorn and Eastham Locks, including the Stanlow Oil Refinery.

In Manchester, the westernmost part of the docks is now home to Salford Quays, a retail and commercial district where tourist attractions include The Lowry art gallery and theatre, and the Imperial War Museum North. There are good views of the canal in this area, while other viewpoints downstream include the Trans Pennine Trail in Warrington and the promenade in Runcorn. However, access is limited beyond Runcorn except near the National Waterways Museum in Ellesmere Port, where there is a pleasant waterside promenade. Chapters 3 and 4 describe the sights at these various locations and Cycle Route #6 follows the banks of the canal part of the way.

▲ Centenary Bridge on the outskirts of Manchester: one of two vertical-lift bridges along the Manchester Ship Canal

The best views of all are from the special cruises operated during the tourist season by Mersey Ferries (www.merseyferries.co.uk). The trips take about six hours and start from Liverpool or Salford with time for sightseeing at the other end before the return journey by coach. The former ferry pier near Eastham Country Park is also a good viewpoint for ships entering and leaving the canal, as described in Chapter 2. Two operators also offer pleasure boat trips in Manchester (www.citycentrecruises.com; www.manchesterrivercruises.com).

A ship passing along the Manchester Ship Canal at Irlam to the west of Manchester, viewed during a Mersey Ferries trip along the canal ▼

Navigation and pilotage

Modern technology provides many aids to help navigate the challenging waters of the Mersey, including marine radar, echo sounders, GPS receivers and satellite-based communications. Crews also benefit from the expertise of the Liverpool Pilotage Service and the two tug companies that operate in the estuary.

Marine radar is particularly valuable in busy shipping lanes, and the Mersey Ferries were the first in the world to use this operationally. The service began in the 1940s, based on radio alerts from a land-based station. Over the years, additional radar stations were built around Liverpool Bay, and in the 1970s a marine control centre was built at Royal Seaforth Dock. Its distinctive square-edged tower is still visible for miles around, although the centre itself is now housed in a modern facility nearby.

Tugs operate under instructions from the pilot or ship's captain and, although small compared to the ships they serve, have enormously powerful engines capable of generating several thousand horsepower. Once a ship is underway, the usual role is to act as a safety net, only making minor adjustments to course, except when a pull is required for a tight turn. Large fenders prevent damage to a ship's hull as it is nudged towards the quayside, sometimes requiring two or three tugs for the largest vessels.

Until the early to mid-19th century, most ships approached the estuary along the north Wirral coastline through the Rock Channel, which is reached from Liverpool Bay from the northwest via the Horse Channel and runs roughly parallel to the shoreline. This route was used commercially until the 1960s by the ferry services that once operated along the north Wales coast but was abandoned due to siltation. A slightly more northerly approach – the New Rock Channel – is still used by small craft.

For vessels approaching from the north, another option was to enter the

Razorbill, one of the latest pilot vessels operated by Liverpool Pilotage Service ▼

Formby Channel, just offshore from Formby Point, but the entrance has since largely disappeared under the sands. The remainder of the channel to the south is now the main shipping lane into the estuary. Called Crosby Channel, it is reached via Queens Channel, which runs roughly east-west. This requires a sharp turn right as the vessel approaches the coast. From the beaches near Formby Point, this sometimes creates the optical illusion that ships are heading straight for dry land, before turning south towards Liverpool.

▲ A pilot vessel passes Liverpool waterfront

Both channels are indicated by a line of marker buoys that, due to the fast-moving tides, are significant structures in their own right, meriting their own identifiers for use on marine charts and radar displays. For example, the key buoy at the entrance to Queens Channel is called Bar Racon, where the Bar or Mersey Bar is a submerged sandbank to the west that has long been a potential hazard, and Racon an abbreviation for radio beacon.

In 1906 work started on building training or revetment walls to help stabilise the channel sides, primarily by dropping limestone blocks into the water from hopper dredgers. This was a huge task only completed about 100 years later. The walls extend for several miles and their tops are sometimes visible at low tide, a most unusual sight in open water. However, despite this effort, dredging is still required, as it is further inland in the approach channels to the Manchester Ship Canal and the Port of Garston.

A pilot vessel overtakes a ship leaving the Mersey Estuary ▼

The pilotage service was established in 1766 by the first Pilotage Act for the Port of Liverpool and is one of the oldest in the country. Perhaps surprisingly, sailing ships were used until the late 1890s before being replaced by steamships and then diesel-electric cutters. The last of the cutters – the *Edmund Gardner* – is now on display near Merseyside Maritime Museum and sometimes open to the public. The fleet now consists entirely of high-speed launches, which were first introduced in the 1980s.

In addition to the Port of Liverpool, other locations served include the Port of Garston, Mersey Wharf and the channel to Eastham Locks, from where the Manchester Ship Canal pilotage service takes over.

Incoming ships are usually boarded near Bar Racon, which is sometimes a challenge in stormy weather and more

▲ Ships in the Crosby Channel often seem to pass surprisingly near the shore, although not as close as suggested by the telephoto lens in this view of the *Another Place* statues on Crosby Beach

sheltered alternatives include Douglas Harbour on the Isle of Man and Point Lynas on Anglesey. In contrast, for the outward journey the pilot remains on board until it is safe and convenient to disembark.

A tug approaches a container vessel, viewed from near Fort Perch Rock in New Brighton ▼

THE THREE QUEENS EVENT

In 2015, Liverpool Pilotage Service played a key role in the success of the Three Queens event, held to celebrate the 175th anniversary of the Cunard Line. Three cruise liners, Queen Mary 2, Queen Elizabeth and Queen Victoria, entered the Mersey in line astern, and then performed a remarkable side-by-side formation display in the Narrows between Liverpool and Birkenhead. This required meticulous planning and advanced ship-handling skills, given the confined space and the influence from the wind and tides. More than a million people lined the shores of the Mersey in one of the biggest spectacles in the region in recent years.

▲ The three cruise ships approaching New Brighton at the start of the event and passing Liverpool waterfront ▼

◄ The fountains made by a tug's firefighting equipment provide a spectacular way to welcome visiting ships, seen here during the Three Queens event, featuring all three ships (below) and Queen Mary 2 (left) ▼

A tug alongside Queen Mary 2 as she leaves Pier Head during the Three Queens event in 2015

Mersey Estuary lighthouses

Lighthouses were once a key navigation aid around the estuary. The best known is that at New Brighton, a much-photographed landmark, last used in 1973. This replaced an earlier structure consisting of a beacon on a wooden tripod known as a perch, so the alternative name Perch Rock Lighthouse is still sometimes used.

Other lighthouses around the estuary included those at Formby, Crosby, Bootle, Garston, Hale Head, Bidston Hill, Ellesmere Port, Ince and Weston Point, with coastal stations at Hoylake and Leasowe on the Wirral. Several lightships were also stationed in Liverpool Bay, with the last operated at Bar Racon until the 1970s.

Leasowe was a particularly important site (www.leasowelighthouse.co.uk). Here, there were two structures called the Sea Lights indicating the way into the Horse Channel, part of the old approach route to the estuary. The primary lighthouse was built in 1763 and named the 'Upper Mockbeggar Light' after Mockbeggar Wharf – a sandbank stretching along the north Wirral coastline – while the other was a few hundred metres offshore.

After the lower structure was destroyed in a storm in 1771, it was replaced by a lighthouse on Bidston Hill more than two miles inland, which still has a strong claim to be the world's most inland lighthouse (www.bidstonlighthouse.org.uk).

The Lighthouse at Hale Head ▲

This became the upper light, while the original inner light became the outer one. Due to the distance from the shore, an unusually powerful beam was required, resulting in the first parabolic reflector installed in a lighthouse, another invention by William Hutchinson whose contributions to maritime safety were noted earlier. That structure was itself replaced in 1873 and the current lighthouse – now a private residence – remained in use until 1913, five years after the lamp was last lit at Leasowe.

A similar 'leading light' solution helped with navigation into the Dee Estuary on the opposite side of the Wirral. When lined up, two so-called Lake Lights at Hoylake indicated the way to a sheltered channel just offshore, which was known as Hoyle Lake. For ships heading for the Mersey, these lights had an additional role, as when lined up they indicated that a turn east would lead into the Rock Channel, a now largely silted up channel which followed the north Wirral coastline to port.

In addition to Bidston, Leasowe and New Brighton lighthouses, others whose structures remain include those at Hale Head and Ellesmere Port. The first two are open to the public on some weekends as discussed in Chapter 2 (see Walk #5 and Cycle Route #3, and websites for opening dates), while Hale Head Lighthouse is passed on Walk #3. There is also a viewpoint for the Ellesmere Port Lighthouse at the northern end of the waterside promenade near the National Waterways Museum (again see Chapter 2).

▼ New Brighton Lighthouse

Telegraph systems

As traffic in the estuary increased, reliable ship-to-shore communications became essential. The first formal system was established in the 1760s on Bidston Hill, consisting of a line of signalling masts, each corresponding to a different shipping company. Spotters on the hill would identify the company and vessel from the flags displayed by approaching ships and raise colour-coded flags on the masts to be interpreted by observers in the port.

The system saved time and money by allowing owners to start arranging berths, hiring labourers, and finding buyers for cargo before a ship arrived. More than 100 masts were eventually installed, but the only obvious sign that remains is a hole where a mast once stood: one of the features on a heritage trail around the hill that is followed on Walk #5. However, with some determination the foundations for the remaining masts can be found in the undergrowth.

In 1827 an 'optical telegraph system' based on semaphore signals came into use between Anglesey and Liverpool. Called the Liverpool to Holyhead Telegraph, there were twelve sites in total, including at Hilbre Island and Bidston Lighthouse, and observers would relay messages along the chain. The time taken for a signal to reach Liverpool was typically a few minutes and several messages could be passed along the line at a time without waiting for each to arrive.

The design of the masts was improved over time with the final version using two

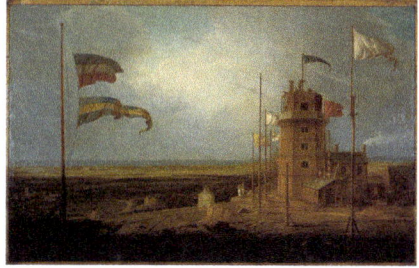

▲ Bidston Lighthouse and signals, 1825, by Robert Salmon (Courtesy National Museums Liverpool). The current lighthouse, now a private residence, dates from 1873

pairs of arms that could be raised, lowered and rotated. The many different combinations of height and angle allowed an extraordinary number of codes to be transmitted; in addition to a ship's name and cargo, these could include time checks, weather reports, pilotage service communications and distress signals. However, a key limitation was the need for good visibility, and in the 1860s the system was replaced by an electrical telegraph, a forerunner of today's radio and satellite communications.

Reminders of the telegraph can still be seen, and perhaps the closest to Liverpool is the old telegraph station at Hilbre Island. This is sometimes open to the public during the Seal Watch and Open Days organised by the Friends of Hilbre, and includes a small display on the history of the system. The island is accessible at low tide, but before attempting the potentially dangerous crossing it is essential to read the warning signs at the start of the route and to check the Friends' website for advice (www.deeestuary.co.uk); see Chapter 6, Wildlife, for more details. Bidston Lighthouse, open to the public on some summer weekends, also has a display on the system (www.bidstonlighthouse.org.uk).

The former optical telegraph station at Hilbre Island ▼

The One O'Clock Gun

Before the days of electronics, navigators relied on highly accurate timepieces called marine chronometers to estimate their bearings. These were normally set using time signals provided by the port authorities, and from the 1840s this task fell to the newly established Liverpool Observatory near Pier Head.

Initially, a signal was provided at 1pm each day by release of the Time Ball, a large sphere mounted on a mast outside the building. However, due to expansion of the port, in 1866 the observatory was transferred to Bidston Observatory on Bidston Hill on the Wirral.

As this was more than two miles from the port, a new approach was required and from 1867 the solution was to fire a cannon called the One O'Clock Gun. This was triggered remotely via an electrical cable connecting it to the observatory.

Located on the waterfront near Morpeth Dock in Birkenhead, the gun was last fired as late as 1969, although with advances in radio communications it could have been abandoned years earlier, if it had not been for public pressure to maintain the service. Several cannons were used over the years; the first is on display at Merseyside Maritime Museum and a replica of the last at its original location in Birkenhead (see Cycle Route #3).

The World Museum in Liverpool features several items from the former observatory, such as a transit telescope used to deduce the time from the passage of the stars and the astronomical regulator clock that kept the time standard for the port. Other highlights include several locally made marine chronometers, for which Liverpool and the nearby town of Prescot were once world famous, and examples of navigational equipment from the days of steamships and sail. See Chapter 1 for more information.

▲ **Upper to Lower:** The One O'Clock Gun at Merseyside Maritime Museum, located on the café terrace alongside Albert Dock / The astronomical regulator clock at the World Museum

Victoria Tower in the northern docks viewed from offshore, was completed in 1848, and had six clock faces and a bell to warn ships' crews of fog and high tides

Tall ship Atyla passing one of the cranes of Liverpool2 (www.atyla.org; @Atyla_ship)

Further Reading

Much has been written about the maritime history of the Mersey Estuary and the following books provide many useful insights:

A Hundred Years of the Manchester Ship Canal, Edward Gray, (Aurora Publishing, 1993)

A Pictorial History of the Mersey and Irwell Navigation, John Corbridge, (E.J. Morten Publishers, 1979)

Albert Dock Liverpool: The Complete Guide, Ron Jones, (Liverpool History Press, 2013)

Discover Liverpool, Ken Pye, (Trinity Mirror Sport Media, 2007)

Faster than the Wind: a History of and a Guide to the Liverpool to Holyhead Telegraph, Frank Large, (Avid Publications, 2001)

From Astronomy to Oceanography: a brief history of Bidston Observatory, J. Eric Jones, (Ocean Challenge, 1999)

Lighthouses of Liverpool Bay, John and Diane Robinson, (The History Press, 2007)

Lighthouses of the Isle of Man and North West England, Tony Denton and Nicholas Leach, (Foxglove Media, 2010)

Liverpool: a history of the 'Great Port', Adrian Jarvis, (Liverpool History Press, 2014)

Liverpool: The First 1000 Years, Arabella McIntyre-Brown, Guy Woodland, (Garlic Press Publishing Limited, 2001)

Liverpool World Heritage City, Ian Wray, John Hinchliffe, Rob Burns, edited by Peter de Figueiredo, (The Bluecoat Press, 2007)

Liverpool: The Story of a City. Museum of Liverpool, (Liverpool University Press, 2012)

Maritime Archives and Library Information sheets, National Museums Liverpool, (www.liverpoolmuseums.org.uk)

Mersey the river that changed the world, Ian Wray (ed.), photography by Colin McPherson, (The Bluecoat Press, 2007)

Mersey Ferries through time, Ian Collard, (Amberley Publishing, 2013)

Mersey Flats and Flatmen, Michael Stammers, (Terence Dalton, 1993)

Old Runcorn, H.F. Starkey, (Halton Borough Council, 1990)

Railways and Waterways to Warrington, 2nd edition, Peter A. Norton, (Cheshire Libraries and Museums, 1984)

River Mersey from source to sea, Phil Page and Ian Littlechilds, (Amberley Publishing, 2014)

Schooner Port: two centuries of upper Mersey sail, H.F. Starkey, (G.W. & A. Hesketh, 1983)

The Canals of North West England, in 2 volumes, Charles Hadfield and Gordon Biddle, (David & Charles, 1970)

The Changing Face of Liverpool 1207–1770, (Merseyside Archaeological Society, 2007)

The Great Mersey Shipping Lines, Peter Elson, (Trinity Mirror Sport Media, 2013)

The River Mersey, Ron Freethy, Photographs by Robert Smithies, (Terence Dalton Ltd., 1985)

The Romans at Wilderspool: The Story of the First Industrial Development on the Mersey, Tim Strickland, (The Greenalls Group, 1994)

See the following websites also: www.bidstonlighthouse.org.uk, www.leasowelighthouse.co.uk, www.liverpoolpilots.com, www.liverpoolmuseums.org.uk, www.merseyferries.co.uk (including '100 Interesting Facts') and wmag.culturewarrington.org.

A red squirrel at the National Trust reserve at Formby Point

chapter 6

WILDLIFE

The nature reserves around the estuary are a great place for waterside and woodland walks.

During winter the mudflats are a haven for wading birds, sometimes performing dazzling aerial displays above the incoming tide.

In recent decades, the reduction in pollution has benefited wildlife and even salmon have returned.

Some traces of the pre-industrial landscape also remain such as peat bogs and saltmarsh.

VISIT IDEAS

See the following chapters for more information on places to visit within the different areas:

Chapter 1 – Lower Estuary (Liverpool)

- Formby Point
- Sefton Coast
- Alt Estuary
- Another Place artwork, Crosby
- Three Graces, Liverpool
- Museum of Liverpool
- World Museum, Liverpool
- Otterspool Promenade, Liverpool
- Speke and Garston Coastal Reserve
- Pickerings Pasture Local Nature Reserve

Some of these places are passed on Cycle Routes #1 and #2 and Walks #1 and #3

Chapter 2 – Lower Estuary (Wirral, Cheshire)

- Hilbre Island
- North Wirral Coastal Park
- Leasowe Lighthouse
- Shorefields Nature Park
- Port Sunlight River Park
- Bidston Hill
- Eastham Country Park

Some of these places are passed on Cycle Routes #3 and #4 and Walks #4 and #5

Chapter 3 – Upper Estuary

- Goyt Valley
- Runcorn Hill Local Nature Reserve
- Wigg Island Community Park
- Spike Island Nature Reserve
- Widnes Warth
- Moore Nature Reserve
- Howley Weir, Warrington
- Warrington Museum & Art Gallery
- Manchester Ship Canal

Some of these places are passed on Cycle Routes #5 and #6 and Walks #7, #8 and #9

Maps are indicative only, and contain OS data © Crown copyright (2019)

FORMBY

Formby Point

Alt Estuary

Crosby Coastal Reserve

Seaforth

NEW BRIGHTON

Leasowe

Egremont

LIVERPOOL

Hoylake

Bidston Hill

Albert Dock

West Kirby

BIRKENHEAD

New Ferry

Otterspool Promenade

Shorefields Nature Park

Port Sunlight River Park

Speke and Garston Coastal Reserve

Wirral Country

Dibbinsdale Nature Reserve

Eastham Country Park

M57

M53

ELLESMERE PORT

Burton Mere

WILDLIFE

Huge improvements have been made to water quality in the Mersey Basin in recent decades with large parts of the estuary designated as protected areas.

The nature reserves that dot the shoreline provide a variety of habitats, including saltmarsh, woodland and floodplain meadows.

The cleaner waters have helped fish populations to recover and salmon have returned, migrating into the upper parts of the basin, and seals sometimes reach Warrington on the incoming tide.

However, it is perhaps for waterbirds that the estuary is best known, gathering in large numbers to feed on the mudflats exposed at low tide.

0   5   10km

M6

M62

Risley
Moss

Paddington
Meadows

WARRINGTON

Woolston
Eyes

Fiddlers Ferry

Howley Weir

WIDNES

Widnes Warth

Spike Island

Moore Nature
Reserve

Pickerings
Pasture

Wigg
Island

Hale
Head

RUNCORN

Runcorn Hill

M56

Frodsham
Marsh

FRODSHAM

Gowy Meadows

Habitat

The Mersey Estuary lies in a wide, glacier-scoured valley between low sandstone hills. After the last Ice Age, the predominant vegetation was arctic grassland but this gave way to swamps and forests as the climate warmed. The tidal influence began from about 6500 BC as sea levels rose, with mudflats and sandbanks forming due to the ebb and flow of the tides, and saltmarsh at the margins.

Some of the earliest signs of human habitation are at Formby Point where footprints from several thousand years ago are sometimes visible at low tide. These are preserved in stratified silt beds and the oldest date from Neolithic times. A replica is on display at the Museum of Liverpool and research suggests that – perhaps surprisingly – some adults may have stood more than 6 feet tall (www.nationaltrust.org.uk). Other footprints in the area include those of deer, wild boar, wolves, cranes and aurochs, a type of wild ox, now extinct. The museum also has several examples of flint tools found in the region, dating from about 6,000 years ago.

The first permanent farmsteads appeared in about 1,000 BC, but even after the Roman, Anglo-Saxon and Viking invasions, much of the land remained undisturbed. Farming and fishing were the main way of life. Salmon were plentiful and, for the more privileged,

> **THE MUDFLAT DIET**
> The Mersey is one of Britain's top ten estuaries for birds, and they come for food. Mersey mud is teeming with small worms, snails and shellfish; the equivalent in calories of 5 chocolate bars, or 10 helpings of chips, in each square metre – the size of a coffee table!
> *From an Environment Agency and Groundwork Mersey Valley interpretation panel at Hale Head*

locally caught venison and oysters were part of the diet. The main towns were Warrington – long a strategic crossing point – and Liverpool, although the populations of each were still only a few thousand by the end of the 17th century, and little more than 100 at Birkenhead a century later.

In the 18th century, as the industrial revolution gathered pace, docks and factories sprang up around the estuary bringing social and economic gains. This also marked the start of a long decline in water quality that continued until the 1970s, affecting both people and wildlife. However, in recent years there has been a remarkable turnaround, in particular due to the work of the Mersey Basin Campaign and its successor, the Mersey Rivers Trust and, as a result, the water is cleaner than it has been in many years.

The campaign ran from 1985 to 2010 and brought together government, local authorities,

> **WIRRAL IN THE 1830S**
> We sailed majestically between the ships which lay at anchor, and from whose masts the flags of all nations floated. The headland at Birkenhead was dotted with a few residences. Beyond that nature had possession and covered the slopes with verdure; for in those days the town of Birkenhead and the vast expanse of buildings to New Brighton had no existence, and from the few scattered cottages to the Rock Lighthouse, which reared its massive form against the sky, was one unbroken vista.
> *From a mariner's 1890 account of a voyage from Manchester to Liverpool by sailing Flat in 1839; quoted in A Pictorial History of the Mersey and Irwell Navigation by John Corbridge*

businesses and communities to tackle water pollution and promote waterside development. Its achievements are described in Chapter 4, Rivers and Tides, and included creating new wildlife areas on disused industrial land.

Since 1991, the Mersey Forest Partnership has also been expanding woodland and green spaces around the estuary as part of its wider remit for Merseyside and North Cheshire (www.merseyforest.org.uk).

Nowadays, the various parks and reserves around the shoreline shelter a wide range of habitats. Types include woodland, lakes, heathland, meadows, sand dunes, and mudflats plus saltmarsh and peat bogs, which are becoming increasingly rare at a national level. Fish populations are also recovering, as discussed later.

Nature reserves and parks around the estuary

The estuary begins to the east of Warrington. In the uppermost reaches it is a tranquil river meandering past woods and floodplain meadows, rarely affected by the tide. The nature reserves at Woolston Eyes and Paddington Meadows lie alongside, while Risley Moss to the north features two rare types of habitat once common in the Mersey Valley: wet woodland and lowland peat bogs.

The tidal limit is normally at Howley Weir close to the centre of Warrington, although the weir is overtopped on the highest tides. About half a mile downstream the channel is contained between flood defences; water levels here can vary several metres in a day due to the effects of the tides. Waterside meadows soon reappear, with the first mudflats around Fiddler's Ferry just to the west of the town. Moore Nature Reserve lies to the south and the bird hides of Widnes Warth a short way beyond.

Approaching the Runcorn Gap, the channel is almost a mile across. The reserves at Spike Island and Wigg Island are at the shoreline, and Runcorn Hill a short way inland.

▲ **Upper to Lower:** Bluebells at Eastham Country Park, a refuge for the native British species / Saltmarsh at Hale Head

LOCATION	HABITAT AND WHERE TO LOOK FOR MORE INFORMATION
North Wirral Coastal Park	Sand dunes and common land; sandy foreshore exposed at low tide; Leasowe Lighthouse Chapter 2; Cycle Route #3; www.visitwirral.com
Seacombe to New Brighton	Waterside promenade overlooking a sandy foreshore exposed at low tide with areas of rock pools, shingle, rock pavement and mussel beds Chapter 2; Cycle Route #3; Walk #4; www.visitwirral.com
Shorefields Nature Park	A grassy area above low sandstone cliffs overlooking a wide bay where mudflats are exposed at low tide Chapter 2
Port Sunlight River Park	Wildlife lake; low cliffs; wildflower meadows; the Summit viewpoint; views of the mudflats offshore from Shorefields Nature Park; heritage centre with café Chapter 2; www.thelandtrust.org.uk
Bidston Hill	Heritage trail through woods, grassland and heathland; sandstone outcrops with rock carvings; urban farm with café; Bidston Lighthouse; Bidston Windmill Chapter 2; Walk #5; www.bidstonhill.org.uk
Brotherton Park and Dibbinsdale Nature Reserve	Parkland, walled garden and fishing pond alongside the River Dibbin; visitor centre Chapter 4; www.dibbinsdale.co.uk
Eastham Country Park	Low sandstone cliffs alongside mudflats exposed at low tide; ancient woodlands; a garden frequented by woodland birds; rare native bluebells in spring; visitor centre; tea garden Chapter 2; Cycle Route #4; www.visitwirral.com
Gowy Meadows Nature Reserve	Floodplain meadows alongside the River Gowy; management includes raising longhorn cows and Hebridean sheep Chapter 4; www.cheshirewildlifetrust.org.uk
Frodsham Marsh	Extensive area of marshland cut off from the estuary during construction of the Manchester Ship Canal more than a century ago; several large ponds (tanks) related to dredging on the canal www.cawos.org

LOWER ESTUARY (WIRRAL)

Swans at Paddington Meadows, Warrington

ENVIRONMENTAL DESIGNATIONS

Given the importance of the Mersey for wildlife, much of the estuary is protected via national and international legislation.

At a national level, one option is to designate an area as a Site of Special Scientific Interest (SSSI) and there are several in the basin. The first was the Mersey Estuary SSSI, created in 1951 in the Inner Estuary, while others downstream and at the coast include the Mersey Narrows, New Ferry, and North Wirral Foreshore SSSIs. Further upstream, examples include the Woolston Eyes and Risley Moss SSSIs near Warrington and the Goyt Valley SSSI in the headwaters (www.gov.uk).

SSSI status is not linked to any specific type of habitat, whereas the international Ramsar Convention on Wetlands of 1971 specifically considers wetlands such as marshes, peatland and open water. The Mersey Estuary Ramsar Site was created in 1995 with the Mersey Narrows and North Wirral Foreshore added in 2013 (www.ramsar.org).

▲ Sandbank in Garston Channel, near Liverpool

At a European level, rare and vulnerable birdlife is covered by the Birds Directive of the European Commission and there are two Special Protection Areas in the estuary: the Mersey Estuary (from 1995) and the Mersey Narrows and North Wirral Foreshore (from 2013) (www.jncc. defra.gov.uk). Species cited include curlew, lapwing, pintail, redshank, shelduck, teal and wigeon.

Another European directive – the Habitats Directive – addresses rare and valued types of habitat and species, such as the Manchester Mosses Special Area of Conservation (SAC) for the remaining degraded raised bog and related habitat between Warrington and Manchester. Local authorities can also create Local Nature Reserves; examples around the estuary include those at Paddington Meadows in Warrington, and Runcorn Hill and Pickerings Pasture near the Runcorn Gap.

▲ North Wirral foreshore seen from Hilbre Island

Marine Life

The tidal influence means that both freshwater and marine creatures are found in the estuary, including the occasional seal, dolphin and porpoise.

The closest seal colonies are in the Dee Estuary on the western shores of the Wirral and at Walney Island in Cumbria. Those seen in the Mersey are probably from the Dee, where the population reaches several hundred in summer. However, by early winter most have left for west Wales where the rocky coastline is more favourable to raising pups. Most are Atlantic grey seals and are larger than the other type seen around the UK – harbour or common seals – with some adult males weighing more than 200 kilograms and over 2 metres from snout to tail.

Although they are inquisitive animals, the most likely reason for swimming into the Mersey is in pursuit of fish. Indeed, seals will sometimes travel more than 100 miles in search of prey and remain at sea for several days. Cod and sand eels are particularly favoured, although they eat most types of fish and crustaceans, including squid and octopus.

Sightings are most common around the mouth of the estuary, but sometimes

▲ A seal swimming near the northern tip of Hilbre Island

the chase continues beyond the Runcorn Gap. For example, in 2014 an adult grey seal made the local news when it was rescued from a farmer's field near Newton-le-Willows having swum into Sankey Brook, a tributary of the Mersey. Similarly, a seal pup made the headlines in 2016 when it reached the area above Howley Weir in Warrington during unusually high tides, remaining there for several weeks.

Several other sightings of adult seals and pups have been reported from the town in recent years, but this is not a new phenomenon and one of the taxidermy exhibits at Warrington Museum & Art Gallery is an adult male seal trapped in the town in 1908.

A telephoto view of sea anglers at New Brighton ▼

AN INCREDIBLE JOURNEY

Until the 19th century, Atlantic salmon were common in the Mersey and a staple in the diet for local communities, with some used as animal feed. Some of the earliest evidence is from a letter written in 1697 by a Warrington-based industrialist, Thomas Patten. Its opening lines were:

I am informed that there is a design to bring a bill into the house of Commons against fish wears that hinder Navigation, in Navigable Rivers, and that take, and destroy fish, and the fry of fish. You very well know the mischief that is done in the River Mercy, or at least have frequently heard, what vast numbers of Salmon Trout are taken, so as to supply all the Country, and Market Towns 20 miles round, and when the Country is cloyed, or when they cannot get sale for them, they give them to their swine...

This letter is reproduced in the *The Norris Papers* and was part of a request to Richard Norris of Speke for his support in lobbying for the bill.

Following a long decline, recent decades have seen a rebound in numbers due to improvements in water quality, the installation of fish passes to help fish negotiate weirs, and – as Patten proposed all that time ago – removing weirs that prevent migration. Recent sightings in Stockport and the River Goyt mean that fish must have swum through Warrington and south Manchester on the way there.

These migrations begin when fish leave their spawning grounds for the sea, where they remain before returning to spawn, often in the same river. This remarkable feat of navigation is thought to be by 'smell' or 'taste' based on the chemical and biological composition of the estuary waters. The advantage of this seemingly dangerous survival strategy is that the upland rivers provide suitable food, shelter and habitat for the small fry and parr, while the oceans offer larger prey for the adult fish. However, after spawning, few survive to migrate again.

The caption for this map from the U.S. Fish & Wildlife Service notes that Atlantic salmon travel thousands of miles to their North Atlantic feeding grounds (arrows), usually near western Greenland. They remain for one to three years before returning to their home river to reproduce.

Atlantic salmon migration routes (credit: U.S. Fish and Wildlife Service) ▼

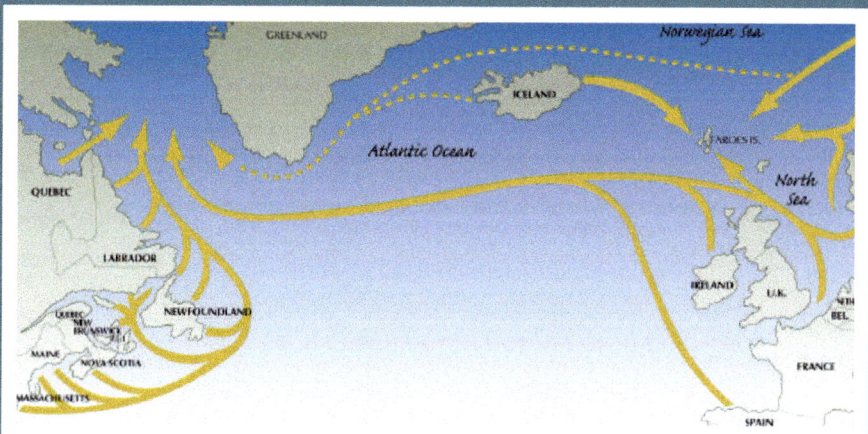

▲ A distant view of basking seals from Hilbre Island

Dolphins are sometimes also seen in the estuary, primarily in the Narrows and at the coast. For example, reports compiled by the Sea Watch Foundation list sightings from Woodside and Seacombe ferry terminals and Egremont near New Brighton (www.seawatchfoundation.org.uk). Harbour porpoises are occasionally spotted upstream, and in 2016 one was stranded on mudflats close to Pickerings Pasture near Widnes. There is an interesting account on the Friends of Pickerings Pasture website of the multi-agency rescue effort required to return it to the water, and of other sightings from the reserve, which occur in most years (www.thefriendsofpickeringspasture.org.uk).

Remarkably, there have also been sightings in the Manchester Ship Canal, including a report in the Guardian newspaper of a dolphin near Runcorn Docks in 2000 and a BBC report of a porpoise in Warrington in 2006. Whales have also been sighted, but this is much less common, although examples have included an orca (killer whale) which was washed up onto a sandbank near Speke in 2001, and a minke whale rescued near Hale Head in 1998, according to RSPCA and Liverpool Echo reports.

Whether the number of seals, dolphins and porpoises has increased along with improvements in water quality is an interesting question but difficult to answer without reliable data on sightings stretching back many decades. However, fish populations have undoubtedly recovered, with more than fifty species recorded in the estuary and increasing numbers of invertebrates, such as brown shrimp, shore crab and common starfish.

A sturgeon caught in the Mersey on display at Warrington Museum & Art Gallery ▼

▲ Seal pup photographs taken at South Walney Nature Reserve (© Cumbria Wildlife Trust)

The former lifeboat station at Hilbre Island seen from offshore ▼

One sign of these changes is the popularity of sea angling. Catches in the Narrows routinely include codling, eel and whiting plus flatfish such as plaice, dab and flounder. Indeed, cod weighing more than ten pounds and a metre long have been caught near Pier Head and thornback rays and dogfish are common at the estuary mouth. The mix changes in the Upper Estuary and by Warrington freshwater types dominate such as roach, perch, bream and chub.

Warrington Museum & Art Gallery also contains evidence of a more exotic visitor in

MARINE LIFE IN ALBERT DOCK

We discovered a veritable feast of marine life which one would be forgiven for mistaking as a reef from some far away foreign land. The secret to this diversity is twofold. Firstly, out in the Irish Sea there is a lack of a hard substrate, which the larvae of many species rely on, to settle and begin the next phases of their lives. Therefore, the many walls of Liverpool's docks offer the perfect home. Secondly, life here originates from all over the world, brought here on the bottom of boats and in the ballast water from the shipping industry. Growing on the encrusting bed of mussels were brightly coloured sponges, sea squirts, anemones and bryozoans (moss animals) of many varieties and forms. European eels patrolled the dock walls as moon jellies majestically pulsed along the surface of the water. A closer look revealed shrimps, crabs, worms and the many species of fish hiding in the algae and whizzing past our nets at high speed, evading capture. The highlight of the day was the sheer surprise and delight on everyone's faces when we plucked the day's best find from the water ... a greater pipefish!

From a description by Sally Tapp of a Wildlife Discovery day at Albert Dock as part of the Heritage on the Dock Festival 2016, adapted from Lapwing Magazine, Winter 2016, Lancashire Wildlife Trust (www.lancswt.org.uk)

the past: a two-metre-long sturgeon caught in the Mersey, part of a taxidermy display of fish species from around the world. There is also a 'Northern Streams' display of fish at the Blue Planet Aquarium near Ellesmere Port (www.blueplanetaquarium.com).

Spotting seals, dolphins & porpoises

Realistically, most visitors are unlikely to see seals, dolphins or porpoises around the estuary.

However, chances improve out in Liverpool Bay so, if travelling by ferry to Ireland or the Isle of Man, it could be worth looking out just in case. Indeed, volunteer observers from the Marine Life charity regularly perform surveys from the ferries and the reports make interesting reading (www.marine-life.org.uk). The RSPB Bird Watching & Nature Discovery cruises occasionally operated by Mersey Ferries are another possibility (www.merseyferries.co.uk).

Of the two seal colonies around Liverpool Bay, the one in the Dee Estuary is closest to the Mersey and Hilbre Island is perhaps the best viewing location, although there are some risks from the tides en route; see later. The most likely place to spot seals is when they haul out at low tide on sandbanks in the distance. With luck, they might also be seen bobbing around in the water to the north of the island near the old lifeboat station and slipway.

The chances of a sighting depend on the tides and time of year. Expert advice is useful and the Friends of Hilbre run Seal Watch and Open Days once a month from March to October (www.deeestuary.co.uk). Wirral Sailing Centre also occasionally runs boat trips to Hilbre Island and elsewhere in the Dee Estuary (www.visitwirral.com).

The island can be reached at low tide from Dee Lane slipway next to the Marine Lake at West Kirby although, due to the risks from the tides and quicksand, it is essential to read the prominent warning signs there, and the safety advice on the Friends of Hilbre website, in particular regarding the recommended route. Further information can be obtained from the rangers at Wirral Country Park (0151 648 4371). Take a telescope or binoculars for the best views, or on open days use the telescope set up by the Friends of Hilbre.

The other colony is at South Walney Nature Reserve near Barrow-in-Furness and again numbers depend on the season. For many years the population of about 100 consisted only of adult seals, so when a pup was born in 2015 it raised considerable media interest and several have been born since.

On the highest tides, seals can sometimes be seen swimming around the reserve, while when the tide is out they may be visible in the distance on the main haul-out area. Seal Cam images are streamed to the Cumbria Wildlife Trust website and a display screen in the visitor centre. Other highlights at the reserve include the huge numbers of wading birds at some times of year and its role as a breeding ground for eider duck (www.cumbriawildlifetrust.org.uk).

Seals at Burbo Bank near the mouth of the Mersey ▼

Waterbirds

The Mersey Estuary is an important refuge for wading birds and wildfowl, and numbers have exceeded 100,000 in some years.

It is perhaps for wading birds that the estuary is best known, including nationally significant numbers of black-tailed godwit, curlew, dunlin, golden plover, redshank and turnstone. From autumn to spring these feed in large numbers on the mudflats exposed at low tide.

Often called waders or shorebirds, different species tend to feed together, as their bills are adapted for different types and sizes of prey. For example, the long, curved bill of the curlew is ideal for reaching deep into the mud to catch lugworms, marine snails and crabs, while the much smaller dunlin searches near the surface for molluscs, crustaceans and worms. Turnstone, as the name suggests, have a different strategy, rooting around for almost anything edible at the surface, including mussels in the beds exposed at low tide along the Narrows.

Although sometimes difficult to spot on the ground, many species are beautiful in flight with long tapering wings designed for long-distance travel and bold light and dark markings on the upper surfaces. Migration routes vary widely and range from simply moving to higher ground, such as the Pennines, to travelling much further afield. Destinations include West Africa, the Mediterranean, Iceland, Scandinavia or the Arctic, depending on the species and time of year.

Perhaps the longest non-stop commuter is the bar-tailed godwit which migrates to Scandinavia and Siberia to breed and is a species sometimes seen along the north Wirral coastline. Tracking studies by the US Geological Survey have shown its Alaskan cousin is probably the world's longest travelling land bird. Some have been recorded flying more than 10,000 kilometres across the Pacific to New Zealand, a journey of just a few days. Redshank and sanderling are also known to clock up journeys of 20,000km or more, albeit with several stops.

Other types of waterbird seen in large numbers around the estuary include Canada and pink-footed geese, and ducks such as pintail and teal. There are also increasing numbers of shelduck, often a good sign in

An oystercatcher carrying a snack; these birds feed mainly on cockles and mussels and not oysters as the name suggests (seen near New Brighton) ▼

terms of water quality, as their diet includes small snails which are very sensitive to pollution. Fish-eating birds such as herons and cormorants are also common, and even ospreys have occasionally been spotted flying along the Narrows and in the Outer Estuary, and further upstream, such as at Moore Nature Reserve. Other occasional visitors include seabirds, such as storm petrels, Manx shearwaters and skuas, particularly during strong onshore winds when they seek shelter around the estuary mouth.

Watching waterbirds

In recent years, birdwatching has become one of the most popular outdoor activities in the UK and for waders and wildfowl there is the added benefit of the waterside views. It is also interesting to learn about the behaviour of individual species, such as their courtship displays and the territorial disputes that break out.

Places where waterbirds may congregate include near the shoreline at Pickerings Pasture Local Nature Reserve, Speke and Garston Coastal Park, Shorefields Nature Park and Port Sunlight River Park. Significant numbers can sometimes also be seen from Eastham Country Park, Spike Island Nature Reserve, Wigg Island Community Park and the permit-only reserve at Woolston Eyes. At the coast, possibilities include New Brighton, the Alt Estuary, the member-only reserve at Seaforth, and in particular the north Wirral coastline at Leasowe, Hilbre Island and Hoylake.

The best time of year to visit depends on the species. Most wading birds start arriving in autumn and stay until early spring, although some resident populations remain all year. The tides are another factor, as most

▲ Turnstones on the seawall south of Pier Head

birds retreat to high-tide roosts when feeding grounds are covered. Frodsham Marsh is a prime example of this, and other sites where this behaviour may be observed include Moore Nature Reserve, Pickerings Pasture and Seaforth Nature Reserve. Several visits may therefore be required to understand the characteristics of a site.

In the Upper and Inner estuary, birds often take flight as tidal fronts cross the mudflats, whereas at the coast some species just shuffle up the beach as the tide comes in. The passage of the Mersey Tidal Bore can also provide good viewing opportunities; Chapter 4, Rivers and Tides, includes tips on finding out tide times and viewing the tidal bore.

OYSTERCATCHERS

Oystercatchers are very active, vocal birds and highly entertaining to watch, especially when breeding. Displays, territorial disputes, protection of the nest from predators, feeding their young: all are done with as much fuss and noise as possible. If you're looking for the rowdiest of the waders, you've found it.

From Watching Waterbirds with Kate Humble and Martin McGill

Turnstones feeding among stones and shellfish on the shoreline south of Pier Head; masters of disguise, there are eight birds in this photograph

▲ **Shelducks** on the mudflats near Speke and Garston Coastal Reserve

◄ A **grey heron** takes flight along the Bridgewater Canal in Runcorn

Curlew and **redshanks** near the promenade south of New Brighton ▼

▲ **Canada geese** and gulls south of the estuary viewed from a Mersey Ferries' cruise along the Manchester Ship Canal, with the lighthouse at Hale Head in the distance

Lapwings and **gulls** near Fiddler's Ferry ▶

Sanderlings in flight near the *Another Place* artwork at Crosby Beach ▼

WATERBIRD PHOTOGRAPHY

With their bold markings and colours, waders and wildfowl are often photogenic subjects, especially when in large numbers, and the shoreline locations can make an interesting backdrop.

For larger birds, such as herons or cormorants, a compact camera may suffice, but enthusiasts often use a camera with a zoom or prime lens. Ideally, if budgets allow, lenses would have a focal length of 400–500mm or more, but good results can also be obtained with less expensive equipment. Most photographic shops can provide advice and open days are sometimes held at RSPB and Wildfowl & Wetlands Trust sites to demonstrate different makes of telescopes and binoculars and sometimes digiscoping, in which a camera or smartphone is attached to a telescope.

Some of the best shots are obtained when there is a strong contrast between a bird's plumage and the background, such as black feathers against the sand or a pale underbelly against the blue of the sea. Good lighting helps, ideally with the sun behind the photographer, and this may require an early start or an evening visit, depending on where a site is around the estuary.

Avoiding disturbance is of course a top priority and the Birdwatchers' Code (see later) includes much useful advice, as does The Nature Photographers' Code of Practice published by the Nature Group of the Royal Photographic Society (www.rps.org).

Although it is rewarding to photograph less common species, it is also worth being alert to other photographic opportunities. Even the better known species, such as swans, geese, ducks and gulls, have their own beauty, particularly when in flight. The waterside locations mean that sunsets may be a bonus along with the ever-changing appearance of the mudflats and sandbanks with the tides.

WATER SAFETY INFORMATION

Beware!

On the river, the tides come in very quickly. The river has:
- Strong powerful currents that can sweep you away
- Deep cold water
- Soft mud and hidden objects that can trap you

STAY SAFE
STAY OUT OF THE WATER
YOU ONLY DROWN ONCE!

NO SWIMMING   NO DIVING   NO PADDLING

▲ A Halton Borough Council warning sign at Pickerings Pasture warning of the dangers from the tides

During the migration season, it is worth looking skywards occasionally, as there may be a steady stream of birds passing silently overhead, sometimes for hours at a time. Flyway crossing points include the mouth of the estuary, Hale Head and the Runcorn Gap.

Many of the canals around the estuary are increasingly valued as havens for wildlife. Herons and cormorants are common sights, along with Canada geese, coots and moorhens. The Mersey Ferries' cruises along the Manchester Ship Canal offer the chance to see some areas normally closed to the public, such as the saltmarshes on the southern shores of the estuary (www.merseyferries.co.uk).

When watching birds, most are alert to movements on the horizon so it is best to remain at a distance, move slowly and try to keep out of sight. It is also important to avoid any type of disturbance that causes birds to take flight, because – especially in winter – this uses valuable energy and, in the breeding season, places eggs and chicks at risk from predators. The Birdwatchers' Code described later in this chapter gives useful advice to help avoid these kinds of problems. It is important to consider personal safety too. The fast-moving tides and quicksand can be hazardous, and the RNLI water safety advice in the Introduction to this book should always be heeded.

To learn more about birdwatching, it is worth joining a Wildlife Trust (www. wildlifetrusts.org) or one of the local wildlife groups in the region, such as those affiliated with the RSPB (www.rspb.org.uk). Most arrange evening talks and weekend excursions, and some have access to areas open only to members. Some larger parks and reserves also have visitor centres with experts on hand, such as Eastham Country Park, and the Pickerings Pasture, Risley Moss, and Brotherton Park and Dibbinsdale reserves.

Definitely worth a visit are two of the flagship reserves in the region: the RSPB's Burton Mere Wetlands reserve on the Wirral, and the Wildfowl & Wetlands Trust's Martin Mere Wetland Centre near Ormskirk. Facilities at these larger reserves include visitor centres and hides sheltered from the weather, plus expert staff and volunteers on hand to provide advice.

Wirral Country Park is another interesting destination, with clifftop views over the Dee Estuary and a visitor centre and café (www.wirral.gov.uk). In late summer, the Wirral Wader Festival is held there with two days of talks and guided walks in celebration of these fascinating birds (www.waderquest.org). Another way to brush up on recognition skills is to visit the World Museum in Liverpool or Warrington Museum & Art Gallery, which both have taxidermy displays with examples of local bird species.

Murmurations

In the oceans, fish often shoal together to confuse predators. Some bird species have a similar survival strategy, flying in vast swirling formations that seem to move together as one. These are called murmurations, and perhaps the best-known exponent is the starling. In the Mersey Estuary, one place where this behaviour sometimes occurs is the Runcorn Gap. As elsewhere in the UK, it is most likely seen towards dusk in late autumn and winter.

▲ Starlings at sunset near the Runcorn Gap

Less widely known is that some species of wader have a similar strategy, including two types found around the estuary: the dunlin and the slightly larger knot. Both have a winter plumage of pale undersides with grey-brown upper surfaces. Multiplied across hundreds or thousands of birds, this can lead to the appearance of the flock changing rapidly from dark to light as they twist and turn, almost disappearing when head on. Occasionally, rippling and strobing effects appear and even short-lived patterns such as ovals and alternating bands of white and grey.

These displays are one of the wonders of the natural world. A good place to view them is from Pickerings Pasture Local Nature Reserve, whose website notes that

Dunlin taking flight near Pickerings Pasture Local Nature Reserve

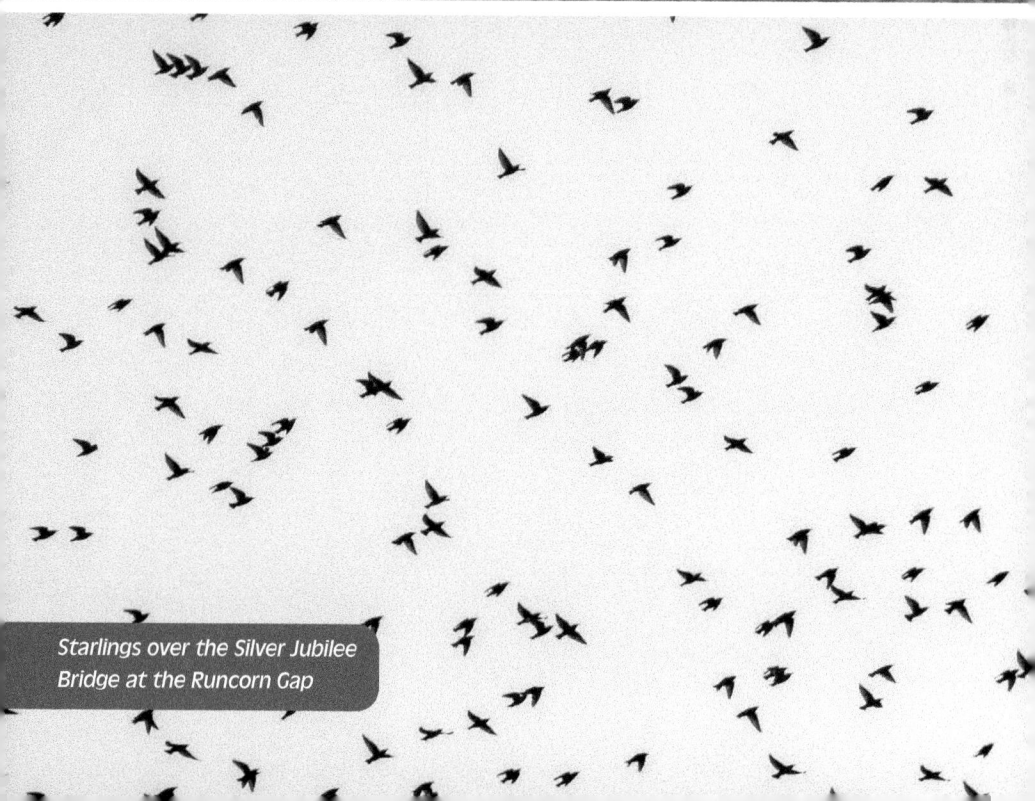

Starlings over the Silver Jubilee Bridge at the Runcorn Gap

A flock of dunlin at Hoylake on the north Wirral coast

flocks of more than 20,000 have been seen here. Another vantage point for both species is along the north Wirral coastline, particularly at Hoylake. Within the estuary, dunlin are the more common and counts have sometimes exceeded 60,000 (www.merseyestuary.org).

Potential triggers include the rush of the incoming tide over the mudflats or foreshore where birds are feeding or the presence of a bird of prey. However, as with any natural phenomenon, predicting when and where it will occur is not an exact science and it may take many visits before conditions are right.

There have been many studies into how this formation flying is possible, with much left to understand. Perhaps the most plausible theory is that individual birds follow a simple set of rules, maintaining a clear space ahead and a roughly equal distance from their nearest half dozen or so neighbours. The noise and pressure variations from all those flapping wings may also play a role, and the intensity of light filtering through the flock.

Although there is no leader, if some birds spot a predator the avoiding actions propagate through the flock. However, many mysteries remain, such as why this behaviour sometimes continues long after any possible threat has passed or begins for no apparent reason.

For starlings, another factor may be that part of the survival strategy is to huddle together overnight for warmth, so the dusk flights help gather up stragglers and generate some heat before settling down for the night. One of the most remarkable aspects of the displays is that at some locations the action stops suddenly as the flock seems to come together as one to drop onto the roost: an act sometimes described as disappearing down a funnel or drain.

The Birdwatchers' Code

Several leading bird organisations, magazines and websites have produced a birdwatchers' code of conduct that puts the interests of birds first and respects other people, whether or not they are interested in birds. See the RSPB website for the full version (www.rspb.org.uk):

Five things to remember

- Avoid disturbing birds and their habitats – the birds' interests should always come first
- Be an ambassador for birdwatching
- Know the law and the rules for visiting the countryside, and follow them
- Send your sightings to the County Bird Recorder and the Birdtrack website (links are available on the RSPB website)
- Think about the interests of wildlife and local people before passing on news of a rare bird, especially during the breeding season.

The interests of birds come first

Birds respond to people in many ways, depending on the species, location and time of year.

Disturbance can keep birds from their nests, leaving chicks hungry or enabling predators to take eggs or young.

During cold weather or when migrants have just made a long flight, repeatedly flushing birds can mean they use up vital energy that they need for feeding. Intentional or reckless disturbance of some species at or near the nest is illegal in Britain.

Whether your particular interest is photography, ringing, sound-recording or birdwatching, remember that the interests of the bird must always come first.

Avoid going too close to birds or disturbing their habitats – if a bird flies away or makes repeated alarm calls, you're too close. And if it leaves, you won't get a good view.

Stay on roads and paths where they exist and avoid disturbing habitat used by birds.

Think about your fieldcraft. Disturbance is not just about going too close – a flock of wading birds on the foreshore can be disturbed from a mile away if you stand on the seawall.

Repeatedly playing a recording of birdsong or calls to encourage a bird to respond can divert a territorial bird from other important duties, such as feeding its young. Never use playback to attract a species during its breeding season. See the RSPB website for information on birds, habitats and the law in the UK.

Be an ambassador for birdwatching

Think about your fieldcraft and behaviour, not just so that you can enjoy your birdwatching, but so others can too.

Respond positively to questions from interested passers-by. They may not be birdwatchers yet, but a good view of a bird or a helpful answer may light a spark of interest. Your enthusiasm could start a lifetime's interest in birds and a greater appreciation of wildlife and its conservation.

Consider using local services, such as pubs, restaurants and petrol stations, and public transport. Raising awareness of the benefits to local communities of trade from visiting birdwatchers may, ultimately, help the birds themselves.

Respect for the countryside

Know the rules for visiting the countryside, and follow them.

Respect the wishes of local residents and landowners, and don't enter private land without permission unless it is open for public access on foot. Follow the codes on access and the countryside for the place you're walking in.

Irresponsible behaviour may cause a land manager to deny access to others (e.g. for necessary survey work). It may also disturb the bird or give birdwatching bad coverage in the media.

In England and Wales, access is to land mapped as mountain, moor, heath and down, and to registered common land. However, local restrictions may be in force, so follow the Countryside Code and plan your visit. In England, the Countryside Code and maps showing areas for public access are on the Government website (www.gov.uk).

LIVER BIRDS

At 18 feet tall, the two Liver Bird statues on top of the Royal Liver Building at Pier Head are one of the most famous sights in Liverpool. Designed and sculpted by the artist Carl Bernard Bartels, they were installed in 1911.

Views differ on what type of bird they represent. A display case at the Museum of Liverpool shows some contenders, including the cormorant, white-tailed sea eagle and heron. An information sheet from National Museums Liverpool begins:

The Liver Bird is part of Liverpool's modern, rather than ancient, folklore. William Enfield, Liverpool's first historian, writing in 1774, speaks of the Liver Bird as existing only in 'fabulous tradition'. People think of the Liver Bird as they think of the Griffin or the Phoenix. [When in] 1911 the Royal Liver Friendly Society crowned its waterfront offices with two huge effigies which bear no resemblance to any real bird, it helped to fix in the popular mind the myth that the Liver was a fabulous bird that once haunted the Pool inlet ...

It concludes:

What then is the Liver Bird? It is an eagle, which was mistaken for a cormorant. Whether one examines the ancient medieval seal, or the seal that was made after the loss of the earlier seal at the time of the Civil War, the bird is quite nondescript, as we have already said and was even thought by one authority to be a dove. Thus it is not surprising that by 1611, the mistake was almost official. Later the cormorant was confused with a bird called, in Dutch, something like LEVER so as to make a play on the name Liverpool. However, since 1797 the emblem of Liverpool has officially been [the] cormorant. It is of interest, however, that when the bishopric of Liverpool took out arms in 1882, the eagle was incorporated, not the cormorant.

Images of the Liver Bird have been widely used around the city on coats of arms, posters and medals, with several examples on display at the museum. The birds also feature on the crests of Liverpool City Council, Liverpool Football Club, and Liverpool Pilotage Service, while the masthead of the Liverpool Echo has a Liver Bird with a copy of the newspaper in its beak.

TEN WATERBIRD SPECIES OF THE MERSEY ESTUARY

▲ **Grey Heron** (large); Often seen waiting patiently at the shoreline to pounce on fish and easy to recognise in flight by its size, sharply curved neck and long trailing legs (New Ferry)

▲ **Cormorant** (large); Near-black plumage and often seen standing at the water's edge – sometimes drying outstretched wings – or flying low above the surface singly or in small groups (New Brighton)

▲ **Shelduck** (large); Beautifully coloured with a red bill, pink legs and white body, bottle-green head and shoulders, black back, and chestnut hoop around the breast; often seen feeding in pairs (Speke and Garston Coastal Reserve)

Great Crested Grebe (large); White and grey plumage with a crest of feathers on the head; performs elaborate courtship displays during the breeding season (Warrington near Howley Weir) ▼

Sanderling (small); Pale-grey upper surfaces with a lighter breast and black bill and legs; tend to run mouse-like along the waterline when feeding (Sefton Coast) ▼

Curlew (large); One of the largest waders with a grey-brown patterned body, downward curved bill and distinctive two-tone call that sounds a little like 'cur-lew'; increasingly endangered (Shorefields Nature Park) ▼

These are just a few examples of the most easily recognised types, and many other species are found around the estuary.

The size entries indicate wingspans – Large >0.7m, Medium 0.4-0.7m, Small < 0.3m.

The descriptions indicate typical winter colours and can change significantly in the breeding season.

They also show where the photographs were taken.

The Further Reading section suggests guides on bird identification and the RSPB website is another useful source of information.

▲ Upper to Lower: **Redshank** (medium); Grey-brown mottled upper sides with pale undersides and bright orange-red legs that are its most distinctive feature when on the ground (New Brighton) / **Dunlin** (small); Grey-brown with a pale underbelly and black and white markings on the upper surface of the wings; famed for its spectacular murmurations (Hoylake)

Oystercatcher (large); Bold black and white coloration, red-pink legs, a loud whistling/piping call and a distinctive orange-red beak often said to resemble a carrot (New Brighton) ▼

Lapwing (large); Black, dark-green and white plumage with a crest of feathers on the head; tend to fly in ragged circling formations and have stubbier wings than most waders; also known as the peewit after its distinctive breeding season call (Fiddlers Ferry) ▼

A bird hide at Widnes Warth

Further Reading

Much has been written about the habitat and wildlife of the Mersey Estuary and the following reports, books and articles provide useful insights:

100 years of the Liverbirds, (Trinity Mirror Sport Media, 2011)

A Frontier Landscape: the North West in the Middle Ages, N.J. Higham, (Windgather Press, 2004)

A Pictorial History of the Mersey and Irwell Navigation, John Corbridge, (E.J. Morten Publishers, 1979)

Birds in Cheshire and Wirral: A breeding and wintering atlas, David Norman, (Liverpool University Press, 2008)

Flocking to the Mersey, Tim Melling (words) and Steve Young, (photographs), Mersey Basin Campaign, www.merseybasin.org.uk, (SourceNW, 2005)

Making the most of the Mersey: a leisure guide to your estuary, Mersey Basin Campaign, (2007)

National Character Area profile: 60 Mersey Valley, Natural England, (2013)

RSPB Handbook of British Birds, Peter Holden and Tim Cleeves, (Bloomsbury, 2014)

The Birds of Lancashire and North Merseyside, Steve White, Barry McCarthy, Maurice Jones, (Hobby Publications, 2008)

The Liver Bird, Information Sheet 21, Maritime Archives & Library, (National Museums Liverpool, 2004)

The Lost World of Formby Point: Footprints on the prehistoric Landscape 5000 BC to 100 BC, Gordon Roberts, www.formby-footprints.co.uk, (The Alt Press , 2014)

The Mersey Estuary, Mersey Estuary Conservation Group, (Hobby Publications, 2006)

The Mersey Estuary Naturally Ours, Mersey Estuary Conservation Group, M.S. Curtis and M. Baker-Schommer (eds.), www.merseyestuary.org, (English Heritage and National Museums Liverpool, 2003)

The Norris Papers, Thomas Heywood (ed.), (The Chetham Society, 1846)

Watching Waterbirds with Kate Humble and Martin McGill, Malcolm Tait (Ed.), (Wildfowl & Wetlands Trust and Think Publishing Ltd., Bloomsbury, 2011)

Water Quality and Fisheries in the Mersey Estuary, England: A historical perspective, P.D. Jones, (Marine Pollution Bulletin, 2006)

Where to Watch Birds: North West England & the Isle of Man, A. Conlin, J.P. Cullen, P. Marsh, T. Reid, C. Sharpe, J. Smith, S. Williams, (Bloomsbury Publishing, 2008)

Wild Mersey, Chris Baines (words) and Colin McPherson and Steve Young (photographs), Mersey Basin Campaign, www.merseybasin.org.uk, (SourceNW, 2009)

Wild Merseyside, John Dempsey, (Trinity Mirror North West and North Wales, 2009)

Wirral Nature Guide: An introduction to coastal wildlife and their habitats, www.visitwirral.com, (Wirral Council, 2009)

The following websites are also useful especially for information on local sites and species:

Friends of Pickerings Pasture (www.thefriendsofpickeringspasture.org.uk)

Mersey Basin Campaign (legacy site) (www.merseybasin.org.uk)

Mersey Estuary Conservation Group (www.merseyestuary.org)

Mersey Rivers Trust (www.merseyriverstrust.org)

Royal Society for the Protection of Birds (www.rspb.org.uk)

A-Z INDEX